BIOSTATISTICS
AND
COMPUTER APPLICATIONS

BIOSTATISTICS AND COMPUTER APPLICATIONS

Dr. Rajeev Goswami

Prints Publications Pvt Ltd
New Delhi

Published by

Prints Publications Pvt Ltd
Viraj Tower-2, 4259/3, Ansari Road,
Darya Ganj, New Delhi-110002
Tel. : +91-11-45355555
Fax: +91-11-23275542
E-mail : contact@printspublications.com
Website : www.printspublications.com

First Edition : 2022 (Hardbound)

ISBN: 978-93-936743-6-4

Price: ₹ 1495/-

Published and Printed by Mr. Pranav Gupta (Director) on behalf of Prints Publications Pvt Ltd, New Delhi.

CONTENTS

PREFACE

The necessity of having a simple, systematized book on Biostatistics has long been felt. This attempt has been made with an object to meet the requirements of a common biology / medical students. Research is going on in every field of biology, i.e. Genetics, Limnology, Microbiology, Environmental Science, Botany, Zoology etc. and Medical Sciences. This book is presented before teachers, research scholars and students of biology and other faculties with a view to rendering effective help in their studies on basics of Statistics.

Collection of data is of no use unless it is analyzed statistically. Statistical analysis makes the data to reach to some information or conclusion.

Computers are available and data storage is no probiem these days. Statistical Analysis Softwares are also available, but the problem is that, which statistical test or analysis is suitable for the data being collected. Examples in this book are well explanatory, easily understandable and confirms the practical-theory relationship.

I have completed statistical analysis work for the teachers, research scholars and students of biology, medical sciences, home science etc. This book, if read thoroughly, will make "Statistical Analysis" friendly.

My special thanks are due to my students who made me feel their difficulties, which was a great incentive for writing this book. I am thankful to Dr. Manoj S. Chandorkar, Late Dr. Arun Bajpai, Dr. Dinesh Parmar, Dr. S.A. Mastan, Dr. Umashankar Sharma for co-operation.

I express my gratitude and indebtedness to my father, Prof. H.K. Goswami, mother, Mrs. Shanti Goswami, my wife, Dr. Anvita Goswami and all family members whose constant co-operation and suggestions made this book completed. At last, I am thankful to my daughter, 9 years old, Miss. Bhuvi Goswami and my son, $3\frac{1}{2}$ years old, Mast. Bhavya Goswami . I express my thanks to my uncle Shri K.K. Goswami for his suggestions.

Finally, I am Obliged to Mr. Pranav Gupta, Director of Prints Publications Pvt Ltd, New Delhi, India for accepting the manuscript and bringing out this book in a graceful manner.

DR RAJEEV GOSWAMI

INTRODUCTION

Definition :

Statistics has been defined differently by different authors from time to time. Application of Statistics in Biology is termed as Bio-Statistics i.e. for analyzing (statistically) the data related to biology.

Statistics is the science which deals with collection, classification and tabulation of numerical facts as the basis for explanation, description and comparison of phenomena. *(Lovitt)*

The science which deals with collection, analysis and interpretation of numerical facts. *(Cronton and Cowdon)*

Statistics and Biology

The association between statistical methods and biological theories was first studied by Francis Galton in his work on Regressions. According to Karl Pearson, the whole theory of heredity rests on statistical basis. In Medical science, the collection and analysis of observed facts relating to cause and occurrence of diseases and of different medicines to prevent diseases indicates wide use of statistics. Statistics has great use in each and every field existing.

Population : The word population is defined as the aggregate of units from which a sample is chosen. The population is sub-divided into suitable units for the purpose of sampling and these are called sampling units. A population of units is said to be finite if the number of units in it is finite.

Sample : One or more sampling units selected from a population according to some specified procedure will constitute a sample. The aim of sampling is to select a fraction of the population in such a way that the information collected for the selected sample will represent the population as close as possible, for the characteristics under study including that of the variability among units in the population and within the resources available to the sampler. A sampling scheme is determined by the size of sampling units, number of sampling units to be used.

Parameter : A function of the values of the units in the population will be called a parameter. The population mean, variance, coefficient of variation, etc are examples of population parameters. Statistical measures computed from the sample observation alone have been termed by Prof R.A. Fisher as STATISTIC.

Estimator : Let the sample observations of size n by x_1, x_2, $x_3 \ldots x_n$. Any function of the sample observations will be called a `statistic'. When a statistic is used to estimate a population parameter the statistic will be called an `estimator'. The sample mean is an estimator of population mean.

Simple Random Sampling

It is the simplest form of sampling and is the basis for many other sampling methods. Simple random sampling is most applicable for the initial survey in an investigation and for studies which involve sampling from a small area where the sample size is relatively small. A sampling procedure such that each of the ^NC_n combinations of n sampling units out of the N has the same chance of being selected is referred to as Simple Random Sampling. This type of sampling is also known as `unrestricted random sampling' or simply as `random sampling'.

Methods of Selecting a Random Sample :

Lottery method of selection : The units in the population are numbered 1 to N. If N identical counters with numberings 1 to N are obtained and one counter is chosen `at random' after shuffling the counters, then the probability of selecting any counter is the same for all the counters. The process is repeated n times without replacing the counters selected. The units which correspond to the numbers on the chosen counters form a simple random sample of size n from the population of N units.

Selection based on printed random numbers : The procedure of selection using the lottery method becomes inconvenient when N is large. To overcome this difficulty table of random numbers is used. Let a simple random sample of any size from a list of 246 compartments, three digited columns of random numbers is used. K^{th} compartment is associated (K=1,2,3.....246) with the four numbers K, K+246, K+492, K+738. In order to give equal chances of selection to all the 246 units, random numbers larger than 983 will be rejected. Thus the serial numbers of the compartments selected for the sample correspond to the numbers obtained as remainders when the three digit figures of random numbers are divided by 246. If the remainder is 0 then the number is taken as 246. If same remainder is repeated more than once, it has to be rejected.

Biostatistics refers to the statistical analysis of the data related to biology/medical sciences. Collection of data and its presentation in the form of frequency distribution is defined in chapter-1. Collection of data is done according to which statistical tool will be used for its analysis. These days every student is aware of making graphs by using the software `Microsoft Excel'. The five basic graphs i.e. bar chart, histogram, line graph, pie chart and pictograph is defined in chapter-2. Several numerical descriptive measures which give an idea of concentration of the observation about central part of distribution i.e. mean, median, mode etc. and positional values are defined in the chapter 3. Numerical descriptive measures which describe the spread or dispersion of a set of observation i.e. range, quartile deviation, standard deviation, variance etc., is defined in chapter-4. Theory of probability is defined in chapter-5. If the random variable (X) takes two values 1 and 0 with probability p and q respectively is called a binomial variate. If the variable under consideration is a binomial variate then the observed data can be fitted to get a binomial distribution which is defined in chapter-6. If probability of success (p) for each trial is very small i.e. $p \to 0$ and number of trials is indefinitely large and $np = \lambda$ is finite follows a poisson distribution then the observed data can be fitted as poisson distributon which is defined in chapter-7.

The properties and fitting of Normal distribution are defined in chapter-8. Degree of association between two random variables X and Y is defined as correlation coefficient. The properties and usefulness of correlation coefficient is defined in chapter-9. Mathematical measure of the average relationship between two or more variables in terms of original data known as regression analysis. Regression analysis by using quantitative and qualitative variables is defined in chapter-10. Analysis of Variance (ANOVA) which is used to test the homogeneity of several means is defined in chapter-11. Three types i.e. one-way, two-way and m observations per cell are mentioned. For analyzing the covariation and testing for differences between slope of lines of regression is defined in chapter-12. Completely randomized design, Randomized block design and Latin square design which is also used to test the homogeneity of several means is defined is chapter-13. Chapter-14 gives a general idea about null hypothesis, alternative hypothesis, one tailed or two tailed hypothesis, type-I and type-II error and various procedure for a test of hypothesis. For testing the significant difference between two independent variables which measure the same characteristics and the two variables which are not independent but paired together for small sample (sample size<=30) is defined in chapter-15.

Chi-square test for testing `goodness of fit', `independence of attributes' and `homogeneity of correlation coefficient' is defined in chapter-16. Different types of tests used to test the significant difference between two variables for large samples (sample size>30) are defined in chapter-17. Nonparametric tests in which numerical value of the characteristics is not found but ranking is done for comparison. Statistics based on ranks of measurements is called rank statistics. These tests are defined in chapter-18. Theory of attributes deal with the study of qualitative characteristics which is defined in chapter-19. A statistic that measures event occurring to a group of people sharing a common demographic experience is defined in chapter-20. Databases are being used in every field of biology to store data. Foxpro application with simple programming techniques to make programs for statistical analysis is defined in chapter-21. Lastly Logarithms are defined.

CHAPTER 1

FREQUENCY DISTRIBUTION

Statistical data is often presented in the form of a frequency distribution.

Frequency

The frequency of a class is equal to the number of observations that fall in that class. The frequency of the class i is equal to f_i.

Relative Frequency

For a given class i, the relative frequency is equal to the proportion of the total number of observations that fall in that class. The formula for calculating relative frequency of class i = f_i/n.

Cumulative Frequency

The cumulative frequency (cf) of class i is equal to the sum of frequencies up to and including the frequency of the class i

$$\text{cf of class i} = f_1+f_2+.....f_i$$

Cumulative Relative Frequency

Cumulative relative frequency is equal to the cf of class i divided by total observations.

crf = cf of class i /n

Raw Data

If the data is not in apparent order i.e. taking the observation and just writing it on a paper. It is also called as statistically unorganized data.

The Array

Raw data is to be rearranged in either ascending or descending order. It consists of a listing of values in order of magnitude from smallest to largest or from largest to smallest.

TABLE 1.0 : Showing Frequency Table

Class Interval	*Frequency (f)*	*Relative frequency*	*Cumulative frequency (cf)*	*Cumulative relative frequency*
1.2-3.2	10	10/50 = 0.20	10	10/50= 0.20
3.2-5.2	14	14/50 = 0.28	24	24/50 = 0.48
5.2-7.2	11	11/50 = 0.22	35	35/50 = 0.70
7.2-9.2	6	6/50 = 0.12	41	41/50 = 0.82
9.2-11.2	4	4/50 = 0.08	45	45/50 = 0.90
11.2-13.2	3	3/50 = 0.06	48	48/50 = 0.96
13.2-15.2	1	1/50 = 0.02	49	49/50 = 0.98
15.2-17.2	1	1/50 = 0.02	50	50/50 = 1.00
	50	1.00		

The Frequency Distribution

1. The representation of numerical facts (data) is known as frequency distribution.
2. The variable (which varies) is usually denoted by X, Y, ... etc.
3. The value corresponding to the existence of the variable is known as frequency, denoted by 'f'.
4. A bar '|' called tally mark is used to denote the frequency in a diagrammatic way. Having occured four times, the fifth occurrence is denoted by a cross tally '\'. Eg. For 7, 卌 | |
5. Two types of frequency distribution occur Discrete(without Class-Intervals) and Continuous (with Class Intervals).
6. To divide the observed range of variables into different classes called 'Class Intervals' and recording frequency for each class is known as grouped frequency distribution.
7. The classes should be mutually exclusive and non-overlapping. The classes should be of equal width. The number of classes should not be less than 5 and not more than 20(upper limit depends on the data). Let a class-

interval be 5 – 10, it means lower limit is 5 and upper limit is 10. It will contain the values =>5 but less than 10. Mid value is calculated by dividing the sum of lower limit and upper limit by 2 i.e. MV = (Lower limit+Upper limit)/2.

8. Dividing the Range(the difference between the greatest and smallest observation) by number of classes to get the magnitude of the class interval.
9. The class interval taken such that each observation will come in either of the class, then it is known as continuous distribution.
10. Cumulative frequency of a class is the total of frequencies up to that class i.e. total number of observation between the lower limit of first class interval and upper limit of that class.

Examples :

Discrete distribution

Enzyme activity obtained by the effect of carbaryl(100 mg/kg bw) on the activity of Lactate Dehydrogenase(LDH) in kidney of Rattus norvegicus for 15 days (period of treatment) as

62.8, 62.8, 62.9, 63.0, 63.1, 63.1, 63.1, 63.2,

Grouped distribution

TABLE 1.1 : Twenty Five Prawns (P. favidens) are distributed according to their length in cms.

Length (X)	*Frequency (f)*
3.5	5
3.8	3
3.9	4
4.2	6
4.5	3
4.7	4
	25

Continuous distribution

The number of classes used in this type of distribution should not be many /too few. The width of the class intervals can be calculated by the formula i = s/4, where s is standard deviation of the distribution. The range of the distribution (Highest value – Smallest value) is divided by the value of i to get the approximate number of classes. The approximate number of the classes(k) can be obtained by the formula given by Struges, $k = 1+3.322 \log_{10} N$

Some points for classification

1. The classes should be clearly defined
2. The classes should be exhaustive i.e. each and every given values should be included in one of the classes
3. The classes should be of equal width. If not, comparable figures can be obtained by dividing the value of frequencies by corresponding widths of the class interval. The ratio obtained is called 'Frequency densities'.
4. The classes should be non-overlapping

Broad class interval will yield rough estimates while for high degree of accuracy small class interval is desirable. By plotting less than cf (Y axis) against the upper limits of ridge counts (X axis), the smooth curve obtained by joining the points is called `less than' Ogive. Similarly, by plotting `more than' cf (Y axis) against the lower limits of ridge counts (X axis), the smooth curve obtained by joining the points is called `more than' Ogive. The point of intersection of the two curves gives the value of Median (at X-axis)

FIG - 1.1

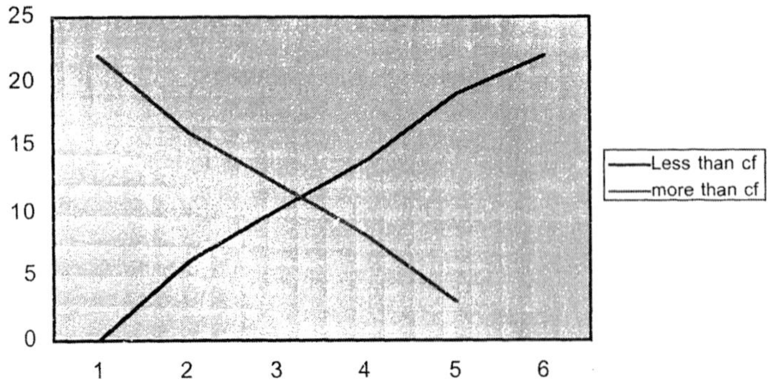

Quantitative Characters

The ridge counts on the first finger in a sample of 89 women from a certain tribe were found to be as follows (S. Narahari, Personal communication) :

TABLE 1.2 : Right Hand

14	10	14	21	18	22	0	8	15	10
9	16	20	16	9	24	8	14	19	15
15	12	18	13	18	17	8	12	10	7
12	13	16	15	14	6	16	14	17	2
13	10	22	0	11	15	16	20	11	14
11	16	20	21	20	21	12	11	20	13
16	13	22	19	11	21	9	19	18	20
15	20	13	13	12	10	22	21	19	18
16	23	19	24	22	21	17	10	2	

Left Hand

16	5	15	23	19	10	1	7	16	6
8	18	17	8	11	23	5	0	15	12
11	8	14	11	13	15	9	15	3	3
15	17	19	11	13	13	13	14	16	2
17	13	18	0	12	7	13	19	14	6
10	16	17	20	12	20	10	22	19	14
15	13	19	22	17	17	17	20	18	15
13	23	6	13	14	10	22	20	19	15
19	20	23	22	14	19	17	12	3	

Frequency	*Right*	*Left*
Smallest	0	0
Largest	24	23
Range(L-S)	24	23

Since the sample size, n, is 89, the minimum number of classes required is K = 303 log 89 = 8(approximately). Hence , an interval of width 3 will be suitable. The number of observations in the various classes can now be found with tally sheet.

TABLE 1.3 : Ridge Count on first finger of 89 women

Ridge Counters Limit	*Class Boundaries*	*Mark*	*Frequency*		*% Frequency*	
			Right	*Left*	*Right*	*Left*
0-2	-2.5	1.0	4	4	4.49	4.49
3-5	2.5-5.5	4.0	0	5	0.00	5.62
6-8	5.5-8.5	7.0	5	8	5.62	8.99
9-11	8.5-11.5	10.0	14	9	15.73	10.11
12-14	11.5-14.5	13.0	18	19	20.22	21.35
15-17	14.5-17.5	16.0	17	20	19.10	22.47
18-20	17.5-20.5	19.0	17	16	19.10	17.98
21-23	20.5-23.5	22.0	12	8	13.48	8.99
24-26	23.5-26.5	25.0	2		2.25	
	Total		89	89	99.99	100.00

Though ridge count is a discrete character, for statistical purposes it is treated as a continuous character, as is indicated by the class boundaries.

The frequency tables show that (1) the counts tend to concentrate around 15, (2) there is a good deal of variation, (3) the counts tend to fall away on both sides, somewhat symmetrically, 15 showing similar frequencies.

The relative (%) frequency tables show that the left hand has comparatively more small and fewer large counts than the right hand. The need for relative frequency tables for such comparison will be greater when the sample sizes differ.

The Less-than and More-than Cumulative Frequency Tables can now be constructed from the frequency tables.

TABLE 1.4 : Cumulative Frequency Tables for Ridge Count

Below	*Less than*		*Above*	*More than*	
	Right	*Left*		*Right*	*Left*
2.5	4	4	0	89	89
5.5	4	9	2.5	85	85
8.5	9	17	5.5	85	80
11.5	23	26	8.5	80	72
14.5	41	45	11.5	66	63
17.5	58	65	14.5	58	44
20.5	75	81	17.5	31	24
23.5	87	89	20.5	14	8
26.5	89		23.5	2	

The frequency polygon is drawn by plotting the frequencies against class marks, the histogram is constructed by erecting rectangles, with heights proportional to the frequencies, over the class intervals (using boundaries), the Ogives are drawn by plotting the cumulative frequencies against the appropriate boundaries.

CHAPTER 2

GRAPHICAL PRESENTATION

'Microsoft Excel' software has 14 types of graphs. Earlier there were only five types of graphs i.e. Bar, Histogram, Line, Pie chart and Pictographs.

Bar Charts : Rectangles are drawn proportionate to the frequency for each value of variable X i.e. length of a ear and variable Y i.e. number of grains in a ear of wheat plant.

FIG - 2.1

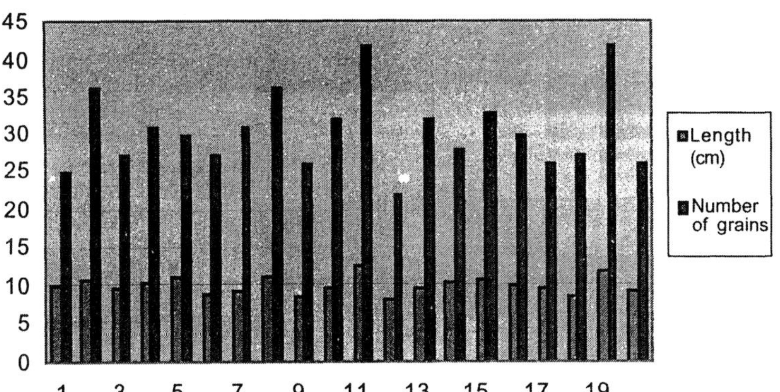

Histogram : For continuous distribution :

X-axis : All the class intervals on a suitable scale

Y-axis : Frequency of that class interval

Sketch : Adjacent rectangular bars (height proportional to the frequency)

Frequency polygon can be drawn by joining the middle points of the upper sides of the adjacent rectangles of the histogram by means of a straight line.

FIG – 2.2

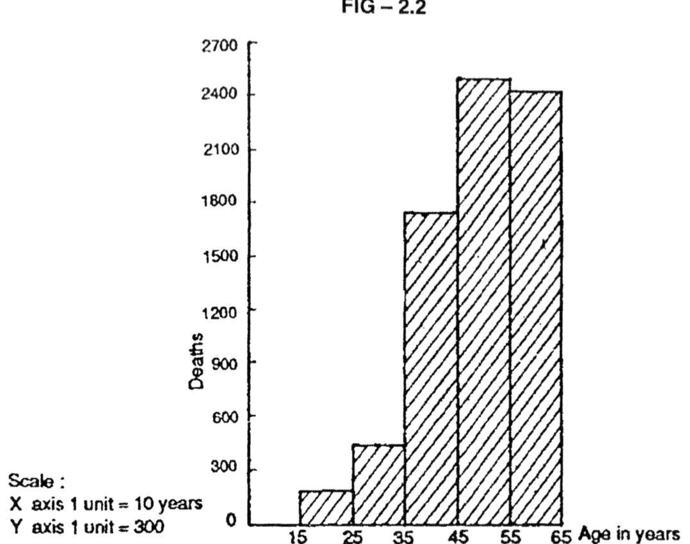

Age-specific and age-adjusted rates of lives lost to cancer in 1985 (per 10,00,000).

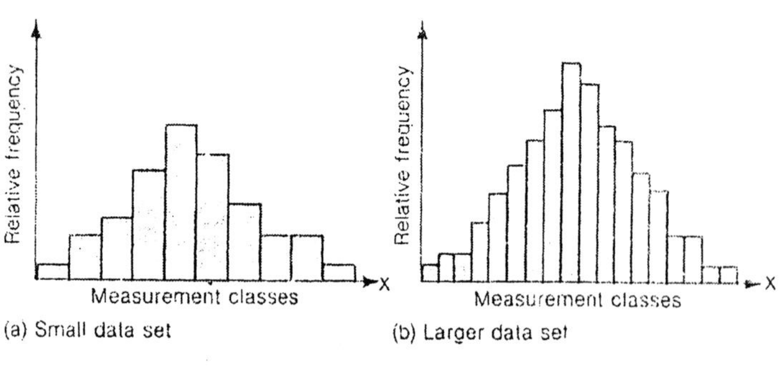

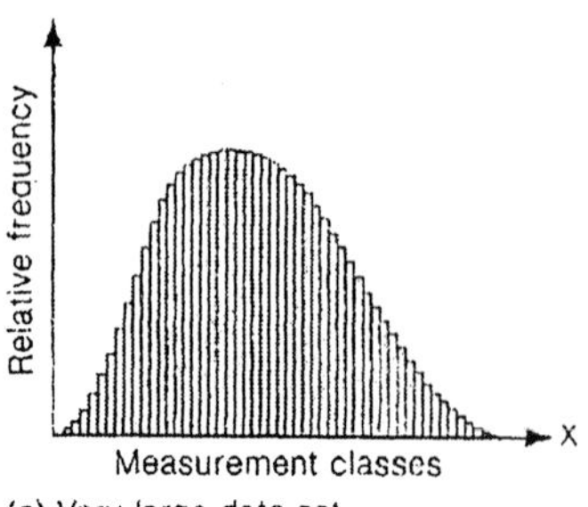

Line Graph : The values of the variable(X) on the X-axis and frequency on the Y-axis. Points are plotted for each combination and then the points are joined by a line. Snout length of three types of fishes are shown below using Line graph.

FIG - 2.3

Morphometric Characters

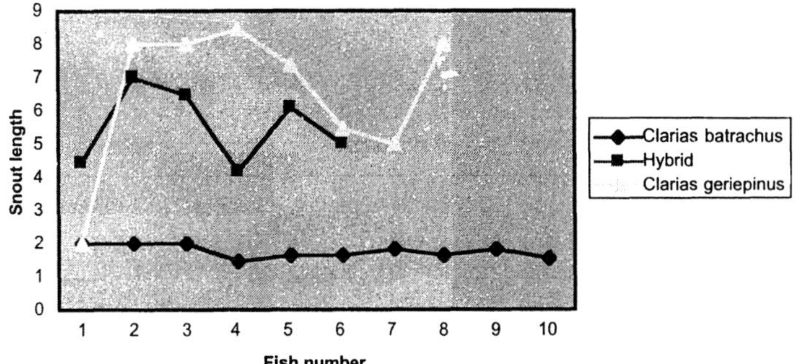

Pie Chart : When it is desired to show the various components as a parts of a whole, pie charts are preferred. It is a circular chart and angle for each component is calculated by multiplying the proportion of that component by 360.

FIG - 2.4

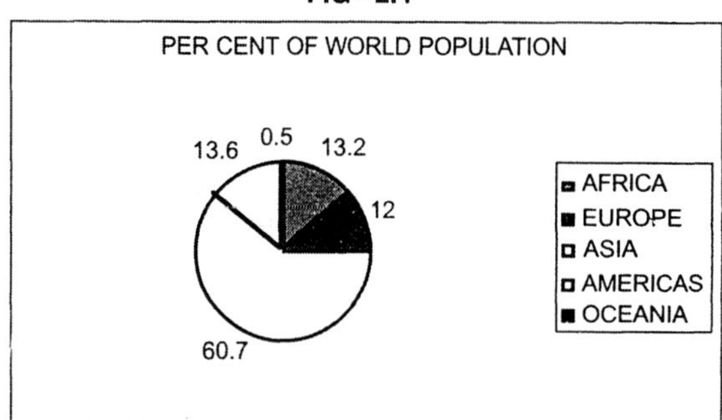

Pictograph : Pictographs usually have the individual pictures in rows, very less in columns ; that the picture should immediately suggest the nature of data shown. The graph predicts a picture as a value so that full frequency can be shown. The frequency of 600 can be shown as * * * , each '*' is having value = 200. Suppose the frequency is 650, the forth '*' is to be drawn according to the value = 50 i.e. ".

CHAPTER 3

MEASURES OF CENTRAL TENDENCY

It gives an idea of the concentration of the observation about the Central Part of the distribution. Several types of numerical descriptive measures have been developed to characterize and help to create a mental picture of the relative frequency distribution of a data set. The two most important of these are *measures of central tendency*, which gives an idea of the concentration of the observation about the Central Part of the distribution and *measures of dispersion* (variation), which describes the spread or dispersion of a set of data.

Five types are :

a. Arithmetic Mean **b.** Median **c.** Mode

d. Geometric Mean **e.** Harmonic Mean

a. Arithmetic Mean (AM) : Arithmetic Mean of a set of discrete observation is their sum divided by total number of observations. Denoted by $\bar{x}$.

$$\bar{x} = \Sigma X_i / n$$

$$= (X_1+X_2+X_3+..........X_n)/n$$

Enzyme activity obtained by the effect of Chlorpyrophos(25 mg/kg bw) on the activity of Alkaline Phosphatase in kidney of Rattus norvegicus for 15 days(period of treatment) as

76.2,76.08,76.15,76.18,76.13,76.10,76.07,76.08,76.10

$$\text{Mean} = \bar{x} = \Sigma X_i / n$$

$$= 685.09/9 = 76.12$$

For the grouped distribution,

$$\bar{x} = \Sigma (f_i * X_i) / \Sigma(f_i)$$

$$= (f_1*X_1+f_2*X_2+f_3*X_3+..........f_n*X_n)/ \Sigma(f_i)$$

TABLE 3.0 : Weight(gms) of 60 L. corrianus collected from a pond.

Weight (X)	*Frequency (f)*	$f_i * X_i$
23	7	161
25	6	150
28	9	252
30	5	150
34	8	272
36	5	180
40	10	400
43	10	430
	60	1995

Mean $= \bar{x} = \Sigma (f_i * X_i) / \Sigma (f_i)$

$= 1995/60 = 33.25$ gms

For continuous distribution,

$\bar{x} = A + \Sigma (f_i * d_i) / \Sigma(f_i)$ where,

A = Assumed Mean (taken from the mid values of class intervals)

$d_i = X_i - A$ and X_i be the mid values of class intervals

TABLE 3.1 : Percentage of alpha chains found in 185 MIC exposed persons.

% of _ chain (X)	*f*	*X (Mid value)*	$X\text{-}A = d_i$	$f_i d_i$
38.0 – 39.5	43	38.75	– 3.0	– 129.0
39.5 – 41.0	39	40.25	– 1.5	– 58.5
41.0 – 42.5	47	41.75	0.0	0.0
42.5 – 44.0	30	43.25	1.5	45.0
44.0 –45.5	26	44.75	3.0	78.0
	185			– 64.5

Assumed Mean A = 41.75

Mean $= \bar{X} = A + \Sigma (f_i * d_i) / \Sigma(f_i)$ where,

$= 41.75 + (-64.5/185)$

$= 41.75 - 0.348 = 41.402$

The d_i values obtained are –3.0, –1.5, 0, 3.0, 1.5. Expressing these values in terms of class intervals, divide these values by class interval i.e. 1.5 the new d_i values will be –2, –1, 0, 1, 2 and use the formula

$$\text{Mean} = \overline{X} = A + \Sigma (f_i * d_i) * i / \Sigma(f_i)$$

% of _ chain (X_i)	f	X_i (Mid value)	$(X_i\text{-}A)/i=d_i$	$f_i * d_i$
38.0 – 39.5	43	38.75	– 2	– 86
39.5 – 41.0	39	40.25	– 1	– 39
41.0 – 42.5	47	41.75	0	0
42.5 – 44.0	30	43.25	1	30
44.0 – 45.5	26	44.75	2	52
	185			– 43

Assumed Mean A = 41.75

Mean = $\overline{X} = A + \Sigma (f_i * d_i) * i / \Sigma(f_i)$ where,

$= 41.75 + [(-43 * 1.5)/185]$

$= 41.75 - (64.5/185) = 41.402$

Mean of a Composite Series

If X_i, (i = 1..k) are the mean of k component series of size n_i, (i = 1..k) respectively then the mean of composite series is given by

$$\overline{X} = (n_1 * X_1 + n_2 * X_2 + n_3 * X_3 + \ldots\ldots\ldots n_k * X_k)/ (n_1 + n_2 + n_3 + \ldots\ldots\ldots n_k)$$

$$\overline{X} = \Sigma (n_i * X_i)/ \Sigma(n_i)$$

Mean of pH of 5 ponds for 12 months are 7.94, 7.8, 7.73, 7.87 and 8.23 respectively. Mean of the composite series will be

$$\overline{X} = (7.94 * 12) + (7.8 * 12) + (7.73 * 12) + (7.87 * 12) + (8.23 * 12)/(12+12+12+12+12)$$

$= 474.84/60 = 7.91$

Weighted Arithmetic Mean

If w_i, (i = 1..n) be the weights attached to the items X_i, (i = 1..n), then the weighted AM

$$\overline{X} = \Sigma (w_i * X_i)/ \Sigma(X_i)$$

b. **Median (Md)** : It is the value of the variable which divides the distribution in two equal parts. It is also called a positional average.

For discerete distribution

1. Arrange the observations either in ascending or descending order.
2. Calculate the number of observations i.e. n.
3. If n = odd number, Median will be $(n+1)/2^{th}$ term.
4. If n = even number, Median will be the mean of $(n/2)^{th}$ and $(n/2)+1^{th}$ terms.

For grouped distribution

1. Calculate N/2 where $N = \Sigma(f_i)$.
2. Find the value of X for which cumulative frequency is just greater that N/2.

It will be the Median.

For Continuous Distribution

The class corresponding to, for which cumulative frequency is just greater than N/2, is called as Median Class. The value of the Median is obtained from the formula,

$$\text{Median} = l + \frac{h}{f}[(N/2) - c]$$

Where, l : lower limit of Median class

h : magnitude of the distribution

f : frequency of the Median class

c : cumulative frequency of the class preceding the median class.

c. **Mode (M_0)** : It is the value of X(variable) for which frequency is maximum. Mode is the value which occurs most frequently in a set of observation.

For grouped distribution

X	1	3	5	6	7	9	11
f	4	9	16	25	15	11	7

The value of x corresponding to the maximum frequency, i.e. 25 is 6. Hence Mode is 6.

For continuous distribution

The class which is having maximum frequency is Modal class.

$$\text{Mode} = l + \frac{h*(f_k - f_{k-1})}{(2f_k - f_{k-1} - f_{k+1})}$$

Where l : lower limit of Mode class

f_k : frequency of modal class

f_{k-1} : frequency of class preceding modal class

f_{k+1} : frequency of class succeeding modal class

For a symmetrical distribution Mean, Median and Mode coincides.

Prof. Karl Pearson's formula for the moderately asymmetrical distribution is

$$\text{Mode} = 3*\text{Median} - 2*\text{Mean}$$

If

1. The Maximum frequency is repeated. Or
2. The maximum frequency occurs at the beginning or at the end of a distribution. Or
3. There are irregularities in data.

Then the method of combination of frequencies is used. The combination of frequencies is done by the formation of different tables by adding different sets of frequencies. The maximum frequency is recorded for each table and the classes used in getting this frequency is noted. The class which is used maximum times for getting these maximum frequencies is the Modal class.

TABLE 3.2

<table>
<tr><th>X</th><th>f</th><th>I</th><th>II</th><th>III</th><th>IV</th><th>V</th></tr>
<tr><td>1</td><td>3</td><td rowspan="2">11</td><td></td><td rowspan="3">26</td><td></td><td></td></tr>
<tr><td>3</td><td>8</td><td rowspan="2">23</td><td rowspan="3">46</td><td></td></tr>
<tr><td>5</td><td>15</td><td rowspan="2">38</td><td rowspan="3">73</td></tr>
<tr><td>6</td><td>23</td><td rowspan="2">58</td><td rowspan="3">98</td></tr>
<tr><td>8</td><td>35</td><td rowspan="2">75</td><td rowspan="3">107</td></tr>
<tr><td>10</td><td>40</td><td rowspan="2">72</td><td rowspan="3">100</td></tr>
<tr><td>11</td><td>32</td><td rowspan="2">60</td><td rowspan="3">80</td></tr>
<tr><td>12</td><td>28</td><td rowspan="2">48</td><td rowspan="3">93</td></tr>
<tr><td>13</td><td>20</td><td rowspan="2">65</td><td rowspan="3">79</td></tr>
<tr><td>15</td><td>45</td><td rowspan="2">59</td><td rowspan="3">65</td></tr>
<tr><td>17</td><td>14</td><td rowspan="2">20</td><td></td></tr>
<tr><td>18</td><td>6</td><td></td><td></td><td></td></tr>
</table>

Maximum frequency is at the 10th place so combination of frequencies is to be done to get the value of Mode. Column I is obtained by adding 2 by 2 frequencies starting from first. Column II is obtained by adding 2 by 2 frequencies starting from second. (leaving 1st).Column III is obtained by adding 3 by 3 frequencies starting from first. Column IV is obtained by adding frequencies 3 by 3 starting from second (leaving 1st). Column V is obtained by adding 3 by 3 frequencies starting from third (leaving 1st & 2nd).

Column No.	*Maximum frequency*	*Combination of frequencies*
f	45	10
I	75	5,6
II	72	6,7
III	98	4,5,6
IV	107	5,6,7
V	100	6,7,8

It is clear from the above table that 6th frequency is used maximum times to get the maximum frequency. The value of x for the 6th frequency will be the Mode. Hence Mode is 10.

TABLE 3.3 : Below are given the mineral found in 58 fishes. Calculate the median and mode of the distribution.

Mineral	*f*
0.5 – 0.7	8
0.7 – 0.9	11
0.9 – 1.1	7
1.1 – 1.3	13
1.3 – 1.5	10
1.5 – 1.7	9
	58

Solution

Mineral	*f*	*cf*
0.5 – 0.7	8	8
0.7 – 0.9	11	19
0.9 – 1.1	7	26
1.1 – 1.3	13	39
1.3 – 1.5	10	49
1.5 – 1.7	9	58
	58	

Median

N/2 = 58/2 = 29

Since the value of cumulative frequency (cf) which is just greater than N/2 = 29 is 39, the median class will be "1.1 – 1.3"

l = 1.1, C = 26, h = 0.2, f = 13

$$\text{Median} = l + \frac{h}{f}\,[(N/2) - c]$$

$$= 1.1 + \frac{0.2}{13}\,(29–26)$$

$$= 1.1 + 0.6/13 = 1.14$$

Mode

Since the highest frequency (13) of the distribution lies in class interval "1.1 –1.3", this will be modal class.

$l = 1.1,\ f_k = 13,\ f_{k-1} = 7,\ f_{k+1} = 10,\ h = 0.2$

$$\text{Mode} = l + \frac{h*(f_k - f_{k-1})}{(2f_k - f_{k-1} - f_{k+1})}$$

$$= 1.1 + \frac{0.2*(13 - 7)}{(26 - 7 - 10)} = 1.1 + 1.2/9 = 1.1+0.13$$

$$= 1.23$$

d. Geometric Mean (GM) : Geometric Mean of a set of n observations is the nth root of their product. The GM of n observation X_i ,(i = 1...n) is given by

$$GM = (X_1*X_2*X_3*\ldots X_n)^{1/n}$$

In the case of frequency distribution,

$$GM = \text{Antilog}[(1/N\{\Sigma\,(f_i*\log x_i)\}]$$

Immunomodulatory Activity

Determination of haegglutination titre value after 15 days of immunization.

Treatment	*Dilution Series*		
	128	256	512
95% Ethanolic Leaf Extract	1	1	4

TABLE 3.4 : To calculate Geometric Mean Titre Value (GMT)

Log G =(Σf*logX)/N

X	*f*	*Log(X)*	*f*Log(X)*
128	1	2.1072	2.1072
256	1	2.4082	2.4082
512	4	2.7093	10.8372
Total	6		15.3526

Log G = 15.3526/6 = 2.5588

G = Antilog (2.5588) = 362.10

Uses : To find the rate of population growth or rate of interest.

e. **Harmonic Mean (HM)** :Harmonic Mean of a set of n observations is the reciprocal of the Arithmetic Mean of the reciprocals of the n observations.

$$HM = \frac{1}{1/n \; \Sigma \; (1/x_i)}$$

In the case of frequency distribution,

$$HM = \frac{1}{1/n \; \Sigma \; (f_i/x_i)}$$

POSITIONAL VALUES : Quartiles, Quintiles, Deciles and Percentiles

Quartiles : The three points which divide the series into four equal parts are called as quartiles.

Q_1 : First (Lower) quartile, 25% of the observation before it i.e. N/4

Q_2 : Second (Middle) quartile, 50% of the observation before it i.e. N/2

Q_3 : Third (Upper) quartile, 75% of the observation before it i.e. $3*N/4$

The lower quartile is the 25th percentile of a data set. The middle quartile is median (M) and the upper quartile is 75th percentile of a data set. The cumulative frequency which is just greater than the value calculated by the given formula will be the respective quartile.

Interquartile range (IQR) is the distance between upper and lower quartiles i.e $Q = Q_3 - Q_1$.

FIG - 3.1

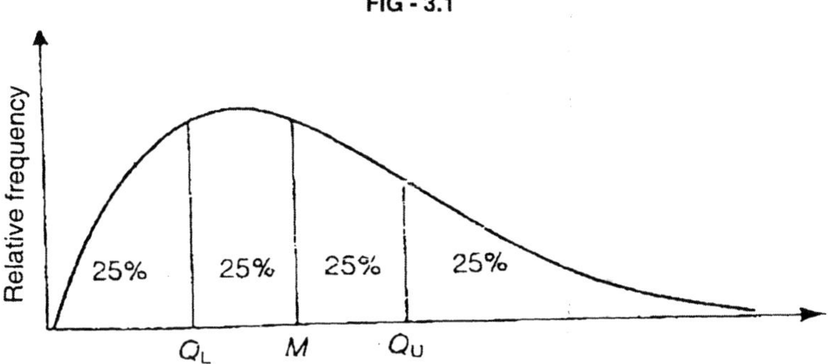

Quintiles : The four points which divide the series in five equal parts are called as quintiles (Qu1, Qu2, Qu3, Qu4).

Deciles : The nine points which divide the series in 10 equal parts are called as deciles.

D_1 : First decile, 10% of the observation before it i.e. N/10

Similarly, D_2, D_3,......D_9 will have 20%, 30%.....90% of observation before it.

Percentiles : The 99 points which divide the observations in 100 equal parts.

P_1 : First percentile : 1% of the observation before it i.e. N/100.

Similarly, P_2,P_3......P_{99} will have 2%, 3% ......99% of the observation before it.

Example : Discrete data

Calculate quartiles, quintiles, 9th decile and 56th percentile from the data set.

14, 21, 28, 33, 18, 37, 23, 49, 45, 43,57,64,53,68,39

By arranging data set in ascending order

14, 18, 21, 23, 28, 33, 37, 39, 43, 45, 49, 53, 57, 64, 68

Quartiles : Q_1 = N/4 th term = (15/4)th term = 3.75th term, since 3.75 is not a natural number, the mean of 3rd and 4th term will be Q_1

3rd term = 21 ; 4th term = 23 ; thus Q_1 = (21+23)/2 = 22

Q_2 = N/2 th term = 7.5th term, similarly the mean of 7th and 8th term will be Q_2

7th term = 37 ; 8th term = 39 ; thus Q_2 = (37+39)/2 = 38

Q_3 = 3N/4 th term = 11.25 th term, 11th term will be Q_3 i.e 49

Quintiles : Qu1 = N/5 th term i.e 3rd term = 28

Qu2 = 2∗N/5 th term i.e 6th term = 33

Qu3 = 3∗N/5 th term i.e 9th term = 43

Qu4 = 4∗N/5 th term i.e 12th term = 53

9th Decile : D_9 = 9∗N/10 th term = 13.5 th term i.e mean of 13th and 14th term

13th term = 57 ; 14th term = 64 ; thus D_9 = (57+64)/2 = 60.5

56th percentile : P_{56} = 56∗N/100 th term = 8.4 th term i.e 8th term = 39

TABLE 3.5 : Muscle weight found in 70 L. corrianus are given below. Calculate Quartiles, D_7 and P_{41}.

Muscle Weight (X)	*Frequency (f)*	*Cumulative Frequency (cf)*
13.5	8	8
14.8	11	19
15.3	10	29
16.8	7	36
17.0	9	45
21.3	10	55
23.0	6	61
25.7	9	70
	70	

N=70

Q_1 = N/4 = 70/4 = 17.5 ; cf just greater than 17.5 is 19 so $Q_1 = 14.8$

Q_2 = N/2 = 70/2 = 35 ; cf just greater than 35 is 36 so Q_2 = Median = 16.8

Q_3 = (3*N)/4 = (3*70)/4 = 52.5 ; cf just greater than 52.5 is 55 so $Q_3 = 21.3$

D_7 = (7*N)/10 = (7*70)/10 = 49 ; cf just greater than 49 is 55 so $D_7 = 21.3$

P_{41} = (41*N)/100 = (41*70)/100 = 28.7 ; cf just greater than 28.7 is 29 so $P_{41} = 15.3$

CHAPTER 4

MEASURES OF DISPERSION

Literal meaning is scatteredness. It gives an idea about homogeneity (less dispersed) or Heterogeneity (more dispersed) of distribution. There are five types of measures of dispersion.

1. **Range**

   Let A and B be the greatest and the smallest observation respectively in a distribution, then its range will be equal to A-B. In other words, the difference between two extreme observations of the distribution. Unreliable measure because it is based on two extreme observations.

2. **Quartile Deviation**

   It is given by $Q = (Q_3\text{-}Q_1)/2$, where Q_1 and Q_3 are first and third quartiles of the distribution respectively. Unreliable measure because it ignores 50% of data. Better than Range.

3. **Mean Deviation**

   Consider a frequency distribution, X_i / f_i , i = 1,2......n, then the Mean Deviation from the average A (Mean or Median or Mode) is given by

   Mean Deviation = $1/N\ \Sigma\ (f_i * |x_i - A|)$, where | | sign denotes the modulus or absolute value, i.e. ignoring –ve sign. Eg. |-7| = 7. It is also not a perfect measure because it ignores –ve values.

4. **Root Mean Square Deviation**

   When deviation has been taken from any arbitrary number A, it is denoted by 's'.

   $$s = \text{SQRT}\ [1/N\Sigma\ f_i*(X_i - A)^2]$$

   $$s^2 = \text{Mean Square Deviation}$$

   Variance is the minimum value of Mean square deviation or standard deviation is the minimum value of Root Mean Square Deviation.

5. **Standard Deviation**

It is the positive square root of the Arithmetic Mean of the squares of the deviation of the given values from their Arithmetic Mean. It is denoted by σ. It is best and most powerful measures of dispersion. The square of the standard deviation is known as Variance, denoted by σ^2.

Ungrouped Data (Discrete) :

$$\sigma = SQRT[1/n*\Sigma (X_i - \overline{x})^2]$$

The deviation of each value from the mean is to be calculated then squared, so that all signs are positive. The squared deviations are then summed and divided by the number of observations. Square root of this value gives the standard deviation 's'.

Another formula can be used for determining standard deviation without calculating mean of the distribution.

$$\sigma = SQRT[\ \Sigma X^2/n - (\Sigma X/n)^2]$$

TABLE 4.0 : Enzyme activity for the effect of Alkaline Phosphatase on the activity of chlorpyrophos in the heart of Rattus norvegicus. Calculate standard deviation and variance.

Enzyme activity : 57.7, 58.1, 57.85, 58.08, 57.8, 57.77, 58.2, 57.97, 57.95, 58.11

Solution

$$\text{Mean} = \overline{x} = \Sigma X_i /n$$
$$= 579.53/10 = 57.953$$

X	$X-\overline{x}$	$(X-\overline{x})^2$
57.70	– 0.253	0.0640
58.10	+0.147	0.0216
57.85	– 0.103	0.0106
58.08	+0.127	0.0161
57.80	– 0.153	0.0234
57.77	– 0.183	0.0335
58.20	+0.247	0.0610
57.97	+0.017	0.0003
57.95	– 0.003	0.0001
58.11	+0.157	0.0247
579.53		0.2553

$$\sigma = SQRT[1/n*\Sigma - (X_i - \overline{x})^2]$$
$$= SQRT(0.2553/10) = 0.1598$$

X	X^2
57.70	3329.290
58.10	3375.610
57.85	3346.622
58.08	3373.287
57.80	3340.840
57.77	3337.373
58.20	3387.240
57.97	3360.521
57.95	3358.203
58.11	3376.772
579.53	33585.758

$$\sigma = SQRT[\Sigma X^2/n - (\Sigma X/n)^2]$$
$$= SQRT\ [(33585.758/10) - (579.53/10)^2]$$
$$= SQRT[3358.576 - 3358.550209]$$
$$= SQRT[0.025791] = 0.1616$$

Grouped Data

$$\sigma = SQRT[1/N*\Sigma\ f_i*(X_i - \overline{x})^2]$$

TABLE 4.1 : Muscle weight found in 70 L. corrianus are given below. Calculate standard deviation.

Solution

Muscle Weight (X)	*Frequency (f)*	$X\text{-}\overline{x}$	$f*(X\text{-}\overline{x})^2$
13.5	8	– 4.7	179.6
14.8	11	– 3.4	130.1
15.3	10	– 2.9	86.4
16.8	7	– 1.4	14.5
17.0	9	– 1.2	13.8
21.3	10	3.1	93.70
23.0	6	4.8	136.0
25.7	9	7.5	501.1
	70		1155.20

$$N = 70$$
$$\sigma = SQRT[1/N*\Sigma f_i*(X_i - \bar{x})^2]$$
$$= SQRT[1155.2/70] = 4.062$$

Continuous Data

TABLE 4.2 : Computation of standard deviation of the frequency distribution of volume of cells in the blood of 100 normal young females.

Volume of cells in Cu.Cm	*f*	*Mid-values*	$d_i = X_i - A$	$f_i d_i$	$X-\bar{x}$	$(X-\bar{x})^2$	$f_i*(X-\bar{x})^2$
35.0 – 36.5	6	35.75	– 4.5	– 27.00	– 5.145	26.471025	158.82615
36.5 – 38.0	8	37.25	– 3.0	– 24.00	– 3.645	13.286025	106.2882
38.0 – 39.5	12	38.75	– 1.5	– 18.00	– 2.145	4.639716	55.676592
39.5 – 41.0	24	40.25	0.0	0.0	– 0.645	0.416025	9.9846
41.0 – 42.5	25	41.75	1.5	37.50	0.855	0.731025	18.275625
42.5 – 44.0	13	43.25	3.0	39.00	2.355	5.546025	72.098325
44.0 – 45.5	10	44.75	4.5	45.00	3.855	14.861025	148.61025
45.5 – 47.0	2	46.25	6.0	12.00	5.355	28.676025	57.35205
	100			64.50			627.111792

Assumed Mean A = 40.25

$$\text{Mean}(\bar{x}) = A + \Sigma (f_i*d_i)/ \Sigma(f_i)$$
$$= 40.25 + 64.5/100 = 40.895$$
$$\sigma = SQRT[1/N*\Sigma f_i*(X_i - \bar{x})^2]$$
$$= SQRT (627.111792/100) = SQRT(6.271117)$$
$$\sigma = 2.50422$$

The same problem can be solved without calculating the Mean of the distribution.

Volume of cells in cu. cm	*f*	*Mid-values*	$d_i = X_i - A$	$f_i d_i$	$f_i d_i^2$
35.0 – 36.5	6	35.75	- 4.5	- 27.00	121.50
36.5 – 38.0	8	37.25	- 3.0	- 24.00	72.00
38.0 – 39.5	12	38.75	- 1.5	- 18.00	27.00
39.5 – 41.0	24	40.25	0.0	0.0	0.0

41.0 – 42.5	25	41.75	1.5	37.50	56.25
42.5 – 44.0	13	43.25	3.0	39.00	117.00
44.0 – 45.5	10	44.75	4.5	45.00	202.50
45.5 – 47.0	2	46.25	6.0	12.00	72.00
	100			64.50	668.25

$$\begin{aligned}\sigma &= \text{SQRT}[\Sigma \{f*(d')^2\}/N - \{(\Sigma f*d')/N\}^2] \\ &= \text{SQRT}\ [(668.25/100) - (64.5/100)^2] \\ &= \text{SQRT}\ [6.6825 - (0.645)^2] \\ &= \text{SQRT}\ [6.6825 - 0.416025] \\ &= \text{SQRT}\ [6.266475] = 2.5033\end{aligned}$$

Variance of a Combined Series :

Consider two frequency distributions (series) F_1 and F_2 with following information

	F_1	F_2
Mean	$\bar{x}_1$	$\bar{x}_2$
St. Dev.	σ_1	σ_2
Sample size	n_1	n_2

Then the standard deviation σ of the combined series is given by

$$\sigma^2 = \frac{[\, n_1*(\sigma_1+d_1^2) + n_2*(\sigma_2+d_2^2)]}{(n_1+n_2)}$$

Where, Mean of the composite series $\bar{x} = \dfrac{n_1*\bar{x}_1 + n_2*\bar{x}_2}{(n_1+n_2)}$

and $d_1 = \bar{x}_1 - \bar{x}$

$d_2 = \bar{x}_2 - \bar{x}$

Standard Error

The standard deviation of the sampling distribution of a statistic is known as its Standard Error. Standard Error of well known statistic, for large samples, n : sample size, σ^2 : Population Variance

Statistic	*Standard Error*
Mean	$\sigma/\sqrt{n}$
s	$\sqrt{(\sigma^2/2n)}$
s^2	$\sigma^2\sqrt{(2/n)}$

Coefficient of Dispersion (CD) :

To compare the variability of two series, which are measured in different units, coefficient of dispersion is calculated.

$$CD = St. Dev. / Mean$$

Coefficient of Variation (CV) :

According to Prof. Karl Pearson , CV is the percentage variation in the mean, st. dev. being considered as the total variation in the mean.

$$CV = 100*CD$$

The series having greater CV is said to be more variable than the other. Lesser CV denotes the more consistent series.

MEASURES OF SKEWNESS

Literally, it means lack of symmetry. It gives the idea about the shape of the curve. A distribution is said to be skewed if,

1. Mean, Median and Mode fall at different points.
2. Quartiles are not equidistant from the median.
3. The curve drawn is streched more to one side than to the other.

Absolute Measure of Skewness

Let M, Md and Mo be the mean, median and mode of a distribution respectively then

1. $S_k = M - M_d$
2. $S_k = M - M_o$
3. $S_k = (Q_3\text{-}M_d) - (M_d\text{-}Q_1)$

Skewness is +ve if $M > M_o$ or $M > M_d$ otherwise –ve.

According to Prof. Karl Pearson, relative measure i.e. independent of units, called as coefficient of Skewness is given by

$$\text{Coefficient of Skewness} = (M\text{-}M_o)/\sigma$$

For any moderately asymmetrical distribution, Coefficient of skewness = $3*(M - M_d)/\sigma$

For any distribution $(M\text{-}M_o)/\sigma$ has a limit : $-1 <= 0 <= +1$

⇨ Limit of Coefficient of Skewness : $-3 <= 0 <= +3$

Coefficient of Skewness Based on Moments

In a Symmetrical distribution all the odd moments about mean i.e. μ_1, μ_3, μ_5 are equal to zero. If they are not equal to zero, it means distribution is skewed. In order to know the skewness, the moments are divided by standard deviation and with the help of α coefficients skewness is measured

$$\alpha_1 = 0$$

$$\alpha_2 = 1$$

$$\alpha_3 = \mu_3/\sigma^3$$

MEASURES OF KURTOSIS

It shows the convexity of the curve. It gives an idea about the flatness or peakedness of the curve. It is measured by the coefficient β_2 or the derivation γ_2.

$$\beta_2 = \mu_4 / \mu_2^2 : \gamma_2 = \beta_2 - 3$$

If $\beta_2 = 3$, Mesokurtic curve : Normal curve (A)

$\beta_2 < 3$, Platykurtic curve : Flatter than the Normal curve (B)

$\beta_2 > 3$, Leptokurtic curve : more peaked than Normal curve (C)

FIG - 4.1

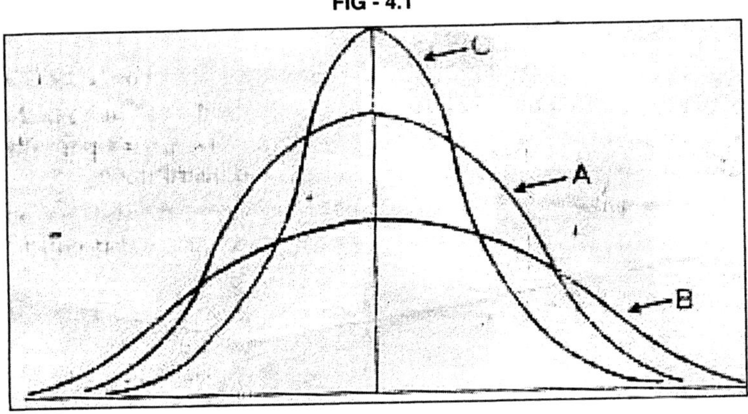

Pearson's β and γ Coefficients

Karl Pearson gave the following 4 coefficients calculated from the moment about mean. These coefficients give an idea about the shape of the curve.

$\beta_1 = \mu_3^2/\mu_2^3$ $\beta_2 = \mu_4/\mu_2^2$

$\gamma_1 = +\sqrt{\beta_1}$ $\gamma_2 = \beta_2 - 3$

In terms of these coefficients the formula for skewness is given by

$$\text{Skewness} = [\sqrt{\beta_1}(\beta_2+3)]/[2X(5\beta_2 - 6\beta_1 - 9)]$$

TABLE 4.3 : Calculate the skewness and kurtosis of the data given below.

Volume of cells in cu.cm	*Number of women*
35 - 36	5
36 - 37	8
37 - 38	12
38 - 39	25
39 – 40	28
40 – 41	13
41 – 42	10
42 - 43	2
	103

A = 38.5 ; $d_i = (X_i - A)$

Volume of cells in cu.cm	*Mid-values*	*f*	*d*	*fd*	*fd^2*	*fd^3*	*fd^4*
35 - 36	35.5	5	– 3	– 15.0	45.0	– 135.0	405.0
36 - 37	36.5	8	– 2	– 16.0	32.0	– 64.0	128.0
37 - 38	37.5	12	– 1	– 12.0	12.0	– 12.0	12.0
38 - 39	38.5	25	0	0.0	0.0	0.0	0.0
39 – 40	39.5	28	1	28.0	28.0	28.0	28.0
40 – 41	40.5	13	2	26.0	52.0	104.0	208.0
41 – 42	41.5	10	3	30.0	90.0	270.0	810.0
42 - 43	42.5	2	4	8.0	32.0	128.0	512.0
Total		103		49.0	291.0	319.0	2103.0

$\bar{x} = A + \Sigma (f_i * d_i) / \Sigma(f_i) = 38.5 + (49/103) = 38.5 + 0.475 = 38.975$

$\Sigma(f_i) = N$

$\upsilon_1 = \Sigma (f_i * d_i) / N = 49/103 = 0.475$

$\upsilon_2 = \Sigma (f_i * (d_i)^2) / N = 291/103 = 2.83$

$\upsilon_3 = \Sigma (f_i * (d_i)^3) / N = 319/103 = 3.10$

$\upsilon_4 = \Sigma (f_i * (d_i)^4) / N = 2103/103 = 20.42$

$\upsilon_1, \upsilon_2, \upsilon_3, \upsilon_4$ pronounced as `nu' are the first, second, third and forth moments about assumed mean

$\mu_1 = 0.0$

$\mu_2 = \upsilon_2 - \upsilon_1^2 = 2.83 - (0.475)^2 = 2.604$

$\mu_3 = \upsilon_3 - 3\upsilon_1\upsilon_2 + 2\upsilon_1^3 = 3.10 - 3*0.475*2.83 + 2*(0.475)^3 = 3.10 - 4.0327 + 0.2142 = -0.7185$

$\mu_4 = \upsilon_4 - 4\upsilon_1\upsilon_3 + 6\upsilon_1^2 \upsilon_2 - 3\upsilon_1^4$

$= 20.42 - (4*0.475*3.10) + (6*2.83*0.2256) - (3*0.050906)$

$= 20.42 - 5.89 + 3.8306 - 0.152718 = 18.2078$

$\mu_1, \mu_2, \mu_3, \mu_4$ pronounced as `mu' are the first, second, third and forth moments about mean

$s = \text{sqrt}(\mu_2) = \text{sqrt}(2.604) = 1.614$

$\beta_1 = \mu_3^2 / \mu_2^3 = (-0.7185)^2 / (2.604)^3 = 0.5162/17.657 = 0.0292$

$\beta_2 = \mu_4 / \mu_2^2 = 18.2078/(2.604*2.604) = 18.2078 / 6.780816 = 2.685$

CHAPTER 5

THEORY OF PROBABILITY

When an experiment is repeated under similar and homogeneous conditions, two types of situation occurs

a. The outcome is unique (deterministic)

   Any derived formula of Physics, Chemistry, Mathematics etc.

b. There may be several possible outcomes (probabilistic)

   In tossing a coin or throwing a dice

Trial and Event

The experiment is known as trial and outcome is known as event.

Exhaustive Event : The total number of possible outcomes in a trial is known as exhaustive events or exhaustive cases. In tossing a coin there are two exhaustive cases i.e. getting a 'head' or 'tail'. In drawing 3 cards from a pack of card, total exhaustive cases $^{52}C_3$.

Favourable Cases : The number of favourable events in a trial is known as favourable cases. In drawing a card which is spade from a pack of cards, favourable cases will be $^{13}C_1 = 13$.

Mutually Exclusive Event : Events are said to be mutually exclusive if the happening of any one of them preludes the happening of other. In tossing a coin getting a 'head' or 'tail' is mutually exclusive event.

Independent Event : Several events are said to be independent if the happening (non-happening) of an event is not affected by next trial. In tossing a coin getting a 'head' is independent of getting a 'head' or 'tail' in another trial.

Mathematical Probability : If a trial results in 'n' exhaustive, mutually exclusive and equally likely cases and 'm' of them are favourable to the happening of event E, the probability of happening of E is given by

$$p = m/n$$

Limits of Probability 0<=p<=1

${}^{n}C_{r}$ = factorial (n) / [factorial (r)*factorial (n-r)] where,

factorial(n) = n*(n-1)*(n-2)*........ 1

A number is chosen from each of two sets A = [1,2,3,4,5,6] and B = [1,2,3,4,5,6]. If p_1 denotes the probability that the sum of the two numbers is 7 and p_2 denotes the probability that their sum is 6, find p_1+p_2.

In each set there are 6 numbers. Total number of ways of choosing one from each will

$$= {}^{6}C_{1} \text{ X } {}^{6}C_{1}$$

Now the ways a sum of 7 can be obtained are (1,6),(2,5),(3,4), (6,1),(5,2),(4,3)

$$= 6 \text{ ways}$$

$$p_1 = 6/\,({}^{6}C_{1} \text{ X } {}^{6}C_{1}) = 6/36 = 1/6$$

similarly, the ways a sum of 6 can be obtained (1,5),(2,4),(3,3), (4,2),(5,1)

$$= 5 \text{ ways}$$

$$p_2 = 5/\,({}^{6}C_{1} \text{ X } {}^{6}C_{1}) = 5/36$$

$$p_1+p_2 = 1/6 + 5/36$$

$$= 11/36 = 0.31$$

A bag contains 3 red, 6 white and 7 blue balls. What is the probability that a ball drawn is white.

Total number of balls = 3+6+7 = 16

One ball can be drawn in ${}^{16}C_{1}$ cases = 16

⇨ total exhaustive cases = 16

Out of 6 white balls one can be drawn in ${}^{6}C_{1}$ cases = 6

⇨ total number of favourable cases = 6

Probability of getting one white ball = 6/16 = 0.37

A bag contains 2 red, 8 white and 10 blue balls. What is the probability that two balls drawn are red and blue.

Total number of balls = 2+8+10 = 20

Two ball can be drawn in ${}^{20}C_2$ cases = (20∗19)/ 2 = 190

⇨ total exhaustive cases = 190

Out of 2 red balls one can be drawn in ${}^{2}C_1$ cases = 2

Out of 10 blue balls one can be drawn in ${}^{10}C_1$ cases = 10

⇨ total number of favourable cases = 2∗10 = 20

Probability of getting one red and one blue ball = 20/190 = 0.105

Algebra of Sets

The Set theory was developed by German mathematician G. Cantor (1845-1918). A SET is a well defined collection of all possible objects having given properties and specified according to a well defined rule. If x is an element of the set A, it is written as $x \in A$. If x is not an element of the set A, it is written as $x \notin A$. If every element of set A belongs to the set B then A is subset of B i.e. $A \subseteq B$. Two sets A and B are said to be equal or identical i.e. A = B or B = A, if $A \subseteq B$ and $B \subseteq A$.

If A, B and C are the subsets of a universal set S, then different laws are :

1.	Commutative Law	$A \cup B = B \cup A$ $A \cap B = B \cap A$
2.	Associative Law	$(A \cup B) \cup C = A \cup (B \cup C)$ $(A \cap B) \cap C = A \cap (B \cap C)$
3.	Distributive Law	$A \cap (B \cup C) = (A \cap B) \cup (A \cap C)$ $A \cup (B \cap C) = (A \cup B) \cap (A \cup C)$
4.	Complimentary Law	$A \cup A = S$; $A \cap A = \emptyset$ $A \cup S = S$; $A \cap S = A$ $A \cup \emptyset = A$; $A \cap \emptyset = \emptyset$
5.	Difference Law	$A-B = A-(A \cap B) = (A \cup B)-B$ $A-(B-C) = (A-B) \cup (A-C)$ $(A \cup B)-C = (A-C) \cup (B-C)$ $A-(B \cup C) = (A-B) \cap (A-C)$
6.	Idempotency Law	$A \cup A = A$; $A \cap A = A$
7.	Involution Law	$\overline{(\overline{A})} = A$
8.	Dualization Law	$\overline{(A \cup B)} = \overline{A} \cap \overline{B}$ $\overline{(A \cap B)} = \overline{A} \cup \overline{B}$

Compound Events : Composition of two or more events. The union of two events A and B is the event that occurs if either A or B or Both occur on a single attempt of the experiment. Denoted as $A \cup B$. The intersection of two events A and B is the event that occurs if both A and B occur on a single performance of the experiment. Denoted as $A \cap B$.

TABLE 5.0 : Percentage of Respondents in Age-Income Classes.

Age	*Income*		
	<25000	*25000-50000*	*>50000*
< 30 yrs	5%	12%	12%
30-50 yrs	14%	20%	14%
>50 yrs	8%	10%	5%

Events A and B are

A : A respondent's income is more than 50000

B : A respondent's age is 30 years or more

P(A) = Since A is defined as income > 50000, it consists of income classification (>50000) and all three age classification within that income class.

$P(A) = 0.12+0.14+0.05 = 0.31$

Similarly, P(B) = It consists of age group(>30 yrs) and all three income groups of column 2 and 3.

$P(B) = 0.14+0.20+0.14+0.08+0.10+0.05 = 0.71$

$P(A \cup B)$ = The union of A and B consists of all simple events in either A or B or both A and B. It consists of all respondents whose income is >50000 or whose age is 30 yrs. or more.

$P(A \cup B) = 0.12+0.14+0.20+0.14+0.08+0.10+0.05 = 0.83$

$P(A \cap B)$ = It consists of all respondents whose income >50000 and whose age is =>30 yrs.

$P(A \cap B) = 0.14+0.05 = 0.19$

Law of Addition of Probabilities : If A and B are two events and A and B have no common point (not disjoint) then, probability of occurrence of at least one of the two events is given by

$$p(A \cup B) = p(A) + p(B) - p(A \cap B)$$

The probability of happening of event A is the sum of the probabilities of happenings of its mutually exclusive forms A_1, A_2, A_3....... A_n. Symbolically,

$$P(A) = p(A_1) + p(A_2) + \ldots\ldots\ldots P(A_n)$$

The probabilities $p(A_1)$, $p(A_2)$, ... $P(A_n)$ of the mutually exclusive forms of A are known as 'partial probabilities'.

If two dice are thrown, what is the probability that their sum is greater than 10.

In throwing two dices total number of exhaustive cases will be 6^2 = 36

Let their sum be S. Probability for S>10 means p(S=11)+p(S=12)

For S=11, combinations will be (6,5),(5,6) = 2

p(S=11) = 2/36

For S=12, combinations will be (6,6) = 1

p(S=12) = 1/36

Total probability p(S>10) = (2/36) + (1/36) = 3/36 = 1/12

Multiplication Law of Probability and Conditional Probability :

If events A and B are so related that the occurrence of B is affected by the occurrence of A, then A and B are called dependent events. For two events A and B,

$$p\,(A \cap B) = p(A) * p(B/A)\ ;\ p(A)>0$$
$$= p(B) * p(A/B)\ ;\ p(B)>0 \text{ where}$$

p(B/A) represents the conditional probability of occurrence of B when the event A has already happened. Conditional probabilities p(B/A) and p(A/B) are defined if and only if p(A) # 0 and p(B) # 0 respectively.

For p(B) >0 ; p(A/B) <= p(A), conditional probability p(A/B) is not defined if p(B)=0.

Independent Events : An event B is said to be independent (or statistically independent) of event A, if the conditional probability of B given A i.e. p (B/A) is equal to unconditional probability of B i.e.

$$P(B/A) = p(B)$$

Or events A and B are independent if

$$P(A \cap B) = p(A)*p(B)$$

The probability of happening of event A is the sum of the probabilities of happenings of its mutually exclusive forms A_1, A_2, A_3....... A_n. Symbolically,

$$P(A) = p(A_1) + p(A_2) + \ldots\ldots. P(A_n)$$

The probabilities $p(A_1)$, $p(A_2)$, ... $P(A_n)$ of the mutually exclusive forms of A are known as 'partial probabilities'.

A bag contains 6 white and 3 black balls. Two balls are drawn at random one after the other without replacement. Find the probability that both balls drawn are black.

Total balls = 9 ; Total white balls = 6 ; Total Black balls = 3

Probability of drawing a black ball in first attempt P(A)

$= {}^3C_1/{}^9C_1$

$= 3/9$

Probability of drawing the second black ball given that the first ball drawn is black

$P(B/A) = {}^2C_1/{}^8C_1$

$= 2/8$

The probability that both balls drawn are black $P(A \cap B)$

$= P(A)XP(B/A)$

$= (3/9)X(2/8)$

$= 1/12$

Let $P(A) = 3/7$, $P(B) = 5/8$ and $P(A \cup B) = 3/4$. Find $P(A/B)$ and $P(B/A)$. Find whether A and B are independent events.

$P(A \cup B) = P(A) + P(B) - P(A \cap B)$

$3/4 = 3/7 + 5/8 - P(A \cap B)$

$\Rightarrow P(A \cap B) = (3/7 + 5/8) - 3/4$

$= 17/56$

$P(A \cap B) = P(A) X P(B/A) = P(B) X P(A/B)$

$17/56 = 3/7 X P(B/A)$

$\Rightarrow P(B/A) = 17/24$

$17/56 = 5/8 X P(A/B)$

$P(A/B) = 17/35$

Since P(B/A) # P(B) and P(A/B) # P(A). The events A and B are not independent.

If two dice are thrown, what is the probability that their sum is greater than 10.

In throwing two dices total number of exhaustive cases will be $6^2 = 36$

Let their sum be S. Probability for S>10 means p(S=11)+p(S=12)

For S=11, combinations will be (6,5),(5,6) = 2

p(S=11) = 2/36

For S=12, combinations will be (6,6) = 1

p(S=12) = 1/36

Total probability p(S>10) = (2/36) + (1/36) = 3/36 = 1/12

A problem in statistics is given to the three students A, B and C whose chances of solving it are $\frac{1}{2}$, $\frac{3}{4}$, *and* $\frac{1}{4}$ *respectively. What is the probability that the problem is solved.*

Let A, B and C denote the events that the problem is solved by students A, B and C respectively. Then

$P(A) = \frac{1}{2}$; $P(B) = \frac{3}{4}$; $P(C) = \frac{1}{4}$

The problem is solved if at least one of them solves it. Thus, the probability of occurrence of at least one of the three events A, B and C is to be calculated, i.e. $P(A \cup B \cup C)$

$P(A \cup B \cup C)$

$= P(A)+P(B)+P(C)-P(A \cap B)-P(A \cap C)-P(B \cap C)+P(A \cap B \cap C)$

$= P(A)+P(B)+P(C)-P(A)P(B)-P(A)P(C)-P(B)P(C)+P(A)P(B)P(C)$

(A, B and C are independent)

= 1/2+3/4+1/4-(1/2)(3/4)–(1/2)(1/4)–(3/4)(1/4)+(1/2)(3/4)(1/4)

= 1/2 + 3/4 +1/4 +3/32 – [3/8+1/8+3/16]

= 51/32 – 11/16 = (51-22)/32 = 29/32 = 0.90625

This problem can also be solved as

$P(A \cup B \cup C) = 1 - P(\overline{A \cup B \cup C}))$

$= 1 - P(\overline{A} \cap \overline{B} \cap \overline{C})$

$= 1 - P(\overline{A})\, P(\overline{B})\, P(\overline{C})$

$= 1 - [(1 - 1/2)]*[(1 - 3/4)]*[(1-1/4)]$

$= 1 -[1/2*1/4*3/4] = 1 - 3/32 = 29/32 = 0.90625$

The odds against A solving a certain problem are 4 to 3 and odds in favour of B solving the problem are 7 to 5. What is the probability that the problem is solved, if they both try independently.

Let E_1 denote the that A solves the problem and E_2 denote the event that B solves the problem.

4 : 3 against ; 7 : 5 favour

Thus

$P(E_1) = 3/(4+3) = 3 / 7$ $\quad$ $P(E_2) = 7/(7+5) = 7 / 12$

$P(\overline{E}_1) = 1 - P(E_1) = 1 - 3/7 = 4/7$;

$P(\overline{E}_2) = 1 - P(E_2) = 1 - 7/12 = 5/12$

The probability that the problem is solved

p = P[at least one of A and B solves it]

= 1 – P[none solves the problem]

$= 1 - P[\overline{E}_1 \cap \overline{E}_2]$

$= 1 - P(\overline{E}_1)\, P(\overline{E}_2)$

$= 1 - (4/7)*(5/12) = 1 - 5/21 = 16/21 = 0.7619$

The chances that doctor A will diagnose a disease X correctly is 60%. The chances that a patient dies by his treatment after correct diagnosis is 40% and chance of death by wrong diagnosis is 70%. A patient of doctor A, who had disease X died. What is the probability that his disease was diagnosed correctly.

Let E_1 : disease X is diagnosed correctly by doctor A

E_2 : patient who had disease X has died

Then, $P(E_1) = 0.6 \Rightarrow P(\overline{E}_1) = 1 - 0.6 = 0.4$

And $P(E_2/E1) = 0.4$ and $P(E_2/\overline{E}_1) = 0.7$

$$P(E_1/E_2) = \frac{P(E_1 \cap E_2)}{P(E_2)}$$

$(E_2 \cap E_1)$ and $(E_2 \cap \overline{E}_1)$ are mutually disjoint events

$$P(E_2) = P[(E_2 \cap E_1) \cup (E_2 \cap \overline{E}_1)]$$

$$= P(E_2 \cap E_1) + P(E_2 \cap \overline{E}_1)$$

thus,

$$P(E_1/E_2) = \frac{P(E_1 \cap E_2)}{P(E_2 \cap E_1) + P(E_2 \cap \overline{E}_1)}$$

$$= \frac{P(E_1)\,P(E_2/E_1)}{P(E_1)P(E_2/E_1)+P(E_1)P(E_2/\overline{E}_1)}$$

$$= \frac{0.6*0.4}{(0.6*0.4)+(0.4*0.7)} = \frac{6}{13} = 0.4615$$

CHAPTER 6

BINOMIAL DISTRIBUTION

It was first discovered by James Bernoulli (1654-1705) in the year 1700.

A random variable X which takes two values 0 and 1, with probability q and p respectively, i.e. $p(X=1) = p$, $p(X=0) = q$; $p+q = 1$, is called a binomial variate and is said to have a binomial distribution.

The probability of x successes and (n-x) failures in n independent trials is given by the compound probability theorem and is equal to

$$p^x q^{n-x}$$

But x successes in n trials can occur in ${}^nC_x$ ways, hence the probability of x successes in n trials in any order is given by the addition theorem of probability

$${}^nC_x\, p^x q^{n-x} \quad (x = 0,1,2\ldots\ldots n)$$

⇨ $(q+p)^n$, binomial expression

Probability Mass Function : A random variable is said to follow a binomial distribution if it assumes only non-negative values and its probability mass function is given by

$$P(X=x) = {}^nC_x\, p^x q^{n-x},\ x = 0,1,2\ldots\ldots ;\ q = 1 - p$$

0, otherwise

n and p, the independent constants are called the parameters of the distribution. N is also called the degree of the distribution.

The mean and variance of a binomial distribution is given by np and npq respectively.

The mean is always greater than the variance. The distribution which shows variance is greater than the mean is 'Negative Binomial Distribution'.

$$\beta_1 = (1-2p)^2 / npq$$

$$\beta_2 = 3 + (1-6pq) / npq$$

Moment generating function (MGF) = $(q + pe^t)^n$

Additive property of a Binomial Distribution

Let two independent variables X and Y be distributed binomially,

$$X \sim B(n_1, p_1)\ ;\ Y \sim B(n_2, p_2)$$

then the random variable (X+Y) is not a binomial variable. But if X_i, (i=1,2....k) are independent binomial variates with parameters (n_i, p), (i=1,2....k), then their sum

ΣX_i is a binomial variate with Σn_i and p as parameters.

Fitting of a Binomial Distribution

In an experiment in which the probability of success for each outcome is same, binomial distribution can be fitted. Some examples where this distribution can be fitted

1. Getting a head/tail in tossing a coin (p=1/2)
2. Getting any number from 1 to 6 in a die throw (p=1/6)
3. Counting for female/male live births (p=1/2)

Recurrence Formula

$$P(x) = {}^nC_x\, p^x\, q^{\,n-x}\ ;\ x = 0,1,..n$$

$$P(x+1) = {}^nC_{x+1}\, p^{x+1}\, q^{\,n-(x+1)}\ ;\ x = 0,1,...n$$

$$\frac{P(x+1)}{P(x)} = \frac{n-x}{x+1} * \frac{p}{q}$$

$$P(x+1) = P(x) * \frac{n-x}{(x+1)} * \frac{p}{q}$$

1. The mean and the variance of the distribution are to be calculated and equated to np and npq respectively to get the values of p and q.
2. Calculate $P(0) = q^n$; the expected frequency $f(0) = N * q^n$
3. The expected frequencies for all X=1,2....n are calculated by using recurrence formula.

TABLE 6.0 : In 103 litres of 4 mice the number of litters which contained 0, 1, 2, 3, 4 females are recorded. Fit a binomial distribution.

Number of Females (X)	*Number of litters (f)*
0	8
1	32
2	34
3	24
4	5
	103

Solution :

$$\text{Mean} = \bar{x} = \Sigma f_i * x_i / \Sigma f_i$$

$$= 192/103 = 1.86$$

$$n*p = 1.86 \Rightarrow p = 1.86/4 = 0.47$$

$$q = (1-p) = 0.53$$

$$p/q = 0.87$$

$$p(0) = q^n = (0.53)^4 = 0.081$$

expected frequency = N*p(x)

x	*f*	*f*x*	*(n–x)*p / (x+1)q*	*p(x)*	*Expected frequency*
0	8	0	3.491	0.081	8.37 = 8
1	32	32	1.309	0.283	29.13 = 29
2	34	68	0.582	0.370	38.16 = 38
3	24	72	0.218	0.215	22.18 = 22
4	5	20	0.000	0.047	4.83 = 5
	103	192			102

A manufacture of cotton pins knows that 5% of his products are defective. If the next 10 pins are tested, what is the probability that 4 of them are defective.

Let x be the number of defective pins, n=10. Then x is a binomial random variable with p, the probability that a single pin is defective,

$$p = 0.05 ; q = 1-p = 0.95$$

The probability distribution of x will be

$$P(x) = {}^{n}C_x\, p^x\, q^{\,n-x} \quad (x = 0,1,2\ldots\ldots 10)$$

we have $n = 10,\ x=4,\ p=0.05$

$$P(4) = {}^{10}C_4\, p^4\, q^{\,10-4}$$

$$= \frac{10.9.8.7}{4.3.2.1}\,(0.05)^4 * (0.95)^6$$

$$= 210*0.00000625*0.735091890625$$

$$= 0.000964808106445$$

Mean = np = 10*0.05 = 0.5

Variance = npq = 10*0.05*0.95 = 0.475

standard deviation = sqrt(0.475) = 0.6892

similarly $P(0) = {}^{10}C_0\, p^0\, q^{\,10-0} = 1.(0.05)^0.(.95)^{10} = 0.598736$

$P(1) = 0.3151247$

$P(2) = 0.0746347$

thus p(x<=2) = p(x=0)+p(x=1)+p(x=2) =0.598+0.315+0.074 = 0.987

also p(x>2) = 1 – p(x<=2) = 1–0.987 = 0.013

CHAPTER 7

POISSON DISTRIBUTION

It was discovered by S.D. Poisson (1781-1840) in 1837. It is a limiting case of binomial distribution under the following conditions

1. The number of trials is indefinitely large i.e. n -> ~
2. The constant probability for success for each trial is indefinitely small i.e. p -> 0
3. np = finite = λ, a positive real number

   $np = \lambda \Rightarrow p = \lambda/n$

Probability Mass Function : A random variable X is said to follow a Poisson distribution if it assumes only non-negative values and its probability mass function is given by

$$P(x) = \frac{e^{-\lambda}\,\lambda^{x}}{x\,!}\ ;\ x=0,1,\ldots\ldots.$$

$$= 0,\ \text{otherwise}$$

The parameter of the distribution is λ and $\lambda>0$.

The mean and variance of the distribution are equal to λ .

$\beta_1 = 1/\lambda\ ;\ \beta_2 = 3 + 1/\lambda\ ;\ \gamma_1 = 1/\lambda\ ;\ \gamma_2 = \beta_2 - 3 = 1/\lambda$

Moment Generating Function (MGF) = $e^{\lambda}\,(e^{t} - 1)$

Additive Property : Sum of independent Poisson variates is also a Poisson variate. If X_i (i=1,2..n) are independent poisson variates with parameters λ_i (i=1,2...n) respectively, then ΣX_i is also a poisson variate with parameter $\Sigma \lambda_i$.

The difference of two independent poisson variate is not a poisson variate.

A manufacturer of cotton pins knows that 2% of his products are defective. If he sells cotton pins in boxes of 200 and guarantees that not more than 5 pins will be defective, what is the probability that a box will have the guaranteed quantity ?

n=200, p=0.02

Mean = λ = nxp = 200x0.02 =4

$e^{-\lambda} = e^{-4} = (1-4+(4^2/2)-(4^3/6)+(4^4/24)-....) = 0.0183$

for the probability x=r<=5,

$$P(x<=5) = \Sigma \frac{e^{-4}\lambda^5}{5!};\ x=0,1,.......$$

$= e^{-4}(1+4+(4^2/2)+(4^3/6)+(4^4/24)+(4^5/120)$

= 0.0183(42.87)

= 0.7845

Fitting of a Poisson Distribution

In an experiment, in which probability of success is very low or tends to 0, obviously for this, n will be large, poisson distribution is fitted.

1. Number of printing mistakes on each page of the book.
2. Number of erythrocytes per square in single blood specimen.

Recurrence Formulae :

$$P(x) = \frac{e^{-\lambda}\lambda^x}{x!};\ x=0,1,.......$$

$$P(x+1) = \frac{e^{-\lambda}\lambda^{x+1}}{(x+1)!};\ x=0,1,.......$$

$$\frac{P(x+1)}{P(x)} = \frac{\lambda}{(x+1)}$$

$$P(x+1) = P(x)\frac{\lambda}{(x+1)}$$

1. Calculate the mean of the distribution i.e. λ
2. Calculate $p(0) = e^{-\lambda} \Rightarrow \log p(0) = -\lambda * \log e$

   $= -\lambda * 0.43429$

   p(0) = antilog (log p(0))

   Expected frequency f(0) = N*p(0)
3. Expected frequencies for all x are then calculated by the use of recurrence formula. (As N is multiplied once for f(0), it is not repeated for all values of x).

TABLE 7.0 : Fit a Poisson distribution to the following data which gives the number of doddens in a sample of clove seeds.

Number of Doddens (X)	*Observed Frequency (f)*
0	56
1	156
2	132
3	92
4	37
5	22
6	4
7	0
8	1
	500

Solution :

Mean $= \bar{x} = \Sigma f_i * x_i / \Sigma f_i$

$= 986/500 = 1.972$

Parameter of poisson distribution $\lambda = 1.97$

$p(0) = e^{-\lambda} = e^{-1.972}$

$\log_{10} p(0) = -1.972 * 0.43429$

$= -0.856419$

$p(0) = 0.139$

Expected frequency $= N * p(x)$

X	*f*	*f*X*	*λ/(x+1)*	*p(x)*	*Expected Frequency*
0	56	0	1.972	0.139	69.59 = 70
1	156	156	.986	0.274	137.05 = 137
2	132	264	.657	0.270	135.08 = 135
3	92	276	.493	0.177	88.70 = 89
4	37	148	.394	0.087	43.63 = 44
5	22	110	.329	0.034	17.14 = 17
6	4	24	.282	0.011	5.59 = 6
7	0	0	.246	0.003	1.55 = 2
8	1	8	.219	0.001	0.37 = 0
	500	986			500

CHAPTER 8

NORMAL DISTRIBUTION

It was discovered by De-Moivre in 1733 as a limiting case of the Binomial distribution. It is a continuous distribution.

Probability Density Function : A random variable X is said to have a Normal distribution with parameters μ (Mean) and σ^2 (Variance) if its density function is given by the probability law :

$$f(x\,;\,\mu,\sigma) = \frac{1}{\sigma * SQRT(2\pi)} \exp\,[-(x-\mu)^2/2\,\sigma^2\,] \qquad -\infty < x < \infty \qquad -\infty < \mu < \infty\,;\ \sigma > 0$$

A random variable X with mean (μ) and variance (σ^2) and follow the normal law is expressed by $X \sim N(\mu\,,\,\sigma^2)$

FIG - 8.1

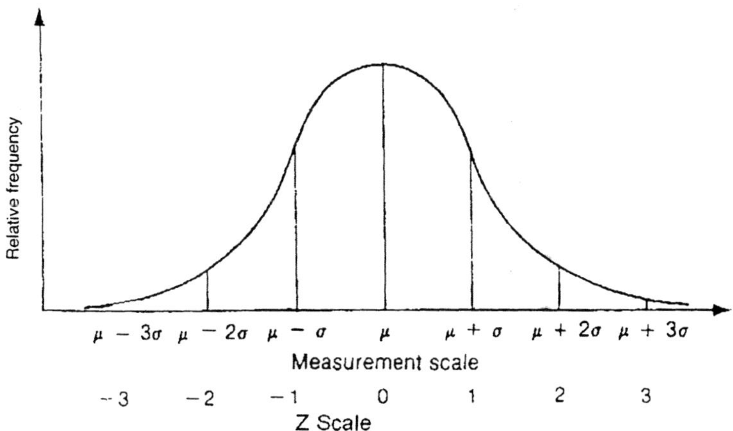

Characteristics

1. If $X \sim N(\mu\,,\,\sigma^2)$ then $Z = (X - \mu)/\sigma$ is a standard normal variate with $E(Z) = 0$ and

$Var(Z) = 1$; $Z \sim N(0,1)$

2. The graph of f(x) is a famous bell shaped curve and symmetrical about line $x=\mu$.
3. The top of the curve is directly above the mean.
4. If σ is large, the curve tends to flatten, otherwise it has a sharp peak.
5. Mean, Median and Mode coincides i.e. mean=median=mode.
6. $\beta_1 = 0$; $\beta_2 = 3$
7. Since f(x) being the probability, it can never be negative so no portion of curve lies below the X axis.
8. Linear combination of independent normal variates is also a normal variate.
9. X-axis is an asymptote to the curve.
10. Area property

$$P(\mu-\sigma < x < \mu+\sigma) = 0.6826$$
$$P(\mu-2\sigma < x < \mu+2\sigma) = 0.9544$$
$$P(\mu-3\sigma < x < \mu+3\sigma) = 0.9973$$

Moment Generating Function (MGF) = $e^{(\mu t + t2\sigma2/2)}$

Important

a. Most distributions eg. Binomial, Poisson can be approximated by Normal distribution.
b. Many sampling distributions eg. Student's 't', chi-square test etc. tend to normality for large samples.
c. The entire theory of small samples tests is based on the assumption that the parent population from which the samples have been drawn follow normal distribution.

Example of Fitting of Normal Distribution

In order to fit Normal distribution to the given data,

first step is to calculate the mean(μ) and standard deviation(σ) from the data.

Second step is to find the standard normal variates corresponding to the lower limit of the class intervals i.e. calculate $z_i = (X_i'-\mu)/\sigma$, where X' is the lower limit of the ith class interval.

Third step is the areas under the normal curve to the left of the ordinate at $z=z_i$ say a_i, are computed from the tables.

Fourth step is the areas for the successive class intervals are obtained by subtraction i.e. $a_{i+1} - a_i$, (i=1.2...).

Finally on multiplying these areas by N, the expected frequencies are obtained.

TABLE 8.0 : Equatorial diameters of homosporous fern, Adiantum capillusveneris L. are given below

Equitorial Diameter(μm)	*f*	*cf*	*snv*	*area*	*diff*	*ef*
30.5-32.5	10	10	–3.08	0.0010		4
32.5-34.5	11	21	–2.57	0.0050	0.0040	14
34.5-36.5	55	76	–2.06	0.0197	0.0147	40
36.5-38.5	43	119	–1.55	0.0606	0.4090	90
38.5-40.5	185	304	–1.03	0.1515	0.0909	150
40.5-42.5	162	466	–0.52	0.3015	0.1500	194
42.5-44.5	262	728	–0.01	0.4960	0.1945	187
44.5-46.5	103	831	0.50	0.3085	0.1875	152
46.5-48.5	120	951	1.01	0.1562	0.1523	91
48.5-50.5	29	980	1.52	0.0643	0.0919	43
50.5-52.5	14	994	2.03	0.0212	0.0431	15
52.5-54.5	3	997	2.54	0.0055	0.0157	4
54.5-56.5	3	1000	3.06	0.0011	0.0044	1
56.5-58.5			3.57	0.0020	0.0090	
	1000					

snv=standard normal variate

Mean = 42.55 ; Median = 42.76 ; Mode = 43.19

Variance = 15.3099 ; Standard Deviation = 3.9128,Kurtosis = 3.276 ; Skewness = –0.21

FIG - 8.2

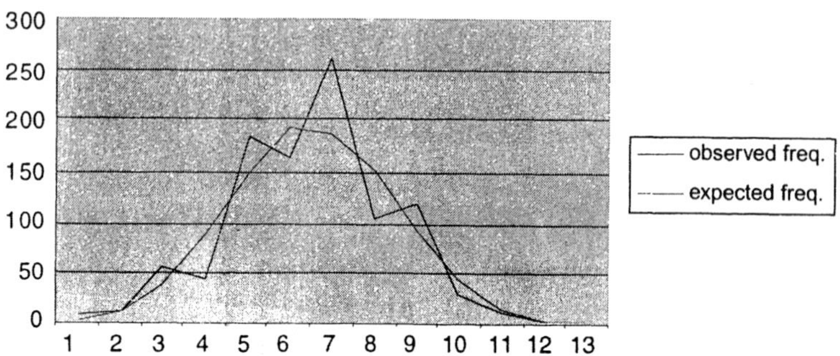

Measures of a Relative Standing

One measure of the relative standing of a particular measurement is its percentile ranking. Let $x_1, x_2 \ldots\ldots x_n$ be a set of n measurements arranged in increasing (or decreasing) order. The pth percentile is a number x such that p% of the measurement falls below the pth percentile and (100-p%) falls above it.

Another measure of relative standing in popular use is the Z-score. The Z-score makes use of the mean and standard deviation of the data set in order to specify the location of a measurement.

The sample Z-score for a measurement x is $Z = (X - \overline{x})/\sigma$

The population Z-score for a measurement x is Z = (X-m)/s. The numerical value of the Z-score reflects the relative standing of the measurement. A large positive Z-score implies that the measurement is larger than almost all other measurements, whereas a large negative Z-score indicates that the measurement is smaller than almost every other measurements. If Z-score is 0 (zero) or near zero, the measurement is located near the middle of the sample or population. In symmetrical distribution, approximately 68% of the measurements will have Z-score between –1 and +1, 95% of the measurements will have Z-score between –2 and +2 and all and almost all the measurements will have a Z-score between –3 and +3.

Example : *Suppose 200 ion workers are selected and annual income of each is determined. The mean and standard deviation are*

Rs. 24000 and 2000. Suppose ankit's annual income is Rs. 22,000, what is his sample Z-score.

Ankit's annual income lies below the mean income

$$Z = (X - \bar{x})/\sigma = (22000\text{-}24000)/2000 = -1.0$$

Ankit's annual income is 1.0 standard deviation below the sample mean or his Z-score is –1.0

CHAPTER 9

CORRELATION

Correlation : Degree of Association

Linear and Non-linear (curvilinear) correlation

The difference between linear and non-linear correlation is based upon the ratio of change between two variables. If the ratio of change in two variables is constant, it is a linear correlation. If the amount of change in one variable does not have a constant ratio of change in other variable, it is a non-linear correlation.

Karl Pearson (1867-1936) developed a formula for Coefficient of Correlation. It is numerical measure of linear relationship between two random variables X and Y and is defined as

$$r(X,Y) = \frac{\text{Covariance } (X,Y)}{\sigma_x \, \sigma_y}$$

$$= \frac{\frac{1}{n}\Sigma\,(X - \bar{x})\,(Y - \bar{y})}{\sqrt{\frac{1}{n}\,\Sigma(X - \bar{x})^2 * \frac{1}{n}\,\Sigma\,(Y - \bar{y})^2}}$$

Limits of correlation coefficient : $-1 <= r(X,Y) <= +1$

FIG - 9.1

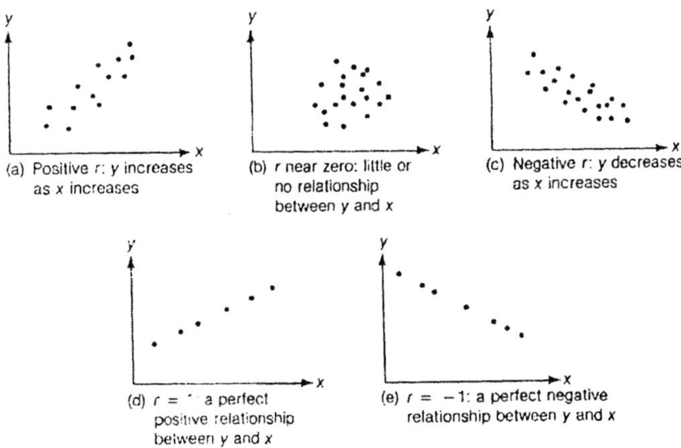

(a) Positive r: y increases as x increases

(b) r near zero: little or no relationship between y and x

(c) Negative r: y decreases as x increases

(d) $r =$ [illegible] a perfect positive relationship between y and x

(e) $r = -1$: a perfect negative relationship between y and x

A high positive correlation indicates that low and high values of one series are respectively associated with low and high values of the other series. A high negative correlation tells us that low and high values of one series are respectively associated with high and low values of the other series.

Characteristics

1. Correlation coefficient is independent of change of origin and scale.
2. Two independent variables are uncorrelated. If X and Y are independent Covariance(X,Y) = 0

Assumption : Pearson's correlation coefficient r is based on the basic assumption that the variables X

If r be the correlation coefficient of n pair of observation (sample) from bivariate normal distribution, Prof. Fisher proved that under null hypothesis

$H_0 : \rho = 0$ i.e. population correlation coefficient is zero.

The statistic

$$t = \frac{r*(n-2)^{1/2}}{(1-r^2)^{1/2}}$$

follows student 't' distribution with (n-2) degree of freedom.

If t_{cal} (calculated) => t_{tab} (tabulated), the correlation coefficient is significant. The Null hypothesis is rejected at certain level of significance, otherwise correlation coefficient is insignificant.

TABLE 9.0: Calculate the correlation coefficient between the temperature of unhusked rice and percentage breakage of grains in milling on the basis of following data

Temp. of unhusked rice(X) 33.9, 34.6, 34.5, 36.9, 37.1, 37.3, 28.8 29.6, 30.7, 31.2, 31.6, 32.2, 33.4, 33.6, 33.6, 33.9

% breakage of grains(Y) 23.3, 29.5, 26.8, 29.5, 30.5, 29.7, 25.6, 25.4, 24.6, 23.6, 26.1, 24.9, 27.0, 25.6, 26.4, 27.2

S.No.	X	Y	$X-\bar{x}$	$Y-\bar{y}$	$(X-\bar{x})^2$	$(Y-\bar{y})^2$	$(X-\bar{x})(Y-\bar{y})$
1	33.9	23.3	.61	–3.31	.37	10.93	–2.0191
2	34.6	29.5	1.31	2.89	1.71	8.37	3.7859

3	34.5	26.8	1.21	.19	1.46	.04	.2299
4	36.9	29.5	3.61	2.89	13.01	8.37	10.4329
5	37.1	30.5	3.81	3.89	14.49	15.16	14.8209
6	37.3	29.7	4.01	3.09	16.05	9.57	12.3909
7	28.8	25.6	–4.49	–1.01	20.19	1.01	4.5349
8	29.6	25.4	–3.69	–1.21	13.64	1.46	4.4649
9	30.7	24.6	–2.59	–2.01	6.73	4.03	5.2059
10	31.2	23.6	–2.29	–3.01	5.26	9.04	6.8929
11	31.6	26.1	–1.69	–.51	2.87	.26	.8619
12	32.2	24.9	–1.09	–1.71	1.20	2.91	1.8639
13	33.4	27.0	.11	.39	.01	.16	.0429
14	33.6	25.6	.31	–1.01	.09	1.01	–.3131
15	33.6	26.4	.31	–.21	.09	.04	–.0651
16	33.9	27.2	.61	.59	.37	.35	.3599
Total	532.9	425.7			97.54	72.77	63.4904

Mean $(\bar{x}) = \Sigma X / n = 532.9/16 = 33.30$

Mean $(\bar{y}) = \Sigma Y / n = 425.7/16 = 26.61$

Standard deviation (X) = $\sqrt{[1/n\ \Sigma(X_i - \bar{x})^2]} = \sqrt{97.54/16} = 2.47$

Standard deviation (Y) = $\sqrt{[1/n\ \Sigma(Y_i - \bar{y})^2]} = \sqrt{72.77/16]} = 2.13$

Covariance (X,Y) = $1/n\ \Sigma (X_i - \bar{x})(Y_i - \bar{y}) = 63.4904/16 = 3.96$

Correlation Coefficient = 3.96/(2.13X2.47) = 3.96 /5.2611 = 0.75

Test for Significance : n = 16 ; n-2 = 14 ; r = 0.75 ; $r^2 = 0.75*0.75 = 0.5625$; $1 - r^2 = 0.4375$

$$t = \frac{r*(n-2)^{1/2}}{(1-r^2)^{1/2}}$$

$$= \frac{0.75*(14)^{1/2}}{(0.4375)^{1/2}} = \frac{0.75*3.71}{0.6614} = \frac{2.7825}{0.6614} = 4.206$$

t_{tab} (14 df) at 5% level of significance is 2.15

Since $t_{cal} > t_{tab}$, Null hypothesis is rejected. The correlation is significant.

RANK CORRELATION

Proficiency in possession of two characteristics A and B, n individuals are given ranks in order of Merit. The rank of characteristic A may differ from that of B for an individual. Let (X_i, Y_i), i=1....n be the ranks of the ith individual in two characteristics A and B respectively.

Pearson's correlation between the ranks X's and Y's is called the rank correlation between A and B for that group of individuals.

Formula Used

$$\bar{x} = \bar{y} = 1/n\ [1+2+.....n) = (n+1)/2$$

$$\sigma_x^2 = \text{SQRT}\ [1/n\ \Sigma\ (X_i - \bar{x})^2]$$

$$= (n^2 - 1)/12 = \sigma_y^2$$

In general, $X_i \# Y_i$ then $d_i = X_i - Y_i$

Let r be the rank correlation coefficient

$$1 - r = (\Sigma\ d_i^2)/2n\ \sigma_x^2$$

$$r = 1 - \frac{6\ (\Sigma\ d_i^2)}{n(n^2-1)}$$

Repeated Ranks : If there is more than one item with the same value in the series, than the Spearman's formula for calculating rank correlation coefficient needs modification. In this case common ranks are given to repeated items. This common rank is the average of the ranks which these items would have assumed if they were slightly different from each other and the next item will get the rank next to the ranks already assumed.

The factor $m(m^2-1)\ /\ 12$ is added to $\Sigma\ d_i^2$, where m is the number of times an item is repeated. This correlation factor is to be added for each repeated value.

TABLE 9.1 : The marks obtained by the students in Mathematics and Biology are given below. Calculate the rank correlation.

Mathematics	65 65 68 63 61 65 60 55 70
Biology	68 68 65 70 70 72 72 58 71

X	Y	$Rank\ X_i$	$Rank\ Y_i$	$D_i = X_i - Y_i$	D^2
65	68	4	6.5	–2.5	6.25
65	68	4	6.5	–2.5	6.25
68	65	2	8.0	–6.0	36.0
63	70	6	4.5	1.5	2.25
61	70	7	4.5	2.5	6.25
65	72	4	1.5	2.5	6.25
60	72	8	1.5	6.5	42.25
55	58	9	9.0	0	0.0
70	71	1	3.0	–2.0	4.0
					109.5

In X, 68 comes three times, the correction factor will be $3*(3^2–1)/12 = 2$

In Y, 68, 70 and 72 comes two times, the correction factor for each will be 0.5

$$\Sigma d_i^2 = 109.5 + 2+0.5+0.5+0.5 = 113$$

$$r = 1 - \frac{6\ (\Sigma d_i^2)}{n(n^2-1)}$$

$$= 1 - \frac{6*113}{9*80}$$

$$= 1 - \frac{678}{720} = 1 - 0.94 = 0.06$$

INTRA CLASS CORRELATION COEFFICIENT

It means within class correlation. In correlation both the variable under consideration measures different characteristics but in Intra Class correlation both the variables measure same characteristics. To examine how the group of members are correlated among themselves with respect to some one of their characteristics, as height of brothers, IQ of twins.

Let F1.......Fn families with K1.....Kn members and Xij (i=1...n ; j= 1.....Ki) denote the measurement on the jth member in the ith family,

The intra class correlation coefficient = $\dfrac{\text{Covariance(X,Y)}}{\sigma_x \sigma_y}$

$$= \frac{\Sigma K_i^2(x_i - x)^2 - \Sigma\Sigma (X_{ij} - x)^2}{\Sigma\Sigma(Ki-1)(X_{ij} - x)^2}$$

where $x_i = \Sigma X_{ij} / K_i$

If Ki = K i.e. if all families have equal members then

$$r' = \frac{1}{k-1}\left\{\frac{K\sigma_m^2}{\sigma^2} - 1\right\}$$

where σ^2 denotes variance of X and σ_m^2 denotes variance of means of the families.

Intra class correlation coefficient

$$r' = \frac{\Sigma(X-\overline{XY})*(Y-\overline{XY})}{Ns^2}$$

$$\overline{XY} = (\Sigma X + \Sigma Y) / 2N$$

$$s^2 = \frac{\Sigma(X-\overline{XY})^2 + \Sigma(Y-\overline{XY})^2}{2N}$$

$$r' = \frac{2\,\Sigma XY - [(\Sigma X+\Sigma Y)^2/2N]}{\Sigma X^2 + \Sigma Y^2 - [(\Sigma X+\Sigma Y)^2/2N]}$$

TABLE 9.2 : Below are given Intelligence Quotients of 13 pairs of identical Male Twins. Calculate intra class correlation.

Pair	*2*	*3*	*4*	*5*	*7*	*10*	*11*	*13*	*17*	*18*	*20*	*22*	*24*
X	97	116	77	126	91	93	76	99	92	84	97	107	117
Y	96	113	83	127	93	95	81	103	99	84	97	100	105

Solution : Intelligence quotients of 13 pairs of Identical male twins

Pair no	*X*	*Y*	*XY*	*X²*	*Y²*
2	97	96	9312	9409	9216
3	116	113	13108	13456	12769
4	77	83	6391	5929	6889
5	126	127	16002	15876	16129
7	91	93	8463	8281	8649

10	93	95	8835	8649	9025
11	76	81	6156	5776	6561
13	99	103	10197	9801	10609
17	92	99	9108	8464	9801
18	84	84	7056	7056	7056
20	97	97	9409	9409	9409
22	107	100	10700	11449	10000
24	117	105	12285	13689	11025
Total	1272	1276	127022	127244	127138

$$r' = \frac{2*(127022) - [(1272+1276)^2/26]}{127244+127138 - [(1272+1276)^2/26]}$$

$$= \frac{254044 - 249704}{254382 - 29704} = \frac{4340}{4678} = +0.9277$$

CHAPTER 10

REGRESSION

It was first used by Sir Francis Galton (British Biometrician), in connection with inheritance of stature. Regression analysis is a mathematical measure of the average relationship between two or more variables in terms of the original data.

Two types of variables are used in regression analysis,

1) The variable whose value is influenced or is to be predicted, called as dependent variable (regressed).

2) The variables used for the prediction, called as independent variable(s) (regressor).

If the variables are related, points in the scatter diagram will cluster round some curve called the "curve of regression". If the curve is straight line, it is called the "line of regression", shows linear regression between variables, otherwise regression is curvilinear.

The line of regression is the line which gives the "best estimate" to the value of one variable for any specific value of the other variable(s).

SIMPLE LINEAR REGRESSION

Let a bivariate distribution (X_i,Y_i) ; $i = 1......n$, where Y is a dependent and X is a independent variable.

Let the line of regression of Y on X be $Y = a + b*X$

According to the principle of least squares, the normal equations to estimate values of a & b are

$$\Sigma Y_i = n*a + b*\Sigma X_i \quad \text{———————} (1)$$

$$\Sigma X_i Y_i = a*\Sigma X_i + b\ \Sigma X_i^2 \quad \text{———————} (2)$$

on dividing equation (1) by n

$$\bar{y} = a + b\,\bar{x}$$

⇨ the regression line of Y on X passes through point ($\bar{x}$,$\bar{y}$), 'b' is the slope of the line of regression of Y on X, the equation is

$$Y - \bar{y} = r\,(\sigma_y/\sigma_x)\,(X - \bar{x})$$

Similarly, equation of the line of regression of X on Y becomes,

$$X - \bar{x} = r\,(\sigma_x/\sigma_y)\,(Y - \bar{y})$$

The point of intersection of the two regression lines is ($\bar{x}$, $\bar{y}$).

There are always two lines of regression. The line of regression of Y on X is used to estimate the value of Y for any value of X i.e. when Y is a dependent variable & X is an independent variable.

Similarly, for the line of regression of X on Y, X is a dependent and Y is an independent variable.

The regression equation of Y on X or X on Y is obtained by minimizing the sum of squares of the errors parallel to Y or X axis respectively.

In the case of prefect correlation i.e. r = 1, the two lines of regression coincides.

Standard Error of the estimate

$$S_{y.x} = SQRT\ \{[\Sigma Y^2 - (a*\Sigma Y + b\ \Sigma XY)]/n\}$$

$$F = \frac{R^2/k}{(1-R^2)/(n-k-1)}$$

where R^2 = squared correlation between X and Y (coefficient of determination) or between a linear combination X_1, X_2, ... and Y; k= number of independent variables{in this case 1} ; n = total sample size.

In the regression analysis , the Null hypothesis, H0 : $R^2=0$, is rejected if calculated value of F is greater than tabulated value at {k, n–k–1} df, the significant F ratio means that the R^2 is statistically significant .

The probability distribution of the random error component, ε. Estimated variance σ^2 of ε ,

$SSE = SS_{yy} - b1*SS_{xy}$

To estimate σ^2, SSE is divided by degrees of freedom for error, n–2.

$s^2=SSE/n-2$; $s=sqrt\ (s^2)$

REGRESSION COEFFICIENTS

"b_{yx}", the slope of the lines of regression of Y on X is called the coefficient of regression of Y on X. It gives the increment in the value of the dependent variable Y(X) corresponding to a unit change in the value of independent variable X(Y).

$$b_{yx} = r\,(\sigma_y / \sigma_x)$$

1. Correlation coefficient is the geometric mean of two regression coefficients.
2. If one regression coefficient is greater than unity, the other must be less than unity.
3. Arithmetic mean of regression coefficient is greater than the correlation coefficient.
4. Regression coefficients are independent of the change of origin but not of scale.

ANGLE BETWEEN TWO LINES OF REGRESSION

If θ be the angle between two regression lines,

$$\theta = \tan{-1}\,\frac{(1-r^2)*(\sigma_x*\sigma_y)}{r*(\sigma_x^2+\sigma_y^2)\}}\quad \theta \text{ will be acute angle}$$

$$\theta = \tan{-1}\,\frac{(r^2-1)*(\sigma_x*\sigma_y)}{r*(\sigma_x^2+\sigma_y^2)\}}\quad \theta \text{ will be obtuse angle}$$

If r = 0, the lines of regression become perpendicular to each other i.e. if the variables are uncorrelated θ = 90°

If r = 1, the lines of regression will coincide i.e. when perfect correlation θ = 0°

TABLE 10.0 : Intravenous injections of Glucose (X) and Glucose retained (Y) both in gm/kg bw /hr for 18 hospital patients are given. Determine the estimating equation.

Case	*X*	*Y*	*X*²	*Y*²	*XY*
1	0.073	0.072	0.005329	0.005184	0.005256
2	0.159	0.154	0.025281	0.023716	0.024486
3	0.222	0.217	0.049284	0.047089	0.048174
4	0.390	0.290	0.152100	0.084100	0.113100

5	0.463	0.458	0.214369	0.209764	0.212054
6	0.512	0.5	0.262144	0.25	0.256
7	0.753	0.686	0.567009	0.470596	0.516558
8	0.926	0.832	0.857476	0.692224	0.770432
9	1.13	0.82	1.2769	0.6724	0.9266
10	1.16	1.04	1.3456	1.0816	1.2064
11	1.193	0.871	1.423249	0.758641	1.039103
12	1.301	1.065	1.692601	1.134225	1.385565
13	1.323	1.132	1.750329	1.281424	1.497636
14	1.46	1.43	2.1316	2.0449	2.0878
15	1.59	1.44	2.5281	2.0736	2.2896
16	1.824	1.307	3.326976	1.708249	2.383968
17	1.964	1.953	3.841600	3.814209	3.827880
18	2.214	1.565	4.910656	2.449225	3.468040
Total	18.655	15.832	26.360603	18.801146	22.058652

$$\overline{X} = 18.655/18 = 1.036 \; ; \; \overline{Y} = 15.832/18 = 0.88$$

To estimate the amount of glucose retained, we use the estimating equation

$$Y = a + b*X$$

The two normal equations will be

$$15.832 = 18a + 18.655b \qquad \text{———I}$$

$$22.058652 = 18.655a + 26.360603b \qquad \text{———II}$$

multiplying equation I by 1.036389 and substracting from equation II

$$22.058652 = 18.655a + 26.360603b \qquad \text{———II}$$

$$16.408111 = 18.655a + 19.333837b$$

$$- \qquad - \qquad -$$

$$5.650541 = 7.026766b$$

⇨ $b = 0.804145$

Substituting the value of 'b' in equation I

$$15.832 = 18a + (18.655)*(0.804145)$$

$$18a = 0.830675$$

⇨ a = 0.046149

Thus, the estimating equation becomes **Y = 0.046 + 0.804 X**

The value of Y′ is calculated by putting the values of X in the estimating equation and both the values i.e. Y and Y′ are plotted to get a line graph.

TABLE 10.1

Y	.072	.154	0.217	.290	.458	.5	.686	.832	.820	1.04
	.871	1.065	1.132	1.43	1.44	1.307	1.953	1.565		
Y'	.105	.174	.224	.360	.418	.458	.651	.791	.955	.979
	1.005	1.092	1.110	1.220	1.324	1.512	1.625	1.826		

Standard Error of the Estimate

$S_{y.x}$ = SQRT {[ΣY² – (a∗ΣY + b ΣXY)]/n}

= SQRT{[18.801146 – (0.046149∗15.832)+(0.804145∗22.058652)]/18}

= 0.136

$S_{y.x}$ = measure of general reliableness of estimates

When X = 1.5, Y = 1.252 + 0.136 = 1.388

Fig - 10.1

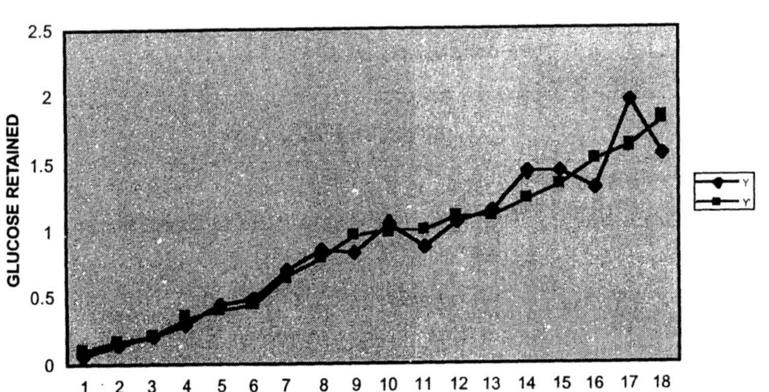

Step 1 : First hypothesize a straight-line probabilistic model to relate (Y) to the (X).

$$Y = a + b1*X + \varepsilon$$

Step 2 : Estimate the unknown parameters

$$SS_{xx} = \Sigma X_i^2 - \frac{(\Sigma X_i)^2}{N} = 26.360603 - \frac{(18.655)^2}{18}$$

$$= 26.360603 - 19.333835 = 7.026$$

$$SS_{yy} = \Sigma Y_i^2 - \frac{(\Sigma Y_i)^2}{N} = 18.801146 - \frac{(15.832)^2}{18}$$

$$= 18.801146 - 13.925124 = 4.876$$

$$SSxy = \Sigma (X_i * Y_i) - \frac{(\Sigma X_i)(\Sigma Y_i)}{N}$$

$$= 22.058652 - \frac{(18.655*15.832)}{18}$$

$$= 22.058652 - 1.40811 = 5.6505$$

The least squares estimate of the slope b and the intercept a are

$$b = \frac{SS_{xy}}{SS_{xx}} = \frac{5.6505}{7.026} = 0.80422$$

$$a = \overline{Y} - b\,\overline{X} = \frac{15.832}{18} - \left[.80422*\frac{18.655}{18}\right]$$

$$= 0.88 - 0.833 = 0.047$$

so the least square equation is **$Y = 0.047 + 0.80422*X$**

Step 3 : The probability distribution of the random error component, ε. Estimated variance σ^2 of ε,

$$SSE = SS_{yy} - b*SS_{xy}$$

$$= 4.876 - (0.80422*5.6505)$$

$$= 4.876 - 4.5442 = 0.3318$$

to estimate σ^2, SSE is divided by the degrees of freedom for error, n-2 thus

$$s^2 = SSE/n\text{-}2 = 0.3318/16 = 0.3318$$

$$s = 0.139$$

Step 4 : A null hypothesis is set H0 : b = 0 i.e. there is no linear relationship between X and Y. To check the usefulness of the hypothesized model i.e. whether X really contributes information for the prediction of Y using a straight-line model,

$$\text{Test statistic } t = \frac{b}{s / SQRT(SS_{xx})} \text{ is tested}$$

For $\alpha = 0.05$, reject H0 if

$$t > t_{\alpha/2} \quad \text{or} \quad t < - t_{\alpha/2}$$

for n=18, df = n-2 = 18-2 = 16 and $t_{0.025} = 2.12$

$$t \text{ statistic} = \frac{0.80422}{0.1439 / \text{sqrt}(7.026)} = \frac{.80422}{0.05428} = 14.816$$

since t_{cal} is much greater than t_{tab}, null hypothesis is rejected. It means X contributes information for the prediction of Y. Additional information about the relationship by forming a confidence interval for the slope b1. A 95% confidence interval is

$$b \pm t_{0.025} * s/\text{sqrt}(SSxx)$$
$$= 0.80422 \pm (2.12)*(0.05428)$$
$$= 0.80422 \pm 0.1150736 = (0.91929, 0.68914)$$

Another measure of the usefulness of the model is the coefficient of correlation r,

$$r = \frac{SS_{xy}}{SQRT(SS_{xx} * SS_{yy})} = \frac{5.6505}{5.8531} = 0.9653$$

The high correlation provides further support that b differs from 0 and the variable Y and X are highly correlated. The coefficient of determination $R^2 = (0.9653)^2 = 0.9318$ which implies 93% of the sum of squares of deviations of the Y values about mean is explained by X. All signs points to a strong linear relationship between Y and X.

Step 5 : This model now can be used for prediction of Y values. Predicted value of Y for the value of $X = X_p = 0.073$ will be

$$Y = a + b * X_p$$
$$= 0.047 + (0.80422)*(0.073)$$
$$= 0.05314$$

for 95% prediction interval,

$$Y \pm t_{0.025} * s * SQRT[1 + (1/n) + [(X_p - x)^2 / SS_{xx}]]$$
$$= 0.05314 \pm (2.12)*(0.139)*SQRT[1+(1/18)+[(0.073-1.036)^2/7.026]]$$
$$= 0.05314 \pm (2.12)*(0.139)*SQRT(1.19199)$$
$$= 0.05314 \pm 0.3217 \text{ or } (0.3748)$$

Fish Length-Weight

$$W = a L^b$$

$$\text{Log } W = \text{Log } a + b \text{ Log } L$$

Normal equations are

$$\Sigma \text{ Log } W = N * \text{Log } a + b * \Sigma \log L \quad \ldots (1)$$

$$\Sigma(\text{Log } W \text{ X Log } L) = \text{Log } a \text{ X } \Sigma \log L + b\, \Sigma(\log L)^2 \quad \ldots (2)$$

$$\text{Log } a = \frac{\Sigma \text{ Log } W \text{ x}(\Sigma(\log L)^2) - \Sigma \log L \text{ x } \Sigma(\log L \text{ x Log } W)}{N \text{ x } \Sigma(\log L)^2 - (\Sigma \log L)^2}$$

$$a = \text{antilog(Log a)}$$

$$b = \frac{\Sigma \text{ Log } W - N \text{ Log } a}{\Sigma \text{ Log } L}$$

TABLE 10.2 : Fish length and weight obtained from a pond of Department of Aquaculture

Length (L)	*Weight (W)*	*Log W*	*Log L*	*Log W × Log L*	*(Log L)^2*
14.6	98.0	1.991226	1.164353	2.318490	1.355718
14.9	110.2	2.042182	1.173186	2.395859	1.376336
15.5	134.4	2.128399	1.190332	2.533501	1.416890
16.3	142.1	2.152594	1.212188	2.609348	1.469399
17.4	169.0	2.227887	1.240549	2.763803	1.538962
17.6	168.5	2.226600	1.245513	2.773258	1.551302
18.5	200.0	2.301030	1.267172	2.915800	1.605724
18.7	210.6	2.323458	1.271842	2.955071	1.617581
18.9	208.4	2.318898	1.276462	2.959984	1.629355
20.7	232.0	2.365488	1.315970	3.112912	1.731778
22.0	241.1	2.382197	1.342423	3.197916	1.802099
22.8	247.3	2.393224	1.357935	3.249842	1.843987
23.3	249.7	2.397419	1.367356	3.278124	1.869662
23.8	253.0	2.403121	1.376577	3.308080	1.894964
24.3	256.3	2.408749	1.385606	3.337577	1.919905
289.30	2920.60	34.062472	19.187464	43.709565	24.623692

$$\text{Log } a = \frac{(34.0624 \text{x} 24.6236) - (19.1874 \text{x} 43.7095)}{15 \text{x} 24.6236 - (19.1874)^2}$$

$$= 0.06725/1.19768 = 0.05615$$

$$\Rightarrow \quad a = 1.138$$

$$b = \frac{34.0624 - (15 \text{x} 0.05615)}{19.1874}$$

$$= \frac{33.2209}{19.1874} = 1.731$$

The equation will be $W = 1.138\ L^{1.731}$

MULTIPLE REGRESSION

Probalistic models that include terms involving X^2, X^3 (or higher order terms), or more than one independent variable are called Multiple Regression Models. The general form of this model is

$$Y = b_0 + b_1 * X_1 + b_2 * X_2 + \ldots\ldots + b_k * X_k \ldots + \varepsilon$$

where Y is the response variable, $b_0, b_1, b_2 \ldots b_k$ are the parameters with unknown values, $X_1, X_2, X_3 \ldots X_k$ are the information contributing variables that are measured without error and ε is a random error component .

The dependent variable Y is written as a function of k independent variables, X_1, $X_2 \ldots\ldots X_k$. The random error term is added to make the model probabilistic rather than deterministic. The value of coefficient bi determines the contribution of the independent variable X_i given that the other X variables are held constant and b0 is Y-intercept.

Estimating equation for three variables

The estimating equation will be

$$Y = a + b\, X_1 + c\, X_2$$

Y = computed value obtained from the given values of X_1 and X_2

a = is the constant in the equation in which Y is estimated by using X_1 and X_2

b = indicates the amount of change in the computed value of Y which accompanies a change of one unit in X_1 when effect of X_2 is also being considered c = indicates the amount of change in the computed value of Y which accompanies a change of one unit in X_2 when effect of X_1 is also being considered a, b, c can also be denoted as $a_{1.23}$, $b_{12.3}$ and $c_{13.2}$

The three normal equations to be solved to get the values of a, b and c will be

$$\Sigma Y = N a + b\,\Sigma X_1 + c\,\Sigma X_2 \quad ...(i)$$

$$\Sigma YX_1 = a\,\Sigma X_1 + b\,\Sigma X_1^2 + c\,\Sigma X_1 X_2 \quad ...(ii)$$

$$\Sigma YX_2 = a\,\Sigma X_2 + b\,\Sigma X_1 X_2 + c\,\Sigma X_2^2 \quad ...(iii)$$

Instead of using Y, X_1, X_2 as variables, y, x_1 and x_2 can be used respectively as they denote the deviations from respective means then the estimating equation becomes

$$Y = a + b\,x_1 + c\,x_2$$

And the normal equations are

$$\Sigma y = N a + b\,\Sigma x_1 + c\Sigma x_2 \quad ...(i)$$

$$\Sigma y\,x_1 = b\,\Sigma x_1^2 + c\,\Sigma x_1x_2 \quad ...(ii)$$

$$\Sigma y\,x_2 = b\,\Sigma x_1x_2 + c\,\Sigma x_2^2 \quad ...(iii)$$

from equation i, a = 0 because $\Sigma y = \Sigma x_1 = \Sigma x_2$

estimating equation becomes $y = bx_1 + cx_2$

and the two constants b & c can be obtained by solving equations A & B

$$\Sigma y\,x_1 = b\,\Sigma x_1^2 + c\,\Sigma x_1x_2 \text{ —— A}$$

$$\Sigma y\,x_2 = b\,\Sigma x_1x_2 + c\,\Sigma x_2^2 \text{ —— B}$$

The sums of the squared deviations and the sums of the products of the deviations are obtained from the following expressions

$$\Sigma y^2 = \Sigma Y^2 - (\Sigma Y)^2/N$$

$$\Sigma x_1^2 = \Sigma X_1^2 - (\Sigma X_1)^2/N$$

$$\Sigma x_2^2 = \Sigma X_2^2 - (\Sigma X_2)^2/N$$

$$\Sigma yx_1 = \Sigma YX_1 - \Sigma Y\,\Sigma X_1/N$$

$$\Sigma yx_2 = \Sigma YX_2 - \Sigma Y\,\Sigma X_2/N$$

$$\Sigma x_1x_2 = \Sigma X_1X_2 - \Sigma X_1\Sigma X_2/N$$

TABLE 10.3 : The two independent variables, length of bones i.e. radius (X1) and ulna (X2) and dependent variable i.e. total height (Y) of 15 young males are given below. All measurements are in cms. The estimating equation is to be determined.

S.No.	Y	X1	X2	YX1	YX2	X1X2	YY	XX1	XX2
1	171	25.30	27.20	4326.30	4651.20	688.16	29241.00	640.09	739.84
2	156	23.20	25.20	3619.20	3931.20	584.64	24336.00	538.24	635.04
3	171	25.20	27.30	4309.20	4668.30	687.96	29241.00	635.04	745.29
4	184	28.40	31.00	5225.60	5704.00	880.40	33856.00	806.56	961.00
5	168	23.40	25.80	3931.20	4334.40	603.72	28224.00	547.56	665.64
6	173	26.00	27.80	4498.00	4809.40	722.80	29929.00	676.00	772.84
7	175	25.00	24.20	4375.00	4235.00	605.00	30625.00	625.00	585.64
8	161	25.70	27.10	4137.70	4363.10	696.47	25921.00	660.49	734.41
9	166	25.30	26.20	4199.80	4349.20	662.86	27556.00	640.09	686.44
10	155	22.40	24.50	3472.00	3797.50	548.80	24025.00	501.76	600.25
11	160	25.10	26.10	4016.00	4176.00	655.11	25600.00	630.01	681.21
12	160	25.20	26.00	4032.00	4160.00	655.20	25600.00	635.04	676.00
13	165	26.30	26.50	4339.50	4372.50	696.95	27225.00	691.69	702.25
14	158	24.50	26.30	3871.00	4155.40	644.35	24964.00	600.25	691.69
15	167	26.10	27.40	4358.70	4575.80	715.14	27889.00	681.21	750.76
Total	2490	377.10	398.60	62711.20	66283.00	10047.56	414232.00	9509.03	10628.30

$$\Sigma y^2 = \Sigma Y^2 - (\Sigma Y)^2/N$$
$$= 414232 - (2490)^2/15$$
$$= 892$$

$$\Sigma x_1^2 = \Sigma X_1^2 - (\Sigma X_1)^2/N$$
$$= 9509.03 - (377.1)^2/15$$
$$= 28.74$$

$$\Sigma x_2^2 = \Sigma X_2^2 - (\Sigma X_2)^2/N$$
$$= 1028.3 - (398.6)^2/15$$
$$= 36.17$$

$$\Sigma yx_1 = \Sigma YX_1 - \Sigma Y \Sigma X_1/N$$
$$= 62711.2 - (2490*377.1)/15$$
$$= 112.6$$

$$\Sigma yx_2 = \Sigma YX_2 - \Sigma Y \Sigma X_2/N$$
$$= 66283 - (2490*398.6)/15$$
$$= 115.4$$

$$\Sigma x_1x_2 = \Sigma X_1X_2 - \Sigma X_1 \Sigma X_2/N$$
$$= 10047.56 - (377.1*398.6)/15$$
$$= 26.76$$

The two simultaneous equations A & B become

$$112.6 = 28.74b + 26.76c \text{ ———— A}$$
$$115.4 = 26.76b + 36.17c \text{ ———— B}$$

Multiplying equation B by 1.074 and subtracting from equation A

$$112.6 = 28.74b + 26.76c$$
$$-123.93 = -28.74b + -38.84c$$

$$-11.33 = -12.08c$$
$$\Rightarrow c = 0.93$$

substituting value of c in equation A,

$$112.6 = 28.74b + 26.76*0.93$$
$$112.6 - 24.88 = 28.74b$$
$$87.72 = 28.74b \Rightarrow b = 3.052$$

the value of 'a' can be calculated by the formula

$$a = [\Sigma Y - b\Sigma X_1 - c\ \Sigma X_2]/N$$

$$a = [2490-(377.1*3.052)-(398.6*0.93)]/15$$

$$a = (2490-1521.6)/15$$

$$a = 968.4/15 = 64.56$$

The estimating equation becomes $Y = 64.56 + 3.052\ X_1 + 0.93\ X_2$

Let $X_1 = 24.2$ and $X_2 = 26.0$, $Y = 64.56 + 3.052*24.2 + 0.93*26$

$$= 64.56+73.85+24.18$$

$$= 162.59$$

Standard Error of the Estimate

$$S\ 1.23 = \text{SQRT}\ \frac{\Sigma Y^2 - (a\ \Sigma Y + b\ \Sigma YX_1 + c\ \Sigma YX_2)}{N}$$

$$= \text{SQRT}\left[\frac{414232 - [(2490*64.56)+(3.052*62711.2)+(0.93*66283)]}{15}\right]$$

$$= \text{SQRT}\ (414232 - 413792.09)/15$$

$$= \text{SQRT}\ (440/15) = \text{SQRT}(29.33) = 5.42$$

Thus 68% of actual height values could be expected to fall with ± 5.42 cm of those obtained from the estimating equation.

Coefficient of Multiple Determination

It is the proportion of total variation that has been explained by use of the multiple estimating equation.

$$R^2_{1.23} = \frac{a\ \Sigma Y + b\ \Sigma YX_1 + c\ \Sigma YX_2 - (\Sigma Y)^2/N}{\Sigma Y^2 - (\Sigma Y)^2/N}$$

$$= \frac{(64.56*2490) + (3.052*62711.2) + (0.93*66283) - (2490)^2/15}{414232 - (2490)^2/15}$$

$$= \frac{160754.4+191394.5+61643.19 - 413340}{414232-413340}$$

$$= \frac{413792.09 - 413340}{892} = \frac{452.09}{892} = 0.51$$

$$R_{1.23} = \text{SQRT}\ (0.51) = 0.71$$

REGRESSION USING QUALITATIVE VARIABLES

TABLE 10.4 : 50 employees of a company were asked to fill a form which contained following variables, quantitative : total absentism in a month(Y), age(X1), number of dependents(X2), qualitative: Alcoholism(X3), education background(X4), Indebtedness(X5) and other earnings(X6). The data were used to obtain a regression equation between dependent(Y) and independent variables(X).

S.No.	*Y*	*X1*	*X2*	*X3*	*X4*	*X5*	*X6*	*YX1*	*YX2*	*YX3*	*YX4*	*YX5*	*YX6*
1	15	50	8	1	1	0	0	750	120	15	15	0	0
2	14	37	7	0	1	0	1	518	98	0	14	0	14
3	12	45	6	0	0	0	1	540	72	0	0	0	12
4	14	47	4	1	1	0	1	658	56	14	14	0	14
5	13	35	8	1	1	0	0	455	104	13	13	0	0
6	12	39	7	0	1	0	1	468	84	0	12	0	12
7	10	36	5	1	0	1	0	360	50	10	0	10	0
8	13	46	4	1	0	0	0	598	52	13	0	0	0
9	15	38	7	0	1	0	1	570	105	0	15	0	15
10	10	41	8	1	0	0	1	410	80	10	0	0	10
11	8	43	6	0	0	0	1	344	48	0	0	0	8
12	5	35	7	0	1	0	0	175	35	0	5	0	0
13	7	38	6	0	0	1	0	266	42	0	0	7	0
14	4	44	6	0	1	1	0	176	24	0	4	4	0

Contd.

S.No.	Y	X1	X2	X3	X4	X5	X6	YX1	YX2	YX3	YX4	YX5	YX6
15	17	35	7	0	1	0	0	595	119	0	17	0	0
16	7	37	4	0	0	1	0	259	28	0	0	7	0
17	15	39	10	0	1	0	1	585	150	0	15	0	15
18	10	32	4	1	0	0	0	320	40	10	0	0	0
19	12	46	6	0	1	0	1	552	72	0	12	0	12
20	9	37	6	1	0	0	0	333	54	9	0	0	0
21	5	35	5	0	1	0	1	175	25	0	5	0	5
22	6	39	4	0	0	0	1	234	24	0	0	0	0
23	8	41	5	1	0	0	0	328	40	8	0	0	0
24	10	45	3	0	1	1	0	450	30	0	10	10	0
25	4	48	5	0	0	1	0	192	20	0	0	4	0
26	12	38	5	0	0	0	0	456	60	0	0	0	0
27	3	26	5	1	0	1	0	78	15	3	0	3	0
28	7	34	8	0	1	0	0	238	56	0	7	0	0
29	15	47	7	0	1	0	1	705	105	0	15	0	15
30	8	45	7	0	1	0	1	360	56	0	8	0	8
31	5	37	6	0	1	0	1	185	30	0	5	0	5
32	10	39	5	0	0	1	0	390	50	0	0	10	0
33	13	49	10	0	1	0	0	637	130	0	13	0	0
34	7	22	2	1	0	0	0	154	14	7	0	0	0

Contd.

S.No.	*Y*	*X1*	*X2*	*X3*	*X4*	*X5*	*X6*	*YX1*	*YX2*	*YX3*	*YX4*	*YX5*	*YX6*
35	8	24	2	1	0	1	0	192	16	8	0	8	0
36	15	31	4	0	0	0	1	465	60	0	0	0	15
37	10	29	4	1	0	1	0	290	40	10	0	10	0
38	5	25	3	1	0	0	0	125	15	5	0	0	0
39	7	33	5	0	0	0	1	231	35	0	0	0	7
40	8	32	3	0	0	0	1	256	24	0	0	0	8
41	9	48	7	1	0	0	0	432	63	9	0	0	0
42	4	37	4	1	0	1	0	148	16	4	0	4	0
43	11	39	6	0	0	1	0	429	66	0	0	11	0
44	8	41	8	0	0	1	0	328	64	0	0	8	0
45	13	43	10	0	1	1	0	559	130	0	13	13	0
46	10	35	2	1	0	1	0	350	20	10	0	10	0
47	15	38	3	0	0	1	0	570	45	0	0	15	0
48	3	36	4	0	0	1	1	108	12	0	0	3	3
49	12	40	7	0	0	1	1	480	84	0	0	12	12
50	8	42	5	1	1	1	0	336	40	8	8	8	0
Total	481	1918	280	18	20	19	19	18813	2818	166	220	157	196
Average	9.62	38.36	5.60	0.36	0.40	0.38	0.38						
Σ^2	5305	75674	1766	18	20	19	19						

S1=481 ; SS1=5305 ; CAL1=(S1*S1)/N = (481*481)/50 = 4627.22

Similarly for S2,S3,S4,S5,S6,S7

Y11=SS1–CAL1 = 5305–4627.22 = 677.78

X11=SS2–CAL2 = 75674–73574.48 =2099.52

Similarly X22,X33.....X66

FOR CROSS PRODUCTS

SS8=18813 ; CAL8=(S1*S2)/N = (481*1918)/50 = 18451.16

SS9=2818 ; CAL9 =(S1*S3)/N = (481*280)/50 = 2693.6

Similarly for S10,S11,S12,S13

YX1=SS8–CAL8 = 18813–18451.16 = 361.84

YX2=SS9–CAL9 = 2818–2693.6 = 124.4

Similarly YX3.....YX6

P1=Y11/N ; P2=X11/N ....P7=X66/N

YS1=SQRT(P1) ; XS2=SQRT(P2)..........XS7=SQRT(P7)

b1 = YX1/X11 ; b2 = YX2/X22 ....b6=YX6/X66

b1=0.1723 ; b2=0.6283 ; b3=–0.6215 ; b4=2.3 ; b5=–2.1885 ; b6=1.1222

a= m1–(b1*m2)–(b2*m3)–...........(b6*m6) = – 0.800594

REGRESSION EQUATION WILL BE

Y=–0.800594+(0.1723*X1)+(0.6283*X2)+(–0.6215*X3)+(2.3*X4)
+(–2.188*X5)+(1.122*X6)

Estimated variance σ^2 of ε, = Y11 – b1*YX1
= 677.78 – (0.1723*361.84)
= 615.4349

SSreg = b1*YX1+b2*YX2+..........b6*YX6 = 279.70

SSres = Y11– SSreg = 398.07

R^2= SSreg/Y1 =0.4126 ; R = 0.6423

R^2 = squared correlation between X and Y or between a linear combination of X1,X2.... and Y. This implies that 41.26% of the variation of the sample Y values about their mean can be explained by the independent variables.

To test whether R^2 is significant or not, the F ratio is calculated. For this, Null Hypothesis H0 : $R^2 = 0$

$$F = \frac{R^2/k}{(1-R^2)/(N-k-1)} = \frac{0.4126/6}{0.5874/43} = \frac{0.0688}{0.0137} = 5.0218$$

where N=total sample size ; k=number of independent variables

this value of F is compared with the tabulated value of F at some level of significance for (k,N-k-1) df. If calculated value of F is greater than tabulated value, reject the Null Hypothesis and conclude that the R^2 is statistically significant and the model is useful.

Since tabulated value of F(6,43) at 5% level of significance is 2.32, the Null hypothesis is rejected. Thus, R^2 is statistically significant.

CHAPTER 11

ANALYSIS OF VARIANCE

The term "Analysis of Variance" was introduced by Prof. R. A. Fisher in 1920. The basic purpose of the analysis of variance is to test the homogeneity of several means. ANOVA consists in estimation of the amount of variation due to each of the independent factors (causes) separately and then comparing these estimates due to assignable factors (causes) with the estimate due to chance factor (error).

The total variation in any set of numerical data is due to :

1. Assignable causes
2. Chance causes

The variation due to assignable causes can be detected and measured. The variation due to chance causes is beyond the control of humans.

Assumptions :

a. The observations are independent.
b. The population from which samples are taken is Normal.
c. Various treatment and environmental effects are additive in nature.

One Way Classification

Let N observations X_{ij} (i = 1.....k) ; (j = 1.....n_i) of a random variable X are grouped, on some basis, into k classes of sizes n_1....n_k respectively. $N = \Sigma n_i$

The total variation in the observations X_{ij} can be split into following components,

1. The variation between the classes, known as treatments.
2. The variation within classes.

The first type is due to assignable causes and the second type is due to chance causes. The main object of analysis of variance technique is to examine if there is significant difference between the class means.

Null Hypothesis : H0 : $\mu 1 = \mu 2 = \mu 3 = \mu 4 ..... = \mu$

The homegeneity of different treatments or to test the equality of the population means.

N = mxn : total number of cells

Total Sum (G) : ΣX_{ij}

Correction factor (CF) : G^2/N

Raw Sum of Squares (RSS) : ΣXij^2

Total Sum of squares (TSS) : RSS-CF

Sum of squares due to treatments (SST) : $\Sigma(T_i^2/n_i) - CF$

Sum of squares due to Error (within varieties) : TSS-SST

ANOVA TABLE

Source of Variation	*df*	*SS*	*MSS*	*Variance Ratio*
Treatments	k-1	SST	MST=SST/k-1	F_t= MST/MSE
Error	N-k	SSE	MSE=SSE/(N-k)	
Total	(N-1)	TSS		

If $F_{cal} > F_{tab}$ at certain degrees of freedom and level of significance, the null hypothesis is rejected otherwise accepted.

The variance is independent of change of origin and scale.

TABLE 11.0 : Below are given the specific growth rate of prawns when type of feed vary in protein %. Test whether % of protein has any significant difference for specific growth rate.

Protein %	*Specific growth rate*			*Total*
15	2.8	2.9	2.9	8.6
20	3.7	3.6	3.7	11.0
25	3.6	3.5	3.7	10.8
30	3.0	3.1	3.0	9.1
35	2.5	2.5	2.6	7.6
40	3.4	3.3	3.4	10.1
45	3.2	3.2	3.3	9.7
50	3.5	3.4	3.5	10.4
				77.3

Null Hypothesis : H0 : m1 = m2 = m3 = m4.....= m

Total Sum = 77.3

Correction factor(CF) = $(77.3)^2 / 24 = 248.97$

Raw sum of Squares(RSS) = 252.21

Total Sum of Squares(TSS) = RSS – CF = 252.21 – 248.97 = 3.24

Sum of Squares due to Treatments(SST) = $(8.6^2 + 11.0^2 + \ldots 10.4^2)/3 - CF = 3.17$

Error Sum of Squares = TSS – SST = 3.24 – 3.17 = 0.07

ANOVA TABLE

Source of Variation	*df*	*SS*	*MSS*	*Variance Ratio*
Treatments	7	3.17	0.4533	108.76
Error	16	0.07	0.0044	
Total	23	3.24		

F_{tab} (7,16) at 5% level of significance = 2.67

Since $F_{cal} > F_{tab}$, null hypothesis is rejected.

Thus treatments have significant difference for specific growth rate of prawns.

Standard error of the difference between any two treatment means is

SE = SQRT(2∗mse/r) = SQRT (2∗0.0044/3) = 0.054

Crtical Difference(CD) = SE∗$t_{0.05}$ for error df

= 0.054∗2.12 = 0.1145

The treatment mean effects, arranged in descending order of magnitude,

Protein %	*Mean value*	*Difference*
20	3.66	
25	3.60	0.06
50	3.46	0.14
40	3.36	0.10
45	3.23	0.13
30	3.03	0.20
15	2.86	0.17
35	2.53	0.33

Two Way Classification

Let m and n be the total number of treatments and blocks(replications) respectively. The yield is expressed in mXn matrix.

Null Hypothesis :

a) There is no significant difference among treatments. H_t : t1=t2=t3.....

b) There is no significant difference among blocks H_b : b1=b2=b3....

Total Observations : N = m x n

Raw sum of squares (RSS) : $\Sigma\Sigma X_{ij}^2$

Total Sum (G) : ΣX_{ij}

Correction factor (CF) : G^2/N

Total Sum of squares (TSS) : RSS-CF

Sum of squares due to treatments (SST) : $1/n\ \Sigma T_i^2 - CF$

Sum of squares due to blocks (SSB) : $1/m\ \Sigma C_j^2 - CF$

Sum of squares due to Error (within varieties) : TSS-SST-SSB

ANOVA TABLE

Source of Variation	*df*	*SS*	*MSS*	*Variance Ratio*
Treatments	m-1	SST	MST=SST/m-1	F_t= MST/MSE
Blocks(Repl-ications)	n-1	SSB	MSB=SSC/n-1	F_b=MSB/MSE
Error	(m-1)(n-1)	SSE	MSE=SSE/(m-1)(n-1)	
Total	(mxn) – 1	TSS		

If $F_{cal} > F_{tab}$ at certain degrees of freedom and level of significance, the null hypotheis is rejected otherwise accepted.

If Null hypothesis is rejected for treatments i.e $F_{t\ cal} > F_{t\ tab}$, Critical Difference(CD) is calculated to find out which treatments differ significantly.

CD(for any two treatment means) : $t_{\alpha\%}$ for error df x Standard Error(SE)

Statndard Error = SQRT(2xMSE/r) ; where r is the total number of blocks

TABLE 11.1 : Effect of Carbaryl(pesticide) on the activity of Alkaline Phosphatase in Brain of Rattus norvegicus.

Dose(mg / kg bw)	*Period of Treatment(hrs)*				
	24	*48*	*72*	*Total*	*Mean*
180	7.60	15.73	22.62	45.95	15.32
275	8.45	16.82	25.13	50.40	16.80
380	8.87	17.33	26.12	52.32	17.44
Total	24.92	49.88	73.87	148.67	

Total Sum = 148.67

Correction Factor = $(148.67^2 / 9) = 2455.86$

Raw Sum of Squares(RSS) = $(7.6^2+15.73^2+ \ldots\ldots +26.12^2) = 2863.95$

Total Sum of Squares (TSS) = RSS – CF

= 2863.95 – 2455.86 = 408.09

Sum of Squares due to Treatments(SST)

= $(45.95^2 + 50.40^2 + 52.32^2)/3$ – CF

= 7.12(Dose)

Sum of Squares due to Blocks/Columns

= $(24.92^2 + 49.88^2 + 73.87^2)/3$ - CF

= 399.40

Sum of Squares due to Error = 408.09 – 7.12 – 399.40 = 1.56

ANOVA TABLE

Source of Variation	*df*	*SS*	*MSS*	*Variance Ratio*
Treatments	2	7.12	3.55	Ft = 9.10
Blocks (Replications)	2	399.40	199.701	Fb = 510.52
Error	4	1.56	0.391	
Total	8	408.09		

Tabulated F(2,4) at 5% level of significance = 6.94

Since Ft and Fb both are greater than Tabulated value.

Conclusion : Treatments(dose) differ significantly for the activity of Alkaline Phosphatase. Blocks (Period) differ significantly for the activity of Alkaline Phosphatase.

TABLE 11.2 : Effect of various spacing and days after sowing on standing crop (g/m²) of Mung.

Row to Row spacing	*Days after sowing*			
	25	*40*	*55*	*Total*
(30 cm)S1	11.29	31.29	196.38	238.96
(45 cm)S2	7.99	29.89	164.44	202.32
(C0 cm)S3	7.96	22.93	131.32	162.21
Total	27.24	84.11	492.14	603.49

Total Sum = 603.49

Correction Factor (CF) = $(603.49^2 / 9) = 40466.68$

Raw Sum of Squares(RSS) = $(11.29^2+31.29^2+ \ldots\ldots +162.21^2)$

= 85503.48

Total Sum of Squares (TSS) = RSS – CF

= 85503.48 – 40466.68 = 45036.80

Sum of Squares due to Treatments(SST)

= $(238.96^2+202.32^2+162.21^2)/3$ - CF

= 982.436(Spacing)

Sum of Squares due to Blocks/Columns

= $(27.24^2 + 84.11^2+ 492.14^2)/3$ - CF

= 42872.75(Number of Days)

Sum of Squares due to Error = 45036.80 – 42872.75 – 982.44 = 1181.61

ANOVA TABLE

Source of Variation	*df*	*SS*	*MSS*	*Variance Ratio*
Treatments	2	982.44	491.218	Ft = 1.66
Blocks(Replications)	2	42872.75	21436.38	Fb = 72.57
Error	4	1181.61	295.403	
Total	8	45036.80		

Tabulated F(2,4) at 5% level of significance = 6.94

Since Ft is less than tabulated value and Fb is greater than Tabulated value.

Conclusion : Treatments(spacing) do not differ significantly for standing crop of Mung.

Blocks(No of days) differ significantly for standing crop of Mung.

ANALYSIS OF VARIANCE (m observations per cell)

To make a test for the interaction effect between two factors A and B, more than one observations per cell are required. Factors A and B are having m and n types respectively. Let there be k observations per cell for each combination of A and B classification. Let X_{ijl} denote the lth observation (l =1,2,...k) in the ith – A classification and j^{th} – B classification.

Null Hypothesis : The factors A and B do not affect the variable whose values are calculated.

Total Observations : N = m x n x k

Raw sum of squares (RSS) : $\Sigma\Sigma\Sigma X_{ijl}^2$

Total Sum (G) : $\Sigma\Sigma\Sigma X_{ijl}$

Correction factor (CF) : G^2/N

Total Sum of squares (TSS) : RSS-CF

Sum of squares due to variable A (S^2A) : $1/n*k\ \Sigma T_i^2$ - CF

Sum of squares due to variable B (S^2B) : $1/m*k\ \Sigma C_j^2$ – CF

Sum of squares due to interaction (S^2AB) :

$(1/k\ \Sigma\Sigma\ T_{ij}^2 - CF) - SSA - SSB$

Sum of squares due to error : TSS – S^2A – S^2B – S^2AB

ANOVA TABLE

Source of Variation	*df*	*SS*	*MSS*	*Variance Ratio*
Factor A	m-1	S^2A	MSA=S^2A/m-1	F_A= MSA/MSE
Factor B	n-1	S^2B	MSB=S^2B/n-1	F_B=MSB/MSE
Interaction AB	(m-1)(n-1)	S^2AB	MSAB = S^2AB/ (m-1)(n-1)	F_{AB} = MSAB/MSE
Error	mn(k-1)	S^2E	MSE=S^2E/mn(k-1)	
Total	(mxnxk) – 1	TSS		

If calculated value of F_A, F_b, F_{AB} is greater than tabulated values, reject the hypothesis.

TABLE 11.3 : Effect of various spacing and days after sowing on standing crop (g/m^2) of Mung.

DAY	COTTON	WIRE	NYLON
	67.0	67.0	47.0
	67.0	67.0	70.0
I	66.0	65.0	71.0
	60.0	65.0	67.0
	60.0	61.0	68.0
	71.0	70.0	55.0
	71.0	65.0	73.0
II	71.0	70.0	69.0
	80.0	53.0	49.0
	77.0	63.0	46.0
	61.0	53.0	66.0
	59.0	50.0	96.0
III	61.0	53.0	69.0
	61.0	50.0	66.0
	60.0	53.0	97.0
	70.0	71.0	99.0
	84.0	70.0	75.0
IV	65.0	77.0	82.0
	67.0	76.0	75.0
	69.0	79.0	80.0

Total observations = 4x3x5 = 60 (4: rows ; 3 : columns ; 5 : observations /cell)

Total Sum (G) = $\Sigma\Sigma\Sigma X_{ijl}$ = 4045.00

Raw Sum of squares of X_{ijl} (RSS) = 280095.00

Correction Factor = GxG/N = 272700.40

Column	*Total*	*Squares*
I	1347.00	1814409.00
II	1278.00	1633284.00
III	1420.00	2016400.00
	4045.00	5464093.00

Row	*Total*	*Squares*
I	968.00	937024.00
II	983.00	966289.00
III	955.00	912025.00
IV	1139.00	1297321.00
	4045.00	4112659.00

Total for Interaction

Interaction	*Total*	*Squares*
R(1,1)	320.00	102400.00
R(1,2)	325.00	105625.00
R(1,3)	323.00	104329.00
R(2,1)	370.00	136900.00
R(2,2)	321.00	103041.00
R(2,3)	292.00	85264.00
R(3,1)	302.00	91204.00
R(3,2)	259.00	67081.00
R(3,3)	394.00	155236.00
R(4,1)	355.00	126025.00
R(4,2)	373.00	139129.00
R(4,3)	411.00	168921.00
	4045.00	1385155.00

Total Variation = RSS – CF = 280095.00 – 272700.40 = 7394.60

Total variation between Column means = (5464093/20) - CF

= 273204.65–272700.40

= 540.25

Total variation between Row means = (4112659.00/15) - CF

= 274177.26 – 272700.40

= 1476.86

Total variations due to Interaction = (1385155/5) - CF - S^2A -S^2B

= 277031.0 – 272700.4 – 540.25 – 1476.86

= 2349.5

Total variation within boxes : TSS - S^2A -S^2B- S^2AB

= 7394.60-1476.86-504.25-2313.49

= 3064.0

ANOVA TABLE

Source of Variation	*df*	*SS*	*MSS*	*Variance Ratio*
Factor A	3	1476.9	492.287	$F_A = 7.712$
Factor B	2	504.2	252.122	$F_B = 3.95$
Interaction AB	6	2349.5	391.582	$F_{AB} = 6.134$
Error	48	3064.0	63.833	
Total	59	7394.6		

CHAPTER 12

ANALYSIS OF COVARIANCE

According to Prof. R. A. Fisher, the analysis of covariance combines the advantages and reconciles the requirements of regression and analysis of variance. It is also a means of analyzing the co-variation. It is of use in testing for differences between slopes of lines of regression.

By applying the method of least squares, a combined analysis of variance and regression equation can be of type

$$Y_{ij} = \mu + \beta(X_{ij} - \overline{X}) + \varepsilon_{ij} \qquad i = 1,2,......r$$

$$j = 1,2,3,...c$$

The quantity Y_{ij} is the dependent variable, μ being the constant, represents a differential that is independent of variation in X_{ij} and may be 0 in any or all of the c classes. X_{ij} is the initial value for which adjustment is to be made, ε_{ij} is a random variable that is normally distributed with mean=0 and the same variance σ^2 for all c classes and all values of $X_{ij.}$ The $\overline{X}$ will be the grand mean of the fixed set of X_{ij}'s. In a random sample of r items from c classes the least square estimates of μ, and β can be calculated by

$$\mu = \frac{\Sigma\Sigma\, Y_{ij}}{n} = \overline{Y}$$

$$= Y_j - \mu - \beta(X_j - \overline{X})$$

$$\beta = \frac{E_{xy}}{E_{xx}}$$

TABLE 12.0 : Below are given the readings of activity of Glutamate Pyruvate Transaminase (GPT) in control (Y) and increase in thé activity by the effect of pesticides (Carbaryl, Dimethoate and Chlorpyrophos ; X) for 15 days in Brain of Rattus

	CARBARYL (100mg/kg bw)		*DIMETHOATE (80 mg/kg bw)*		*CHOLRPYROPHOS (25mg/kg bw)*	
	Y	*X*	*Y*	*X*	*Y*	*X*
	40.27	11.93	41.25	15.15	39.25	10.95
	40.28	11.90	41.20	15.10	39.20	11.05
	40.23	11.98	41.23	15.12	39.25	10.95
	40.25	11.97	41.26	15.14	39.24	10.96
	40.27	11.93	41.25	15.15	39.25	10.98
Total	201.30	59.71	206.19	75.66	196.19	54.89
Mean	40.26	11.942	41.238	15.132	39.238	10.978

GRAND TOTAL Y= 603.68 X= 190.26

GRAND MEAN $\overline{Y} = 40.2453$ $\overline{X} = 12.684$

$r = 5, s = 3$

$K_y = (\Sigma\Sigma Y_{ij})^2/n = (603.68)^2/15$ $K_x = (\Sigma\Sigma X_{ij})^2/n = (19026)^2/15$

$K_{xy} = (\Sigma\Sigma Y_{ij})(\Sigma\Sigma X_{ij})/n = (603.68*190.26)/15$

$C_{yy} = (\Sigma C_{yj}^2)/r - K_y = [(201.3)^2 + (206.19)^2 + (196.19)^2]/15 - K_y$

$C_{xx} = (\Sigma C_{xj}^2)/r - K_x = [(59.71)^2 + (75.66)^2 + (54.89)^2]/15 - K_x$

$C_{xy} = (\Sigma C_{yj} C_{xj})/r - K_{xy} = [201.3*59.71) + (206.19*75.66) + (196.19*54.89)]/15 - K_{xy}$

$S_{yy} = (40.27)^2 + (40.28)^2 + \ldots\ldots\ldots\ldots$

$S_{xx} = (11.93)^2 + (11.90)^2 + \ldots\ldots$

$S_{xy} = (40.27*11.93) + (40.28*11.90) + \ldots\ldots\ldots\ldots$

ANALYSIS OF COVARIANCE TABLE

Source of Variation	*Sum of squares for Y*	*Sum of Cross-Products for X & Y*	*Sum of squares for X*	*Regression Coefficient*	*Amount explained by Regression*	*Adjusted sum of squares for Y*	*Df*	*Mean Square*	*F-ratio*
Between Columns	10.0016	20.6884	47.2685	0.7396	9.0476	0.9540	2	0.477	1152
Residual	00.0058	-0.0040	00.0132	-0.3021	0.0012	0.0046	11	0.004	
Total	10.0074	20.6844	47.2817	0.4375	9.0488	0.9586	13	0.481	

The tabulated value of F(2,11) at 5% level of significance is 3.88. The calculated value is greater than the tabulated value. Thus, the three methods differ significantly.

CHAPTER 13

PRINCIPLES OF EXPERIMENTAL DESIGN

Prof. Ronald A. Fisher invented the study of experimental design. The basic principles of design of experiment are

a. Replication

b. Randomisation

c. Local Control

a. Replication means execution of an experiment more than once. The repetition of the treatments under investigation is known as replication. By replication, the experimenter tries to average out as far as possible the effects due to uncontrolled factors. The error associated with the difference between the average results for two treatments is decreased by the replication of an experiment. If σ^2 is the error variance and there are r replications, the error variance of the difference between the means for two treatments is $2\sigma^2/r$ and the corresponding standard error is $\sigma\sqrt{2/r}$.

Advantages

It serves to reduce the experimental error and thus enables to obtain more precise estimates of the treatment effects. The precision of the experiment is inversely proportional to the square root of the replications. Thus, replication has an important but limited role in increasing the efficiency of the design.

The most important purpose of the replication is to provide an estimate of the experimental error, without which

1. To test the significance of difference between two treatments is not determined.
2. The length of confidence interval is not determined.

b. Randomisation is a process of assigning the treatments to various experimental units in a purely chance manner.

Objectives of Randomisation

1. The validity of the statistical tests of significance. Exp. Analysis of Variance, F-test for testing the homogenity of several means, depends on the fact that statistic under consideration obeys some distribution. Randomising the treatments over the experiment units is a safe action against distribution of experimental results by unanticipated influences. Exp. rise in temp, fertility of soil.
2. Randomisation insures that the different treatments, by the repetition of the experiment on the average are subject to equal environmental effect. Randomization equalises even factors of variation, which is uncontrolled by the experimenter. Randomisation without replication is not sufficient.

c. Local control is a process of reducing the experimental error by dividing the relatively hetrogeneous experimental area (field) in to homogeneous blocks. It increases the efficiency of the design.

In order to separate the soil fertility effects from the experimental units, the whole experimental area (field) is divided in to homogeneous groups (blocks) row wise or column wise (one way eliminator of fertility gradient, RBD, or both) according to the fertility gradient of the soil such that the variation within each block is minimum and between blocks is maximum.

There are many experimental designs which are used under different situations.

When experimental material is homogeneous and limited, completely randomized design (CRD) is used.

When fertility variation of the field is in one direction, randomized block design (RBD) is used.

When fertility variation moves in two directions, latin square design (LSD) is used.

When several factors with different levels are to be studied, factorial design is used.

When several factors are to be tested simultaneously with some of the factors require larger plots and may be studied with different precision, and others require smaller plots, split plot design is used.

COMPLETELY RANDOMISED DESIGN (CRD)

It is the simplest of all designs. In this design, treatments are allocated at random to the experimental units over the entire experimental material. The principle of Local Control is not adopted in this design. The error variance is controlled by selecting a homogeneous set of experimental units. Total variation is divided into two components(treatments and error). Randomisation is done treatment wise. The whole field is divided directly into plots of equal size.

This design is useful in the biological experiments.

Statistical Analysis

Null Hypothesis : a) There is no significant difference among treatments. $H_t : t_1=t_2=t_3.....$

Total Observations : N = m x n

Raw sum of squares (RSS) : $\Sigma\Sigma X_{ij}^2$

Total Sum (G) : ΣX_{ij}

Correction factor (CF) : G^2/N

Total Sum of squares (TSS) : RSS-CF

Sum of squares due to treatments (SST) : $1/n \ \Sigma T_i^2$ - CF

Sum of squares due to Error (within varieties) : TSS-SST

ANOVA TABLE

Source of Variation	*df*	*SS*	*MSS*	*Variance Ratio*
Treatments	m-1	SST	MST=SST/m-1	F_t= MST/MSE
Error	N-m	SSE	MSE=SSE/(N-m)	
Total	N–1	TSS		

TABLE 13.0 : Total dissolved solid (TDS) is obtained for Upper lake, Lower lake, Hataikheda reservoir and Halali Dam. Test whether TDS differ significantly in four water bodies.

Upper Lake (t_1)	*Lower Lake (t_2)*	*Hataikheda Reservoir (t_3)*	*Halali Dam (t_4)*
154	172	152	162
152	170	154	161
156	174	150	163

Null Hypothesis $H_t : t_1=t_2=t_3=t_4$

Total observations = m × n = 3 × 4=12

G (Grand Total) = 1920

Correction Factor (CF) = 307200

Raw sum of squares (RSS) = 307970.0

Total sum of squares (TSS) = 770

Sum of squares due to treatment (SST) = 744

Sum of squares due to error (SSE) = 26

Source	*df*	*ss*	*mss*	*F*
Treatments	3	744	248	76.3077
Error	8	26	3.2500	
Total	11	770		

Tabulated value of F(3,8) =4.07. Since calculated F is greater than tabulated F, the null hypothesis is rejected. Thus, treatments differ significantly.

Critical difference (CD) = 3.091116

The difference between treatment means

d_{12} = −18 d_{13} = 2 d_{14} = −8
d_{23} = 20 d_{24} = 10 d_{34} = −10

The maximum difference is between second and third treatment i.e. d_{23} = 20.00

RANDOMISED BLOCK DESIGN (RBD)

If treatments are applied at random to relatively homogeneous units within each block and replicated over all the blocks, the design is R.B.D. In this, randomisation is restricted and variation among blocks is removed from variation due to error. It provides a method of reducing the effects of trends. The total variation is divided into three components(treatment, blocks and error). First the field is divided into homogeneous blocks equal to number of replications. Then each block is divided into plots equal to the number of treatments. Generally, 4 or 5 replications are sufficient in case of CRD, RBD.

Advantages

1. Accuracy : It is more efficient than C.R.D.(Completely Randomised Design). The elimination of between S.S. from residual S.S. results in decrease of error mean S.S.

2. Flexibility : In R.B.D. no restrictions are placed on the number of treatments.
3. The Statistical analysis is simple and easy.

Disadvantages

1. R.B.D. is not suitable for very large number of treatments.

Statistical Analysis

Let m and n be the total number of treatments and blocks(replications) respectively. The yield is expressed in mXn matrix.

Null Hypothesis :

a) There is no significant difference among treatments. H_t : $t_1=t_2=t_3.....$

b) There is no significant difference among blocks H_b : $b_1=b_2=b_3....$

Total Observations : N = m x n

Raw sum of squares (RSS) : $\Sigma\Sigma X_{ij}^2$

Total Sum (G) : ΣX_{ij}

Correction factor (CF) : G^2/N

Total Sum of squares (TSS) : RSS-CF

Sum of squares due to treatments (SST) : $1/n \ \Sigma T_i^2$ - CF

Sum of squares due to blocks (SSB) : $1/m \ \Sigma C_j^2$ - CF

Sum of squares due to Error (within varieties) : TSS-SST-SSB

ANOVA TABLE

Source of Variation	*df*	*SS*	*MSS*	*Variance Ratio*
Treatments	m-1	SST	MST=SST/m-1	F_t= MST/MSE
Blocks (Replications)	n-1	SSB	MSB=SSC/n-1	F_b=MSB/MSE
Error	(m-1)(n-1)	SSE	MSE=SSE/(m-1)(n-1)	
Total	(mxn) – 1	TSS		

If $F_{cal} > F_{tab}$ at certain degrees of freedom and level of significance, the null hypotheis is rejected otherwise accepted.

If Null hypothesis is rejected for treatments i.e $F_{t\ cal} > F_{t\ tab}$, Critical Difference(CD) is calculated to find out which treatments differ significantly.

CD(for any two treatment means) : $t_{\alpha\%}$ for error df x Standard Error(SE)

Statndard Error = SQRT(2xMSE/r) ; where r is the total number of blocks(replications).

By comparing the differences between the mean yields for different treatments with critical difference, treatments giving significantly high yields can be obtained.

By arranging mean yields of all treatments in ascending order, the best(top) and worst(bottom) treatment can be found.

Efficiency of the RBD relative to its layout as CRD is given by :

$$E = \frac{r(t-1) \times MSE + (r-1) \times MSB}{(rt-1) \times MSE}$$

TABLE 13.1 : An agricultural experiment was conducted to the effects of three varieties for Wheat A, B and C in their yield. Blocks are divided in to three plots and plots of each block were assigned at random to the three varieties. Find out whether three varieties differ significantly.

	RI	*RII*	*RIII*	*RIV*	*RV*		*Total*	*Squares*	*Ave*
A	5	2	1	5	3	|	16	256	3.2
B	4	0	1	4	4	|	13	169	2.6
C	4	3	2	5	4	|	18	324	3.6
Total	13	5	4	14	11	|	47	749	
Squares	169	25	16	196	121	|	527		

Total observations(N) = 3x5 = 15

Total Sum (G) = 47

Raw Sum of Squares (SS) = $5^2+2^2+1^2+5^2+3^2+4^2+........4^2$ = 183.0

Correction factor(CF) = (47x47)/15 = 147.26

Total Sum of Squares (TSS) = 183 –147.26 = 35.74

Sum of squares due to treatments = 1/5 x(749) – 147.26 = 2.54

Sum of squares due to blocks(replication)

= 1/3 x(527) – 147.26 = 28.4

Sum of squares due to error = 35.74 – 2.54 – 28.4 = 4.80

ANOVA TABLE

Source of Variation	*DF*	*SS*	*MSS*	*Variance Ratio*
Treatments	2	2.533	1.267	$F_t = 2.11$
Blocks(Replication)	4	28.4	7.1	$F_b = 11.83$
Error	8	4.8	0.6	
	14			

$F_{tab}(4,8) = 3.84$; $F_{tab}(2,8) = 4.46$

Since $F_{tab}(2,8) > F_{cal}(2,8)$; Treatments do not differ significantly

$F_{tab}(4,8) < F_{cal}(4,8)$; Blocks(Replications) differ significantly

Since treatments do not differ significantly, calculation for Critical Difference is not needed.

Efficiency of RBD over CRD, $E = \frac{5X2X0.6 + 4X7.1}{14X0.6} = \frac{34.4}{8.4} = 4.09$

LATIN SQUARE DESIGN (LSD)

In this design, the number of treatments is equal to number of replications. In the case of m treatments there have to be $mxm=m^2$ experimental units. The whole area is divided into m^2 experimental units (plots) such that each row as well as each column contains m unit. m treatments are then allocated at random to rows and columns such that each treatment occurs only once in each row and each column. This is called mxm Latin Square Design. The total variation is divided into four components (rows, columns, treatments and error). 5 –12 replications are sufficient for LSD.

Advantages

With two way grouping L.S.D. controls more of the variation than R.B.D.

Statistical analysis is simple though it is complicated than RBD.

More than one factor can be investigated simultaneously

It is an incomplete 3-way layout. Its advantage over complete 3-way layout is that instead of m^3 only m^2 units are needed.

Disadvantages

The fundamental assumption that factors act independently may not be true in general.

LSD is suitable for only treatments between 5-10.

In the field layout RBD is much easy to manage than LSD because for latter a square field is needed.

Statistical Analysis

Let m be the total number of treatments and blocks(replications) respectively. The yield is expressed in mxm matrix.

Null Hypothesis :

a) There is no significant difference among treatments. H_t : $t_1=t_2=t_3$.....

b) There is no significant difference among blocks H_b : $b_1=b_2=b_3$....

Total Observations : $N = m \times m = m^2$

Raw sum of squares (RSS) : $\Sigma\Sigma X_{ij}^2$

Total sum (G) : ΣX_{ij}

Correction factor (CF) : G^2/N

Total sum of squares (TSS) : RSS-CF

Sum of squares due to treatments (SST) : $1/m \, \Sigma T_i^2$ - CF

Sum of squares due to columns (SSC) : $1/m \, \Sigma C_j^2$ - CF

Sum of squares due to rows (SSR) : $1/m \, \Sigma Ri^2$ - CF

Sum of squares due to Error (within varieties) : TSS-(SST+SSC+SSR)

ANOVA TABLE

Source of Variation	*df*	*SS*	*MSS*	*Variance Ratio*
Treatments	m-1	SST	MST=SST/m-1	F_t= MST/MSE
Columns	m-1	SSC	MSC=SSC/m-1	F_c= MSC/MSE
Rows	m-1	SSR	MSR=SSR/m-1	F_r= MSR/MSE
Error	(m-1)(m-2)	SSE	MSE=SSE/ (m-1)(n-1)	
Total	(mxm) – 1	TSS		

If $F_{cal} > F_{tab}$ at certain degrees of freedom and level of significance, the null hypotheis is rejected otherwise accepted.

If Null hypothesis is rejected for treatments i.e $F_{t\ cal} > F_{t\ tab}$, Critical Difference(CD) is calculated to find out which treatments differ significantly.

CD(for any two treatment means) : $t_{\alpha\%}$ for error df x Standard Error(SE)

Standard Error = SQRT(2xMSE/r) ; where r is the total number of blocks(replications).

By comparing the differences between the mean yields for different treatments with critical difference, treatments giving significantly high yields can be obtained.

By arranging mean yields of all treatments in ascending order, the best(top) and worst(bottom) treatment can be found.

Efficiency of the LSD relative to its layout as RBD is given by :

$$E = \frac{MSC + (m\text{-}1)\ MSE}{mXMSE}$$, when rows are taken as blocks

$$E = \frac{MSR + (m\text{-}1)\ MSE}{mXMSE}$$, when columns are taken as blocks

TABLE 13.2 : Yields in Kg. Per plot on the Wheat crop carried out for testing the effect of 5 manures A, B, C, D and E are given. Analyse the data.

B 15	A 8	E 17	D 20	C 17
A 9	D 21	C 19	E 16	B 13
C 18	B 12	D 23	A 8	E 17
E 18	C 16	A 10	B 15	D 23
D 22	E 15	B 13	C 18	A 10

Shifting origin to 16

	RI	*RII*	*RIII*	*RIV*	*RV*	*Total*	*Squares*	*Treatment Total*
	–1	–8	1	4	1	–3	9	A : –35
	–7	5	3	0	–3	–2	4	B : –12
	2	–4	7	–8	1	–2	4	C : 8
	2	0	–6	–1	7	2	4	D : 29
	6	–1	–3	2	–6	–2	4	E : 3
Total	2	–8	2	–3	0	–7	25	
Squares	4	64	4	9	0	81		

Total Observations (N) = 5x5 = 25

Total Sum (G) = –7

Raw Sum of Squares (SS) = $(-1)^2 + (-8)^2 + 1^2 + 4^2 + 1^2 + (-7)^2 +$

................$(-6)^2 = 485$

Correction Factor (CF) = (–7)x(–7)/25 = 1.96

Total Sum of Squares (TSS) = 485 –1.96 = 483.04

Sum of squares due to treatments = 1/5 x[$(-35)^2$ + $(12)^2$ +$(8)^2$ + $(29)^2$ +3^2] – 1.96 = 454.64

Sum of squares due to blocks(replication) = (1/5 x 81) – 1.96 = 14.24

Sum of squares due to rows = (1/5x25) – 1.96 = 3.04

Sum of squares due to error = 483.04 – 454.64 – 14.24 – 3.04 = 11.12

ANOVA TABLE

Source of Variation	*DF*	*SS*	*MSS*	*Variance Ratio*
Treatments	4	454.64	113.66	F_t = 122.21
Blocks(Replication)	4	14.24	3.56	F_b = 3.82
Rows	4	3.04	0.76	F_r = 0.817
Error	12	11.12	0.93	
Total	24	483.04		

$F_{tab}(4,12)$ = 4.26 at 1% level of significance

Since $F_{tab}(4,12) < F_{cal}(4,12)$; Treatments differ significantly

$F_{tab}(4,12) > F_{cal}(4,12)$; Blocks(Replications) and Rows do not differ significantly

Since treatments differ significantly, calculation for Critical Difference is needed.

Standard Error of estimate = SQRT(2xMSE/r) = sqrt[(2x0.93)/5] = 0.61

Critical Difference = 0.61x3.055 =1.86

SPLIT PLOT DESIGN

If one set of treatments is assigned to larger plots, i.e. Main Plots, into which a replicate is divided and another set of treatments assigned to Sub-Plots of Main Plots, the design is known as Split Plot Design. In this type of design each block is divided into main plots to be assigned to the levels of first factor randomly, then each main plot is divided into Sub Plots to be assigned to the levels of second factor randomly. The Split Plot design are more useful when treatments like sowing dates, spacing, ploughing, etc. are involved, as these can be assigned to larger plots. The design results in saving of experimental area. The comparisons between main plot treatments is made with much less precision than in Randomised design because it is calculated exclusively from differences between main plots.

Statistical Analysis

Main Plot

Main plot treatments are summed (sub plot values) according to blocks/replication.

Blocks Main plot treatments

	c1	c2	c3	......	Total
I	v1	v2	v3		tr1
II	v6	....			tr2
III	....				tr3
Total	tc1	tc2	tc3	......	Grand total

Where v1,v2.... are the sums of subplots for c1, c2... respectively for each blocks.

If there are k subplots for each n main plot treatments and there are m blocks then,

$$\text{Correction Factor(CF)} = \frac{(\text{Grand Total})^2}{\text{mxnxk}}$$

$$\text{Total Sum of Squares (TSS)} = \frac{v1^2 + v2^2 + \ldots}{k} - CF$$

$$\text{Sum of Squares for Blocks} = \frac{tr1^2 + tr2^2 + \ldots}{kxn} - CF$$

$$\text{Sum of squares for main plot treatment} = \frac{tc1^2 + tc2^2 + \ldots}{kxm} - CF$$

Sum of squares for main plot error = TSS – SSB – SST

Degrees of freedom for TSS = (mxn) – 1

SSB = (m-1)

SST = (n-1)

SSE = [(mxn)-1] – (m-1) – (n-1)

Sub-Plots

Sub-plot treatments are summed for each main plot treatments from all blocks/replicates.

Main plot treatments

Sub plot treatments	c1	c2	c3	......	Total
m1	v1	v2	v3		tr1
m2	v6	....			tr2
m3	....				tr3
Total	tc1	tc2	tc3	......	Grand total

ANOVA TABLE

Source	*Degrees of Freedom*	*Sum of Squares*	*Mean Sum of Squares*	*Fcal*
Block (Replication)	(b-1)	II	MSS_b=II/(b-1) ….(a)	(a)/e1
Main Treatment	(c-1)	III	MSS_{t1}=III/(c-1)..(b)	(b)/e1
Error A	(b-1)(c-1)	IV	MSE_a=IV/(b-1)(c-1)..e1	
Minor Treatment	(r-1)	V	MSS_{t2}=V/(r-1)……(c)	(c)/e2
Interaction	(c-1)(r-1)	VI	MSS_i=VI/(c-1)(r-1)..(d)	(d)/e2
Error B	Total– [(b-1)+(c-1)+(b-1)(c-1) +(r-1)+(c-1)(r-1)]	VII	MSE_b=VII/df	
Total	(b * c * r)-1	I′		

TABLE 13.3 : To conduct analysis of variance for split plot design from the given data : 4 major treatments, 3 minor treatments and 6 replication.

Replication 1

s2	m3	7.7	s3	m2	4.2	s4	m1	6.9	s1	m1	6.8
	m1	5.1		m1	1.3		m2	2.1		m2	6.9
	m2	2.6		m3	1.4		m3	0.4		m3	5.3

Replication 2

s3	m2	8.3	s4	m1	1.3	s1	m3	7.3	s2	m1	5.5
	m1	5.4		m2	1.0		m1	7.8		m3	2.6
	m3	8.3		m3	1.3		m2	6.4		m2	2.1

Replication 3

s3	m3	4.4	s1	m3	3.1	s2	m2	4.4	s4	m2	0.3
	m2	4.0		m2	2.9		m1	3.5		m1	0.8
	m1	3.7		m1	2.8		m3	1.2		m3	1.4

Replication 4

s2	m3	4.2	s4	m2	2.6	s1	m1	16.9	s3	m1	8.8
	m1	7.3		m1	4.5		m3	10.0		m2	6.1
	m2	7.5		m3	4.0		m2	9.5		m3	5.9

Replication 5

s1	m1	22.1	s3	m3	5.3	s4	m1	6.3	s2	m1	4.9
	m2	19.0		m1	6.3		m3	3.9		m2	4.0
	m3	14.9		m2	4.3		m2	1.6		m3	5.1

Replication 6

s4	m3	1.5	s3	m2	2.5	s1	m2	4.9	s2	m3	1.3
	m1	2.0		m1	2.0		m3	2.2		m2	0.9
	m2	2.1		m3	2.9		m1	3.3		m1	2.3

date of sowing *replication*		*S1*	*S2*	*S3*	*S4*
I	19.0	15.5	6.9	9.4	R1=50.8
II	21.5	10.2	22.0	3.6	R2=57.3
III	8.8	9.1	12.1	2.6	R3=32.6
IV	36.4	19.0	20.8	11.1	R4=87.3
V	56.0	14.0	15.9	11.8	R5=97.7
VI	10.4	4.5	7.4	5.6	R6=27.9

T1=152.1 T2=72.3 T3=85.1 T4=44.1 Total=353.6

Correction Factor (CF) = (Grand Total $)^2$ / (m*n*k)

= $(353.6)^2$ / 6x4x3

= 125032.96/72 = 1736.57

Total Sum of Squares (TSS) = $(19^2+15.5^2+..........5.6^2)/3$ - C.F.

= (361+240.25+47.61+.....31.36)/3 - C.F.

= 8294.28/3 - 1736.57 = 2764.76 - 1736.57

= 1028.19 -----I

Sum of Squares due to Blocks (SSB)

= $(50.8^2+57.3^2+......27.9^2)/12$ - C.F.

= (2580.64+3283.29+......778.41)/12 - C.F.

= 24871.68/12 – 1736.57

= 2072.64 – 1736.57 = 336.07 --------II

Sum of Squares due to Main Treatments(SST1)

= $(152.1^2+72.3^2+....44.1^2)/18$ - C.F.

= 37548.52/18 – 1736.57

= 2086.03–1736.57 = 349.46------III

Sum of Squares due to Error (SSEA) = I-(II+III)

= 1028.19 – (336.07+349.46)

= 1028.19 – 685.53 = 342.66 --------IV

For analysis of Interaction of Major and Minor Treatments

Major Treatments / Minor Treatments	S1	S2	S3	S4	Total
m1	59.7	28.7	27.5	21.9	137.8
m2	49.6	21.5	29.4	9.7	110.2
m3	42.8	22.1	28.2	12.5	105.6
Total	152.1	72.3	85.1	44.1	353.6

Sum of Squares due to Minor Treatment (SST2)

= $137.8^2+110.2^2+105.6^2/24$ - C.F.

= (18988.84+12144.04+11151.36)/24 - C.F

= 1761.84 – 1736.57 = 25.27 ------V

TSS' = $(59.7^2+28.7^2+27.5^2+21.9^2+49.6^2+.........12.5^2)/6$ - CF

= (3564.09+823.69+.........156.25)/6 – 1736.57

= (12776.24/6) – 1736.57 = 2129.37 – 1736.57

= 392.8

Sum of squares due to interaction = TSS' - (III + V)

= 392.8 - (349.46+25.27)

= 18.07 ----------------------- VI

I'(Sum of squares of all sub-plots)

$= (7.7^2+5.2^2+2.6^2+6.9^2+2.1^2+......+1.3^2+0.9^2+2.3^2)$- C.F.

= 2920.68 – 1736.57

= 1184.11

Sum of squares due to Error B = I' - (II+III+IV+V+VI)

= 1184.11 – (336.07+349.46+342.66+25.27+18.07)

= 112.58 ---------------------------VII

ANOVA TABLE

Source	*df*	*Sum of Squares*	*MSS*	*Fcal*
Blocks(replication)	(6–1)=5	336.07	67.214	2.942
Main Treatment	(4–1)=3	349.46	116.487	5.099
Error A	(5X3)=15	342.66	22.844	
Minor Treatment	(3–1)=2	25.27	12.635	0.273
Interaction	(3X2)=6	18.07	3.017	0.065
Error B	40	112.58	2.81	
Total	(6X4X3)–1=71	1184.11		

The mean square between planting dates is compared against mean square for the main plot error [Error (a)]for significance and those for the main response to methods of planting and the interaction, planting dates X methods of planting, being effects belonging to sub plots, are tested against the mean square for the sub-plot error [Error (b)]. Both the main effects are significant.

STRIP PLOT DESIGN

Two different sets of treatments can be tried in large plots with one set of plots superposed over the other set at right angles. A block may be divided into strips in one direction to be allotted to one set of treatments and into another set of strips, in a direction at right angles to the first, to be allotted to the second set of treatments. This type of arrangement is called Strip-Plot design. A separate error variance is to be calculated corresponding to each plot size as in Split Plot design.

Statistical Analysis

blocks : m ; Dates of planting : n ; Manures : k

Correction Factor (CF) = (Grand Total)^2/(m*n*k)

Sum of squares of data of all replications (I') = ΣX_{ij}^2 - CF

Analysis of Table 1 (Blocks and Dates of Planting)

1) Total Sum of Squares (TSS1) = (Sum of Squares of all Data)/n - CF
2) Sum of Squares due to Blocks (SSB) = (R_1^2+........R_b^2)/(n*k) - CF
3) Sum of Squares due to treatments(SST1) = (D_1^2+...D_k^2)/(m*n)
4) Sum of squares due to Error(A) = TSS1-(SSB+SST1)

   Analysis of Table 2 (Blocks and Different manures)
5) Total Sum of squares(TSS2) = (Sum of squars of all data)/k - CF
6) Sum of squares due to different manures(SST2) = (M_1^2+....M_n^2)/(m*k) - CF
7) Sum of squares due to Error (B) = TSS2 - (SSB+SST2)

   Analysis of Table 3 (Dates of planting and Different manures)
8) Total Sum of Squares(TSS3) = (Sum of squares of all data)/(total number of plots) - CF
9) Sum of squares due to interaction = TSS3-(SST1+SST2)
10) Sum of squares due to Error (C) = I' - (2+3+4+6+7+9)

Complete ANOVA Table

Source	*Degrees of Freedom*	*Sum of Squares*	*Mean Sum of Squares*	*F-val*
Replication	m-1	II	II/(m-1)= a′	a′/c′
Date of Planting	n-1	III	III/(n-1)= b′	b′/c′
Error (A)	(m-1)*(n-1)	IV	IV/(m-1)(n-1) = c′	
Manure	k-1	VI	VI/(k-1)=d′	d′/e′
Error (B)	(m-1)(k-1)	VII	VII/(m-1)(k-1) = e′	
Interaction	(n-1)(k-1)	IX	IX/(n-1)(k-1) =f ′	f ′/g′
Error (C)	Total-(all dfs)	X	X/df = g′	
Total	(m*n*k)- 1			

TABLE 13.4 : To conduct analysis of variance from the given data of an experiment involving paddy at different treatments such as dates of planting(3) and different types of manures(3).

	Replication 1				*Replication 2*				*Replication 3*		
	d1	d3	d2		d2	d1	d3		d2	d1	d3
m2	110	137	144	m1	165	119	148	m2	150	104	140
m1	116	143	149	m3	160	116	145	m3	145	101	131
m3	107	130	134	m2	162	122	154	m1	154	116	143

	Replication 4				*Replication 5*				*Replication 6*		
	d2	d3	d1		d3	d1	d2		d2	d3	d1
m3	124	100	60	m1	137	110	142	m3	147	134	104
m1	141	131	89	m3	124	100	128	m2	153	142	107
m2	131	119	84	m2	130	107	140	m1	156	146	119

Grand Total = (110+137+......119) = 6950

Correction Factor = $(6950)^2/(6*3*3)$ = 48302500/54 = 894490.74

I' = $(110^2+137^2+144^2+...............119^2)$ - CF

= (919430 – 894490.74) = 24939.26

Analysis of Table 1(each value is a total of 3 plots)

Date of Planting->	*d1*	*d2*	*d3*	
Replication				
I	333	427	410	R1=1170
II	357	487	447	R2 =1291
III	321	449	414	R3 = 1184
IV	233	396	350	R4 = 979
V	317	410	391	R5 = 1118
VI	330	456	422	R6 = 1208
Total	1891	2625	2434	6950

TSS1 = (110889+182329+168100+........178084)/3 - CF

= (2751778)/3 – 894490.74 = 917259.33 – 894490.74

= 22268.59 ----1

SSB = (1368900+1666681+.....1459264)/9 - CF

= (8105066)/9 – 894490.74 = 900562.89 – 894490.74

= 6072.15 --- 2

SST1 = (3575881+6890625+5924356)/(3∗6) - CF
= (16390862)/18 – CF = 910603.44 – 894490.74
= 16112.70 ------3

Sum of squares due to Error (A) = 1 - (2+3)
= 22268.59 – (6072.15+16112.70)
= 83.74 ------ 4

Analysis of Table 2 (each value is a total of 3 plots)

Different level of manures	*m1*	*m2*	*m3*	
Replication				
I	408	391	371	R1=1170
II	432	438	421	R2=1291
III	413	394	377	R3=1184
IV	361	334	284	R4=979
V	389	377	352	R5=1118
VI	421	402	385	R6=1208
Total	2424	2336	2190	6950

TSS2 = (166464+152881+........148225)/3 - CF
= (2707586)/3 - CF = 902528.67 – 894490.74 = 8037.93 ------ 5

SST2 = (5875776+5456896+4796100)/(6∗3) - CF
= (16128772)/18 - CF
= 896042.89 – 894490.74 = 1552.15 ----- 6

Sum of squares due to Error (B) = 5 – (2+6)
= 8037.93 – (6072.15+1552.15)
= 413.63 ------ 7

Analysis of Table 3 (each value is a total of 6 plots)

Date of planting		*d1*	*d2*	*d3*	*Total*
Manure	m1	669	907	848	2424
	m2	634	880	822	2336
	m3	588	838	764	2190
Total		1891	2625	2434	6950

TSS3 = (447561+822649+.......583696)/6 - CF

= (5473038)/6 – 894490.74 = 17682.26 ------- 8

Sum of squares due to interaction

= 8 – (3+6)

= 17682.26 – (16112.70+1552.15)

= 17.41 ------ 9

Sum of squares due to Error (c) = I' – (2+3+4+6+7+9)

= 24939.26 –(6072.15+16112.7+83.74+1552.15 +413.63+17.41)

= 687.48

Complete ANOVA Table

Source	*Degrees of freedom*	*Sum of squares*	*MSS*	*Fcal*
Replication	(6–1)=5	6072.15	1214.43	145.02
Date of Planting	(3–1)=2	16112.70	8056.35	962.06
Error(A)	(5∗2)=10	83.74	8.374	
Manure	(3–1)=2	1552.15	776.08	18.76
Error (B)	(5∗2)=10	413.63	41.363	
Interaction	(2∗2)=4	17.41	4.35	0.1266
Error (C)	=20	687.48	34.37	
Total	53	24939.26		

The mean square for dates of planting is tested against error (a); for manuring is tested against error (b)and that for interaction against error (c).

CHAPTER 14

TESTS OF HYPOTHESIS

The problem of estimation is more often encountered in surveys. In experimentation, the more common problem is the comparison of a factor with a standard or the comparison of two or more factors. This is the second type of inferential problem.

Suppose we want to compare the effectiveness of two drugs A and B in reducing blood pressure. We take two samples and test one drug on each sample. The samples are assumed to have come from two different populations of patients, each population imagined to have been tested with one of the drugs. We want to test whether A is more effective than B.

We assume that blood pressure is normally distributed and also that the variability of the blood pressure is same in the two populations. Now, what we want to know is whether the mean of population A is smaller than that for population B. Such a statement about the population in terms of the parameters is called a Hypothesis.

The hypothesis as stated above is vague since we are not specifying by how much the two means differ. Such vague hypothesis does not permit us to obtain sampling distributions and hence cannot be directly tested. A hypothesis which specifies this difference is called a Null Hypothesis. In example stated above, the null hypothesis (H_0) becomes as "there is no significant difference between two means".The actual hypothesis whose truth we want to know is called the Alternate Hypothesis, denoted by H_1.

The null hypothesis completely specifies the population distribution, both by form and by parameters. A statistic called the Test Criterion (T.C.), whose sampling distribution is known when the Null hypothesis is true, is now chosen and its value computed from the sample observations. It is now possible to get, from the sampling distribution, the probability that the test criterian takes the computed value or more extreme value (unfavourable to Null hypothesis). If the probability is small, it could be due to two reasons 1) we have an unrepresentative sample, or 2) the Null hypothesis is false. The sample is always taken as representative hence the second reason is accepted, the Null hypothesis is rejected and the Alternative hypothesis is accepted. If the probability is large, the Null hypothesis is accepted and the Alternative hypothesis is rejected. While testing Null hypothesis, we come across two situations

	Decision	
	Accept	*Reject*
Null Hypothesis		
True	No Error	Type I error
False	Type II error	No error

Type I error is the error committed when the Null hypothesis is wrongly rejected and arises only when the Null hypothesis is true. Type II error is committed when the Null hypothesis is wrongly accepted and arises only when the Null hypothesis is false. It is not possible to reduce both types of errors simultaneously, except by increasing the sample size or/and reducing the variability in the population.

The probability of committing Type I error is called the Level of Significance, and the Null hypothesis is said to be accepted or rejected at this level. It is conventionally taken as 1% or 5%. The probability of not committing Type II error is called the Power of a test and is dependent on the form of the Alternative hypothesis. As in the case of of obtaining a good estimator, the Test Criterion is chosen, using some statistical principles, so as to maximize the power of a test under certain conditions.

We can mark out regions under the tails of the sampling distribution corresponding to the chosen significance level. These are called as Critical Regions. The values of the Test Criterion demarcating the critical regions are called Critical values. These are usually obtained by reference to standard statistical tables. If the computed value of the Test Criterion is more extreme than a Critical value, the Null hypothesis is rejected at the corresponding level of significance.

Various steps in the procedure for a Test of Hypothesis are :

1. Assume the form of the population distribution on the basis of the character type.

2. Formulate the hypothesis which we want to test(Alternative hypothesis H_1) in terms of population parameters.
3. Formulate the hypothesis which we will test (Null hypothesis H_0).
4. Specify the Test Criterion(T.C.) and compute its value from the sample observations.
5. Choose the level of significance and obtain the critical values from the table for the sampling distribution of the chosen criterion.
6. If the computed value is more extreme than the critical value, reject the Null hypothesis and accept the Alternate hypothesis. Otherwise, accept the Null hypothesis and reject the Alternative hypothesis.

It is necessary to specify the hypothesis, the assumptions, the test criterion and its sampling distribution for any particular test to be carried out.

Select the alternative hypothesis as that which the sampling experiment is intended to establish.

Let a building specification in a certain city requires that the average breaking strength of residential pipe be more than 2000 pounds/foot of length

One tailed, upper tailed	$H_a : \mu > 2000$
One tailed, lower tailed	$H_a : \mu < 2000$
Two tailed	$H_a \neq 2000$

Select the Null hypothesis, which will be specified as the parameter value closest to the alternative in one tailed tests, and as the complementary value in two-tailed tests

$$H0 : \mu = 2000$$

Rejection regions for common values of α

Alternative hypothesis

	Lower tailed	*Upper tailed*	*Two tailed*
$\alpha = 0.01$	$Z < -2.33$	$Z > 2.33$	$Z < -2.575$ or $Z > 2.575$
$\alpha = 0.05$	$Z < -1.645$	$Z > 1.645$	$Z < -1.96$ or $Z > 1.96$
$\alpha = 0.1$	$Z < -1.28$	$Z > 1.28$	$Z < -1.645$ or $Z > 1.645$

CHAPTER 15

't' DISTRIBUTION

If 'n', the sample size is small exact sample tests given by W. S. Gosset (1908) (pen name `student') later developed by Prof R. A. Fisher (1926) is used. The exact sample tests can also be applied to large samples though the converse is not true.

Let Xi (I=1,2,....n) be a random sample of size n from a normal population with mean μ and variance σ^2. Then student `t' is defined by the statistic

$$t = \frac{\overline{x} - \mu}{S/n^2}$$

Where $\overline{x} = \Sigma X_i / n$ is the sample mean and

$S^2 = \frac{1}{n-1} \Sigma (X_i - \overline{x})^2$ is an unbiased estimate of population variance σ^2, and it follows

student `t' distribution with (n-1) degrees of freedom.

Application of 't' distribution

1. 't' test for single mean

To test a Random sample X_i (i=1...n) of size n has been drawn from a Normal population with a specified mean μ_0. Or, if the sample mean (x) differs significantly from the hypothetical value μ_0 of the population mean.

Null Hypothesis (H_0) : The sample has been drawn from the population with mean μ_0 or there is no significant difference between sample mean x and population mean μ_0.

The statistic

$$t = \frac{\overline{x} - \mu_0}{s/\sqrt{n}}$$ follows 't' distribution with (n-1) df.

If t_{cal} (–ve sign ignored) > t_{tab}, Null hypothesis is rejected at a certain level of significance otherwise accepted.

2. 't' test for difference of means

Formula used : $t = \dfrac{\overline{X} - \overline{Y}}{\sqrt{(S^2(1/n_1+1/n_2))}}$

$$S^2 = \frac{[\ \Sigma(X-\overline{X})^2 + \Sigma(Y-\overline{Y})^2]}{(n_1+n_2-2)}$$

TABLE 15.0 : Below are given the gain in weight(in lbs) of fishes fed on two diets A and B. Test whether two diets differ significantly as regards their effect on increase in weight.

Diet A : 12 , 14, 9, 11, 12, 15, 8, 12, 17, 13, 14

Diet B : 15, 13, 18, 8, 17, 9, 14, 12

Null Hypothesis (Ho) : There is no significant difference between the mean increase in weight due to diets A and B

Diet A Mean = 12.45 $\Sigma(X-\overline{X})^2 = 66.7275$

Diet B Mean = 13.25 $\Sigma(Y-\overline{Y})^2 = 87.5$

$$S^2 = \frac{[66.7275+84.5]}{11+8-2}$$

$= 8.87$

$S = 2.98$

$$t = \frac{(13.25-12.45)}{2.98X0.464}$$

$= 0.579$ for 17 df

Tabulated value of t at 5% level of significance for 17 df = 2.11

Result : Since calculated vale of t is less than the tabulated value , the null hypothesis is accepted.

There is no significant difference between Diet A and B as regard to increase in weight.

3. PAIRED 't' test

If the sample sizes are same i.e. $n_1=n_2=n$ and the two samples are not independent but the sample observations are paired together.

Increments $d_i=X_i-Y_i$, (i=1,........n) are calculated for all i=1,....n

the statistic $t = \dfrac{|\ \overline{d}\ |}{S/\sqrt{n}}$

Where $\bar{d} = \Sigma d_i / n$ and $S^2 = \frac{1}{n-1} \Sigma (di - \bar{d})^2$

follows student's 't' distribution with n-1 degrees of freedom.

TABLE 15.1 : In a certain experiment to compare two types of Fish food A and B, the following results of increase in weights were observed in fishes :

Fish Number	*1*	*2*	*3*	*4*	*5*	*6*	*7*	*8*
Diet A (X)	49	53	51	52	47	50	52	53
Diet B (Y)	52	55	52	53	50	54	54	53

Test whether the two diets differ significantly, also is food B is better than food A. The same set of 8 fishes were used.

Null Hypothesis : There is no significant difference between the two foods.

Fish Number	*X*	*Y*	*d (X-Y)*	d^2
1	49	52	– 3	9
2	53	55	– 2	4
3	51	52	– 1	1
4	52	53	– 1	1
5	47	50	– 3	9
6	50	54	– 4	16
7	52	54	– 2	4
8	53	53	0	0
Total	407	423	– 16	44

$$\bar{d} = \Sigma d/n = -16/8 = -2$$

$$S^2 = \frac{1}{n-1} [\Sigma d^2 - (\Sigma d)^2/n)] = 1.714$$

$$t = |-2|/\text{sqrt}(1.714/8) = 4.32$$

Tabulated value of t for 7 df at 5% level of significance = 1.90

Since calculated value is greater than tabulated value, the hypothesis is rejected.

Conclusion : There is significant difference between food A and food B.

Since mean of increase in weight for food B is greater than food A, food B is superior to food A.

CHAPTER 16

CHI - SQUARE DISTRIBUTION

Chi-square variate

The square of a standard normal variate is known as chi-square variate with 1 degree of freedom.

If $X \sim N(\mu, \sigma^2)$ then $Z = (X_i - \mu)/\sigma$ is a standard normal variate with $E(Z) = 0$ and $Var(Z) = 1$; $Z \sim N(0,1)$

and $Z^2 = [(X_i - \mu)/\sigma]^2$ is a chi-square variate with 1 degree of freedom.

In general, if X_i, I=1,2...n are n independent Normal variates with mean μ_i and variance σ_i^2 then

$$\chi^2 = \Sigma \left(\frac{X_i - \mu_i}{\sigma_i}\right)^2$$

is a chi-square variate with n-1 degree of freedom.

The sum of independent chi-square variates with n_i degree of freedom (i=1...k) respectively is also a chi-square variate with Σn_i

Application of Chi-square variate

1. To test the Goodness of fit
2. Independence of attributes
3. Homogeneity of correlation coefficient

1. $\chi 2$ test for Goodness of Fit

In 1900, Prof. K. Pearson introduced a test for testing disagreement between theory and experiment. Let O_i, (i =1...n) be the set of observed (experimental) frequencies and Ei is the corresponding set of expected(theoretical) frequencies, then K. Pearson's chi-square is given by

$$\chi^2 = \Sigma \frac{(O_i - E_i)^2}{E_i}$$

follows a chi-square distribution with n-1 df.

Null Hypothesis : The Experimental results support the Theory.

Conditions for the validity of Chi-square test

a. The sample observation should be independent.
b. $\Sigma O_i = \Sigma E_i$
c. No theoretical cell frequency should be less than 5.
d. N, the total number of frequency should be large =>50.

If any cell frequency is less than 5, then it is pooled with either the preceding or succeeding frequency so that pooled frequency is greater than 5 and degree of freedom is adjusted accordingly. If 2 frequencies are pooled, it will finally loss 2 degree of freedom.

Theory predicts the proportion of beans in the 4 groups A, B, C and D be 9:3:3:1. In an experiment among 1600 beans, the numbers in the four groups obtained are 882, 313, 287 and 118 respectively. Does the experimental result support the theory ?

Null Hypothesis (Ho) : Experimental result supports the theory.

Total number of beans = 882+313+287+118=1600

E(882) = (9×1600)/16 = 900 ; E(313) = (3×1600)/16 = 300

E(287) = (3×1600)/16 = 300 ; E(118) = (1×1600)/16 = 100

$\chi^2 = (882-900)^2/900 + (313-300)^2/300 + (287-300)^2/300 + (118-100)^2/100 = 4.7266$

χ^2 tabulated value at (4-1)=3 df at 5% level of significance = 7.815

Result : Since calculated χ^2 value is less than the tabulated χ^2 value. The hypothesis is accepted. Experimental result supports the theory.

TABLE 16.0 : Observed frequencies of cotton plants in F2. These are two types of plants with leaf shape 1) narrow and 2) broad and colour 1) yellow and 2) white

Ratio obtained are

	Yellow	*White*
Narrow	717	249
Broad	236	80

Does segregation ratio depend upon leaf shape ?

Null Hypothesis : The segregation ratio does not depend on leaf shape.

For 2×2 contingency table direct formula can also be used

$$\chi^2 = \frac{(|ad - bc| - N/2)^2 ¥N}{(a+c)(a+b)(b+d)(c+d)}$$

Yellow	*White*	*Total*
717 (a)	249(b)	(a+b)=966
236(c)	80(d)	(c+d)=316
(a+c)=953	(b+d)=329	(a+b+c+d) =N =1282

$$\chi^2 = \frac{(|57360-58764| - 1282/2)^2 \times 1282}{953\times966\times329\times316}$$

$$= \frac{(1404-641)^2\times1282}{95709050472} = \frac{746340658}{95709050472} = 0.0078$$

Tabulated value for 1 df = 3.841. Since tabulated value is greater than calculated value, the null hypothesis is accepted. The segregation ratio are independent and does not depend on leaf shape.

2. Independence of Attributes

Contingency Table

Let there are two attributes X and Y, X is divided into r classes and Y is divided into s classes. (A_i) is the number of persons possessing the attribute A_i (i=1,2...r), (B_j) is the number of persons possessing the attribute B_j (j=1,2,...s) and (A_iB_j) is the number of persons possessing both the attributes A_i and B_j, (i=1,2,...r ; j=1,2,....s). Also the total frequency is equal to N,

$$\sum_{i=1}^{r} (A_i) = \sum_{i=1}^{s} (B_j) = N$$

Expected frequencies (E_i) are calculated as

Attribute Y

		1	2 ...... s		Total
Attribute X	1	(X_1Y_1)			(X_1)
	2				(X_2)
	3				
	⋮				
	r			(X_rY_s)	(X_r)
	Total	(Y_1)	(Y_2)	(Y_s)	N

This is s X r contingency table

Expected frequency of $(X_1Y_1) = (X_1)*(Y_1)/N$

Expected frequency of $(X_rY_s) = (X_r)*(Y_s)/N$

The coefficient of contingency is given by $C = sqrt(\chi^2/(N+\chi^2))$ with limits as $0<=C<=1$

Similarly all expected frequencies are calculated and chi-square is obtained by the formula :

$$\chi^2 = \Sigma \frac{(O_i - E_i)^2}{E_i}$$

Null Hypothesis : The attributes X and Y are independent

If chi-square calculated is greater than chi-square tabulated for certain degrees of freedom and at certain level of significance, the null hypothesis is rejected meaning that the two variables are dependent.

TABLE 16.1 : To test whether presence of malaria parasites in the blood film is dependent on enlarged spleen.

		Enlarged spleen		*Total*
		Yes	*No*	
Presence of malaria parasites	Yes	740	743	1483
In blood film	No	1287	2731	4018
	Total	2027	3474	5501

Expected frequency of 740 = 1483*2027/5501 = 546.5

Expected frequency of 743 = 1483*3474/5501 = 936.5

Expected frequency of 1287 = 4018*2027/5501 = 1480.5

Expected frequency of 2731 = 4018*3474/5501 = 2537.5

Oi	*Ei*	*Oi-Ei*	*(Oi-Ei)2*	*(Oi-Ei)²/Ei*
740	546.5	193.5	37442.25	68.5
743	936.5	193.5	37442.25	40.0
1287	1480.5	193.5	37442.25	25.3
2731	2537.5	193.5	37442.25	14.8
5501	5501.0			148.6

since calculated chi-square is much greater than tabulated (6.635) at 1% level of significance. The null hypothesis is rejected, meaning presence of malaria parasites in blood film is dependent to enlargement of spleen.

Yates Correction

In a 2X2 contingency table, having degrees of freedom = (2-1)X(2-1) = 1, if any cell frequency is less than 5, we pool our data and the degrees of freedom is reduced by 1 which means degrees of freedom becomes 0, this is meaningless. According to Prof. F. Yates (1934), add 0.5 to the cell frequency which is less than 5 and then adjusting for the remaining cell frequencies accordingly. The chi-square test is applied without pooling method.

If N is large, the Yates's correction will make very little difference.

It is recommended by many authors that Yate's correction be applied to every 2X2 contingency table, even if no theoretical frequency is less than 5.

3. Homogeneity of Correlation Coefficient

Let $r_1, r_2, \ldots r_k$ be k estimates of correlation coefficients from independent samples of sizes $n_1, n_2, \ldots n_k$ respectively. To test the hypothesis that the sample correlation coefficients are the estimates of same correlation coefficient ρ from a normal population.The values of $z_1, z_2, \ldots z_k$ are calculated by using

$$z_i = 1.15129*\log\left(\frac{1+r_i}{1-r_i}\right)$$

These z_i's are normally distributed about a common mean

$\xi = 1.15129*\log(1+\rho)/(1-\rho)$ and

variance = $1/(n_i-3)$

the estimate $\bar{z}$ is therefore

$$\bar{z} = \frac{\Sigma\, z_i(n_i-3)}{\Sigma\,(n_i-3)}$$

so that $(z_i - \bar{z})(n_i - 3)^{1/2}$; i = 1,2,.....k are independent standard normal variates. Hence

$\Sigma\,(z_i-\bar{z})^2\,(n_i - 3)$ is a chi-square variate with (k-1) df

If χ^2 value obtained is greater than tabulated value of χ^2 at 5% level of significance for (k-1) df, the hypothesis of homogeneity of correlation coefficients is rejected otherwise the correlation coefficients are said to be homogeneous. The estimate of population correlation coefficient ρ is calculated by the formula

$$\rho = \frac{e^{2z} - 1}{e^{2z} + 1}$$

The correlation between length and weight of fish catla catla on the basis of observation taken on 10, 14, 16, 20, 25, 28 fishes at six ponds were found to be 0.512, 0.621, 0.582, 0.672, 0.813 and 0.759. Test whether these correlation coefficients can be considered as homogeneous ? If yes, calculate the common correlation coefficient.

H0 : The given values of correlation coefficients are homogeneous.

Z_i values are calculated by the formula $z_i = 1.1512*\log\frac{1+r_i}{1-r_i}$

$$r_1 = 0.512 \; z_1 = 1.1512*\log\frac{1+0.512}{1-0.512} = 1.1512*\log\frac{1.512}{0.488}$$

$$= 1.1512*\log 3.098$$

$$= 1.1512*0.4911 = 0.5653$$

similarly, z_2 =0.7266, z_3 = 0.6653, z_4 = 0.8142, z_5 = 1.1356 and z_6 = 0.9937

$$\bar{z} = \frac{\Sigma\, z_i(n_i-3)}{\Sigma\,(n_i-3)}$$

$$= \frac{0.5653*7+0.7266*11+0.6653*13+0.8142*17+1.1356*21+0.9927*25}{7+11+13+17+21+25}$$

$$= \frac{83.1051}{94} = 0.8841$$

$$\bar{z} = 0.8841$$

$$\chi^2 = \Sigma\,(z_i-\bar{z})^2*(n_i-3)$$

$$\chi^2 = (0.5653-0.8841)^2\times7+(0.7266-0.8841)^2\times11+(0.6653-0.8841)^2\times13$$
$$+(0.8142-0.8841)^2\times17+(1.1356-0.8841)^2\times21+(0.9937-0.8841)^2\times25$$
$$= 3.3195$$

Tabulated value of chi-square for (6-1)=5 degrees of freedom at 5% level of significance is 11.070. Since calculated value is less than the tabulated value the null hypothesis is accepted. Thus, the sample correlation coefficients are homogeneous.

The estimate of population correlation coefficient

$$\rho = \frac{e^{2z} - 1}{e^{2z}+1}$$

$$= \frac{e^{1.7682} - 1}{e^{1.7682}+1} = \frac{5.8603-1}{5.8603+1} = 0.7084$$

CHAPTER 17

LARGE SAMPLE TESTS

a) Test of Proportion

Let X_1 and X_2 be the number of persons possessing the given attribute A in random samples(large) of sizes n_1 and n_2 from the two populations respectively. The sample proportions are given by

$$P_1 = X_1/n_1 \qquad P_2 = X_2/n_2$$

Null Hypothesis : $P_1 = P_2$; there is no significant difference between sample proportions.

The formula used :

$$Z = \frac{P_1 - P_2}{\text{Sqrt}\,[\,P\,Q\,(1/n_1+1/n_2)]}$$

Where $P = \frac{X1+X2}{n1+n2}$ an unbiased estimate of population proportion based on both the samples and Q=1-P

TABLE 17.0 : 139 and 227 adults from control and MIC affected areas respectively have been examined for the content of the foetal haemoglobin (10 HbF%) in the adult haemoglobin. Test whether MIC gas effected persons for the presence of foetal haemoglobin.

	Sample size	*persons having 10% HbF (FH)*
Control area	139	5
MIC affected area	227	58

Null Hypothesis : MIC gas does not effect the presence of foetal haemoglobin

P_1 = 5/139 = 0.0359 ; P_2 = 58/227 = 0.255

P = (X1+X2)/(n1+n2) = (5+58)/(139+227) = 63/366 = 0.172

Q = 1 – P = 0.828

|Z | = (0.0359–0.255)/ sqrt[0.172X0.828 {(1/139)+ (1/227)}]

= 5.4775

Z tab = 1.96 at 5% level of significance for large sample

Result : Since calculated Z is greater than tabulated Z , null hypothesis is rejected.

MIC gas affected the presence of Foetal Haemoglobin (10% HbF)

b) Test of Significant for Difference of Means

Let X be the mean of a sample of size n_1 from a population with mean μ_1 and variance σ_1^2 and let Y be the mean of an independent sample of size n_2 from another population with mean μ_2 and variance σ_2^2

Since sample sizes are large i.e. sample size >30,

$$X \sim N(\mu_1, \sigma_1^2/n_1) \text{ and } Y \sim N(\mu_2, \sigma_2^2/n_2)$$

Under Null Hypothesis H0 : $\mu_1 = \mu_2$ i.e. there is no significant difference between two means.

$$\text{Formula used : } Z = \frac{\overline{X} - \overline{Y}}{\text{Sqrt } (\sigma_1^2/n_1 + \sigma_2^2/n_2)}$$

TABLE 17.1 : In two reservoirs the value of pH was calculated each month for two years.

	Sample size	*Mean*	*Standard Deviation*
Reservoir A	24	8.01	0.4176
Reservoir B	24	7.70	0.3397

Test whether average pH of two reservoirs are equal. t-tabulated at 1% level of significance for large sample = 2.58

Null Hypothesis : The sample means do not differ significantly

Since (n_1+n_2-2) df = 24+24-2=46, large sample test of difference of mean is to be used.

$\sigma_1^2 = (0.4176 * 0.4176) = 0.17438976$; $n_1 = 24$

$\sigma_2^2 = (0.3397 * 0.3397) = 0.11539609$; $n_2 = 24$

$\overline{X} = 8.01$; $\overline{Y} = 7.70$, $\overline{X}-\overline{Y} = 8.01-7.70 = 0.31$

Z = (0.31/0.10988362) = 2.8211

Since t-calculated > t-tabulated, null hypothesis is rejected.

Coclusion : Average pH of two reservoirs differ significantly.

c) Test of Significance for Difference of Standard Deviations

If S_1 and S_2 are the standard deviations of two independent samples, then under Null Hypothesis

H0 : $\sigma_1 = \sigma_2$ i.e. the sample standard deviations do not differ significantly.

The statistic

$$Z = \frac{S_1 - S_2}{S.E.\ (S_1 - S_2)} \sim N(0,1) \text{ for large samples}$$

But for large samples, S.E. $(S_1 - S_2) = \text{sqrt}[(\sigma_1^2/2n_1)+(\sigma_2^2/2n_2)]$

Since σ_1^2 and σ_2^2 are not known usually, for large samples their estimates are used given by corresponding sample variances.

Formula used $$Z = \frac{S_1 - S_2}{\text{Sqrt}[(S_1^2/2n_1)+(S_2^2/2n_2)]}$$

For large samples 't' tabulated values are 1.96, 2.58 and 3.29 at 5%, 1% and 0.1% level of significance respectively.

CHAPTER 18

NONPARAMETRIC TESTS

Techniques for comparing two or more populations that are based on an ordering of the sample measurements according to their relative magnitude relates to nonparametric tests. In nonparametric tests, less stringent assumptions are required about the nature of the probability distributions of the population. Many nonparametric methods use the relative ranks of the sample observations rather than their actual numerical values. These tests are particularly valuable when we are unable to obtain numerical measurements of some phenomena but are able to rank them in comparison to each other. Statistics based on ranks of measurements is called rank statistics. If the executives A and B are evaluated by each of 10 observers, the probability distributions for two populations of ratings one for A and another for B can be compared. `t' test would be inappropriate because the only data recorded is preferences.

Wilcoxon Rank Sum Test for Independent Samples

It was developed by Sir Frank Wilcoxon.

Assumptions : 1. The two samples are random and independent.

2. The two probability distributions from which the samples are drawn are continuous.

Average of the ranks are assigned if tied measurement occurs. For example if third and fourth ranked measurements are tied, assign each a rank of (3+4)/2 =3.5

One Tailed Test

H0 : Two sampled populations have identical probability distribution

Ha : The probability distribution of population A is shifted to the right of that for B

Test Statistic : The rank sum, T, associated with the sample with less measurements (if sample sizes are equal, either rank sum can be used). Null hypothesis is rejected if $T_A \Rightarrow T_U$ where T_A is the rank sum of smaller sample and T_U is the upper value given by Appendix X for the chosen one tailed α value.

Two Tailed Test

H0 : Two sampled populations have identical probability distribution

Ha : The probability distribution of population A is shifted to the left or to the right of that for B.

Test Statistic : The rank sum T, associated with the sample with less measurements (if the sample sizes are equal, either rank sum can be used). The null hypothesis is rejected if $T <= T_L$ or $T => T_U$ where T_L is the lower value given by Appendix X for chosen two-tailed α value, T_U is the upper value from Appendix X.

Appendix X gives the values of T_L and T_U for sample sizes n_1 and n_2 less than or equal to 10. When both the sample sizes are 10 or larger, the sampling distribution of T_A can be approximated by a normal distribution with mean and variance

$$\text{Mean} = n_1(n_1+n_2+1)/2$$

$$\text{Variance}(T_A) = n_1n_2(n_1+n_2+1)/12$$

WILCOXON RANK SUM TEST FOR LARGE INDEPENDENT SAMPLES

One Tailed Test

H0 : Two sampled populations have identical probability distribution.

Ha : The probability distribution of population A is shifted to the right of that for B

Let $R_1 = n_1(n_1+n_2+1)/2$

$R_2 = n_1n_2(n_1+n_2+1)/12$

Test Statistic $Z = \dfrac{T_A - R_1}{\sqrt{R_2}}$

Rejection Region : $Z > Z\alpha$

Two Tailed Test

H0 : Two sampled populations have identical probability distribution.

Ha : The probability distribution of population A is shifted to the left or to the right of that for B

Let $R_1 = n_1(n_1+n_2+1)/2$

$R_2 = n_1n_2(n_1+n_2+1)/12$

Test Statistic $Z = \frac{T_A - R_1}{\sqrt{R_2}}$

Rejection Region : $Z > Z_{\alpha/2}$ or $Z < -Z_{\alpha/2}$

TABLE 18.0 : Six government economists and 7 professors of economics are randomly selected for the prediction of next year's percentage change in cost of living as compared with this year's figure. The objective is to compare the government economist's prediction to the professor's.

A		*B*	
Government Economist		*Economics Professor*	
Prediction	*Rank*	*Prediction*	*Rank*
3.1	4	4.4	6
4.8	7	5.8	9
2.3	2	3.9	5
5.6	8	8.7	11
0.0	1	6.3	10
2.9	3	10.5	12
10.8	13		

$T_A=25$ $T_B=66$

Test the hypothesis that the economics professor's prediction of the next year's percentage change in cost of living tends to be higher than the government economist's.

Ranking of sample observation is done as they were all drawn from the same population.

H0 : The probability distributions corresponding to the government economist and economics professor's prediction of inflation rate are identical.

Ha : The probability distribution of economics professor prediction lies above (to the right of) that for the government economist's prediction.

Test Statistic : Since sample size of government economist (n_1=6) is less, the test statistic is T_A, the rank sum of government economist's prediction.

$T_A=25, n_1=6, T_B=66, n_2=7$

The sum of T_A and T_B will always equal n(n+1)/2 where $n=n_1+n_2$ = 7+6=13

T=13(13+1)/2 = 91

Since T_A+T_B is fixed, a small value of T_A implies a large value of T_B (and vice versa) and a large difference between T_A and T_B. The smaller the value of one of the rank sums, the greater is the evidence to indicate that the samples were selected from different populations.

Rejection Region : Since the test is one sided, by consulting Appendix X for the rejection region corresponding to α=0.05. H0 will be rejected only when $T_A <= T_L$ (since we are testing that the distribution of government economist's prediction lies below the distribution of professor's prediction.)

$T_A=25$ and $T_L=30(n_1=6, n_2=7)$

Sine $T_A<T_L$; null hypothesis is rejected

Conclusion : Economics professor's prediction tends to exceed the government economist's prediction.

Wilcoxon Signed Rank Test for the Paired Difference Experiment

Difference between the measurements is analyzed because it is a paired difference experiment. Ranks of the absolute values of the differences between the measurements are calculated (the ranks of the differences after removing minus signs). Tied absolute differences are assigned the average of the ranks they would receive if they were unequal but successive measurements. After the absolute differences are ranked, the sum of the ranks of the positive differences, T+ and the sum of the ranks of the negative differences, T- are computed. If the alternative hypothesis is that the probability distribution for A is shifted to the left of B, T+ is used as test statistic and reject H0 if T+ <=T0. If the difference of ranks is zero, that pair is eliminated from the calculation of the test statistic and n is adjusted accordingly (subtracting number of zeros from n).

Assumptions : 1) The sample of differences is randomly selected from the population of differences.

2) The probability distribution from which the sample of paired differences is drawn is continuous.

One Tailed Test

H0 : Two sample populations have identical probability distribution.

Ha : The probability distribution for population A is shifted to the right of that for population B.

Test Statistic : T-, the negative rank sum (differences are computed by subtracting each paired B measurements from the corresponding A measurement).

Rejection Region : T-<=T0, where T0 is found in Appendix XI for the one tailed significance level α and the number of matched pairs.

Two Tailed Test

H0 : Two sampled populations have identical probability distribution.

Ha : The probability distribution for population A is shifted to the right or to the left of that for population B.

Test Statistic : T, the smaller of the positive and negative rank sums, T+ and T-.

Rejection Region : T<=T0, where T0 is found in Appendix XI for the two tailed significance levels.

TABLE 18.1 : Ten judges are given a sample of two products that are to be compared. Each judge rates the softness of each product on a scale from 1 to 10, with higher ratings implying a softer product.

Judge	*Product*		*Difference*	*Absolute value*	*Rank of the*
	A	*B*	*(A-B)*	*of difference*	*absolute value*
1	6	4	2	2	5
2	8	5	3	3	7.5
3	4	5	–1	1	2
4	9	8	1	1	2
5	4	1	3	3	7.5
6	7	9	–2	2	5
7	6	2	4	4	9
8	5	3	2	2	5
9	6	7	–1	1	2
10	8	2	6	6	10

H0 : Two sampled populations have identical probability distribution.

Ha : Probability distribution of A is shifted to the right or to the left of population B.

T+ sum of positive ranks = 5+7.5+2+7.5+9+5+10 = 46

T– sum of negative ranks = 2+5+2 = 9

The rejection region for T can be obtained from Appendix XI. The values of T0 are tabulated for both , one tailed and two tailed test. For a two tailed test with $\alpha = 0.05$, null hypothesis is rejected if T <= T0 for n=10 pairs of observations. Since T0=8 with n=10 and $\alpha = 0.05$, the smaller rank sum T=T– =9, does not fall within the rejection region. The null hypothesis is accepted and it can be concluded that experiment does not provide sufficient evidence to indicate that the two paper products differ with respect to their softness ratings . If a significance level of α =0.01, the rejection region would have been T<=11, the null hypothesis is rejected concluding the samples do provide evidence that the probability distributions of the softness ratings differ at α=0.01.

Wilcoxon Signed Rank Test for a Paired Difference Experiment (Large sample)

Assumption n=>25

One Tailed Test

H0: Two sampled populations have identical probability distributions

Ha : The probability distribution for population A is shifted to the right of that for population B.

Test Statistic : Let $R_1 = n(n+1)/4$

Let $R_2 = \sqrt{(n(n+1)(2n+1)/24)}$

$Z = (T+ - R_1)/R_2$

Rejection region : $Z > Z\alpha$

Two Tailed Test

H0 : Two sampled populations have identical probability distributions

Ha : The probability distribution for population A is shifted to the right or to the left of that for population B.

Test Statistic : Let $R_1 = n(n+1)/4$

Let $R_2 = \sqrt{(n(n+1)(2n+1))/24}$

$Z = (T+ - R_1)/R_2$

Rejection region : $Z > Z_{\alpha/2}$ or $Z < - Z_{\alpha/2}$

Kruskal - Wallis H Test for a Completely Randomised Design

Completely randomized design is one in which independent random samples are selected from each p populations (treatments) to be compared. Analysis of variance and the F-test are used to compare the means of p populations. In this design, it is assumed that populations have normal probability distributions with equal variances. But Kruskal-Wallis H-test is a nonparametric test which requires no assumptions concerning the population probability distribution to compare p populations.

Assumptions :
1. The p samples are random and independent
2. There are 5 or more measurements in each sample
3. The p probability distributions from which samples are drawn are continuous.

H0 : The p probability distributions are identical.

Ha : At least two of the p probability distributions differ.

Test Statistic :

$$H = 12/n(n+1)\, \Sigma\, R_j^2/\, n_j - 3\,(n+1)$$

Where n_j : number of measurements in sample j

R_j : Rank sum of sample j, where the rank of each measurement is computed according to its relative magnitude in the totality of data for the p samples

n : Total sample size = $n_1+n_2+\ldots..n_p$

Rejection region : $H > \chi^2_\alpha$ with p-1 degrees of freedom

The H statistic measures the extend to which the p samples differ with respect to their relative ranks. The approximation distribution of the test statistic H is a χ^2 distribution with (p-1) degrees of freedom. Entries in Appendix V give an upper tail value of χ^2 such that $P(\chi^2>\chi^2_\alpha) = \alpha$. The columns of the table identify the value of α associated with the tabulated value of χ^2_α and rows correspond to degrees of freedom.

TABLE 18.2 : Number of employees are compared in companies representing each of three different business classifications IT, agriculture, service. Ten companies of each type are selected and number of employees are noted.

IT		*Agriculture*		*Service*	
Empl.	*Rank*	*Empl.*	*Rank*	*Empl.*	*Rank*
10	5	244	25	17	9.5
350	27	93	19	249	26
4	2	3532	30	38	15
26	13	17	9.5	5	3
15	8	526	29	101	20
106	21	133	22	1	1
18	11	14	7	12	6
23	12	192	23	233	24
62	17	443	28	31	14
8	4	69	18	39	16

The ranks are calculated for each observation according to relative magnitude of the measurements when all p samples are combined. Total of ranks for each business classification is calculated as R_1(IT) = 120 , R_2 (Agri.)=210.5 and R_3(service)=134.5.

H0 : All the three populations have identical probability distribution.

Ha : At least two of the three population probability distribution differ.

n = 30 ; $H = 12/(30)(31)\,[(120^2/10) + (210.5^2/10) + (134.5^2/10)] - 3(31)$

$H = 99.097 - 93 = 6.097$

Thus for α=0.05 and degrees of freedom = 2, the null hypothesis that the three probability distributions are the same is rejected if $H > \chi^2_{0.05}$

Since calculated H = 6.097 and tabulated $\chi^2_{0.05}$ (2 df) =5.99147

Null hypothesis is rejected.

Conclusion : At least two of the three sampled business type differ.

The Friedman F_r Test for a Randomized Block Design

Assumptions :

1. The treatments are randomly assigned to experimental units within the blocks
2. Either the number of blocks (b) or the number of treatments (p) should exceed 5 for the chi-square approximation to be adequate.
3. The p probability distributions from which the samples within each block are drawn are continuous.

H0 : The probability distributions for the p treatments are identical.

Ha : At least two of the probability distributions differ in location.

Test Statistic :

$$F_r = 12/bp(p+1)\ \Sigma\ R_j^2 - 3\ b(p+1)$$

where

b = number of blocks

p = number of treatments

R_j = Rank sum of the jth treatment, when the rank of each measurement is computed relative to its position within its own block.

Null hypothesis is rejected if $F_r > \chi^2_\alpha$ with (p-1) degrees of freedom

TABLE 18.3 : Suppose a marketing firm wants t compare the relative effectiveness of three different modes of advertising ; direct mail, newspaper advertising and magazine advertising. For 15 companies all three modes are used over a 1-year period, and the marketing firm records the year's percentage response to each type of advertising. That is, the firm divides the number of responses to a particular type of advertising by the total number of potential customers reached by the advertisement of that type.

Company	*Direct Mail*	R_1	*Newspaper Ad.*	R_2	*Magazine Ad.*	R_3
1	7.3	1	15.7	3	10.1	2
2	9.4	2	18.3	3	8.2	1

3	4.3	1	11.2	3	5.1	2
4	11.3	2	19.1	3	6.5	1
5	3.3	1	9.2	3	8.7	2
6	4.2	1	10.5	3	6.0	2
7	5.9	1	8.7	2	12.3	3
8	6.2	1	14.3	3	11.1	2
9	4.3	2	3.1	1	6.0	3
10	10.0	1	18.8	3	12.1	2
11	2.2	1	5.7	2	6.3	3
12	6.3	2	20.2	3	4.3	1
13	8.0	1	14.1	3	9.1	2
14	7.4	2	6.2	1	18.1	3
15	3.2	1	8.7	3	5.0	2

B =15 (blocks ; companies)

P = 3 (treatments : type of advertising)

$\Sigma R_1 = 20, \quad \Sigma R_2 = 39, \quad \Sigma R_3 = 31$

H0 : The probability distributions of the response rates are identical for the three modes of advertisement.

Ha : At least two of the three probability distributions differ in location.

$$F_r = 12/bp(p+1)\ \Sigma\ R_j^2 - 3\ b(p+1)$$
$$= 12/(15)(3)(4)\ [20^2+39^2+31^2] - 3(15)(4)$$
$$= (400+1521+961)/15 - 180$$
$$= 192.13 - 180 = 12.13$$

tabulated $\chi^2_{0.01}$ for 2 df = 9.21034

Since Fr > $\chi^2_{0.01}$ for 2 df, null hypothesis is rejected.

Conclusion : At least two of the response rate probability distribution for the three modes of advertising differ in location.

Spearman's Nonparametric Test for Rank Correlation Coefficient

One Tailed :

H0 : $p_s = 0$; There is no population correlation between ranks

Ha : p_s # 0 ; There is a population correlation between ranks

Formula Used : $r_s = 1 - 6\Sigma d_i^2/n(n^2-1)$

$d_i = U_i - V_i$ (difference of ranks of the ith measurement for sample 1 and 2)

The sign of r_s indicates the nature of the relationship between the two variables, positive values indicate a tendency for the variables to increase together, and negative values indicate a tendency for one variable to increase while the other decreases.

TABLE 18.4 : Bank manager wants to determine whether to aim its advertisement at a broad spectrum of potential borrowers or to concentrate on a specific income group. Ten non-commercial customers are chosen and their present income and total amount each has borrowed over last one year.

Customer	*Income*	*Rank U_i*	*Borrowed*	*Rank V_i*	*D_i*	*D_i^2*
1	14,800	5	4300	7	–2	4
2	8,900	1	4800	8	–7	49
3	83,600	10	500	2	8	64
4	22,100	8	3300	5	3	9
5	18,200	7	5500	9	–2	4
6	13,700	4	3700	6	–2	4
7	41,800	9	0	1	8	64
8	9300	2	3200	4	–2	4
9	12,700	3	6100	10	–7	49
10	16,100	6	1800	3	3	9
						260

$$r_s = 1 - 6\Sigma d_i^2/n(n^2-1)$$
$$= 1 - 6(260)/10(100-1)$$
$$= 1 - 1.576 = -0.576$$

To determine rejection region, Appendix XII is consulted. The entries in the table are values for an upper tail rejection region, since only positive values are given. Thus for n=10 and α=0.05, the value 0.564 is boundary of the upper tailed rejection region, so that p(rs >0.564) = 0.05 if infact H0 is true. The two tailed rejection region is

$r_s > 0.564$ or $r_s < -0.564$ and the α value is therefore double the table value i.e. $\alpha = 2(0.05) = 0.1$.

Thus, rejection region : $r_s < -0.564$ or $r_s > 0.564$ for $\alpha = 0.1$, since calculated value of rs = –0.576 which is less than –0.564, the null hypothesis is rejected at $\alpha = 0.1$ and conclude that the population rank correlation coefficient differs from 0. It appears that the bank customers at lower income levels tend to borrow more than those at higher income levels. The bank will aim its loan advertising at those in the middle and lower income groups.

CHAPTER 19

THEORY OF ATTRIBUTES

Literally an attribute means a quality or characteristic. There are some characteristics which cannot be measured quantitatively (eg. drinking, smoking, honesty etc.) The theory of attributes deals with the study of qualitative characteristics. By the presence and absence of the attribute, population is to be divided and then frequencies for all combinations calculated.

Notations :

Let the population be divided into two classes according to the presence or absence of the attribute.

Positive Class : The class which denotes the presence of the attribute (denoted by Roman letters, as A, B, etc.)

Negative Class : The class which denotes the absence of the attribute (denoted by Greek letters, as α,β, etc.) If A denotes smokers then α will denote non-smokers.

Complimentary Classes : A and α are said to be the complimentary classes.

Contrary Class : The combination of negative and positive classes is called contrary class, as $A\beta C$.

Order : The number of observation assigned to a class is called class frequency. It is denoted by using '()'. As '(A)' is the frequency of order 1. A class represented by n attributes is called a class of nth order.

The total number of members of the population i.e. N, without any specification of attributes is frequency of 'zero' order.

The combination of the attributes are denoted by grouping together the attributes concerned.

Let the attributes A,B and C denote drinking, sickness and male respectively. Then (ABC) denote the males who drink and are sick.

[() indicates frequency] or (AβC) denotes the males who drink and are healthy.

The classification in which the population has only two complementary classes and no more is known as DICHOTOMOUS class. In this type of classification with respect to n attributes, the number of class frequencies of order r is equal to

$$^{n}C_{r} * 2^{r}$$

The total number of class frequencies of all orders, for n attributes is equal to

$$\sum_{r=0}^{n} {}^{n}C_{r} * 2^{r} = 3^{n}$$

Relation between class frequencies

All the class frequencies of various orders are dependent on each other and any class frequency can always be expressed as a set of some frequencies.

$$N = (A) + (\alpha) = (B) + (\beta)$$
$$(A) = (AB) + (A\beta) ; (B) = (AB) + (\alpha B)$$
$$(\alpha) = (\alpha B) + (\alpha\beta) ; (\beta) = (A\beta) + (\alpha\beta)$$

The class of highest order is known as ultimate class and its frequency as ultimate frequency.

Symbolic expressions

(AβC, αBC)

Let A.N = (A) and α .N = (α)

Adding both, A.N + α.N = (A) + (α)

⇨ $A + \alpha = 1$

Thus, in symbolic expressions A & B can be replaced by (1-α) and (1-β)

Similarly

$$(\alpha\beta) = \alpha\beta \,.\, N$$
$$= (1-A)(1-B)*N$$
$$= N - [(A)+(B)]+(AB)$$

Condition for consistency of data

For a single attribute A : (A) => 0 ; (B) => 0

⇨ (A) <= N

For two attributes A,B : (AB) => 0 ; (A β)=> 0

⇨ (AB)<=(A)

(α B)=> 0

⇨ (AB) <=(B)

(αβ)=>0

⇨ (AB) => (A)+(B)-N

Height and weight measurements were made on a thousand husbands and their wives. If measurements of husbands exceed their wives in 900 cases for height, 750 cases for weight and 660 cases for both, calculate in how many cases both measurements on wives exceed the measurements on husbands.

Let attribute A : husband's height exceed their wives

B : husband's weight exceed their wives

Given (A) = 900 ; (B) = 750 ; (AB) = 660 ; (αβ) = ?

$$(\alpha\beta) = N - [(A)+(B)]+(AB)$$
$$= 1000 - [900+750] + 660$$
$$= 10$$

There are 10 cases where both measurements of wives exceed their husbands.

Independence of Attributes

Two attributes are said to be independent if there exists no relation between them of any kind. If A, B are independent ;

$$(AB)/(B) = (A\beta)/(\beta)$$
$$\Rightarrow \quad (AB)/(B) = (A)/(N)$$

If the attributes A and B are independent, the proportion of AB's in the population is equal to the product of proportions of A's and B's in the population.

$$(AB)/N = (A)/N*(B)/N$$

Association

The two attributes A, B are said to be associated if they are not independent but related in some way.

If

a. (AB) > [(A)*(B)]/N ; positively associated

b. (AB) < [(A)*(B)]/N ; negatively associated

c. (AB) = (A) or (AB) = (B) ; completely associated

d. (AB) = 0 or ($\alpha\beta$)=0 ; complete dissociation

e. [(A)*(B)]/N tends to zero ; association by chance

Let [(A)*(B)]/N = $(AB)_0$

Which is the value of (AB) under the hypothesis that A and B are independent.

Let d = (AB) – $(AB)_0$

Yule's coefficient of association

G.U. Yule gave the coefficient of association as,

$$Q = \frac{(AB)(\alpha\beta) - (A\beta)(\alpha B)}{(AB)(\alpha\beta) + (A\beta)(\alpha B)}$$

$$= \frac{N*d}{(AB)(\alpha\beta) + (A\beta)(\alpha B)}$$

limits of Yule's coefficient : –1 <= Q <= +1

TABLE 19. 0 : Investigate the association between height of father and son (age=>24 & <=30), good height (>5'6") and satisfactory height (>5'2" <= 5'6")

		Father's height	
		Good	*satisfactory*
Son's height	Good	92	70
	Satisfactory	65	105

Let A : Father with good height

B : Son with good height

Then (AB) = 92, ($A\beta$) = 65, (αB) = 70, ($\alpha\beta$) = 105

$$Q = \frac{(92*105) - (70*65)}{(92*105) + (70*65)} = +0.59$$

fairly good association. Height is a hereditary character.

CHAPTER 20

POPULATION STUDIES

Cohort Measure

A statistic that measures events occurring to a cohort (a group of people sharing a common demographic experience) who are observed through time. The most common cohorts are Birth cohort, Marriage cohort etc.

Proportion

The relation of a population subgroup to the entire population.

Example : The proportion of Malaysia's population(urban) was 0.57 or 57%.

Ratio

The relation of one population subgroup to the total population or to another subgroup.

Example : Sex ratio in Iran in 1996 was 103 males per 100 females.

Rate

The frequency of demographic events in a population during a specified time period (probably a year) divided by the population at risk of the event occurring during that time period. Most rates are expressed per 1000 population. Rates can be age-specific, sex-specific, race-specific etc.

Sex Ratio

It is the ratio of males to females in a given population.

$$\frac{\text{Number of Males}}{\text{Number of Females}} \times 100$$

Age Dependency Ratio

It is the ratio of persons in the "dependent" ages (usually under 15 and over 64) to those in the "economically productive" ages (15-64 years).

$$\frac{\text{Population under age 15 years + Population over age 64 years}}{\text{Population ages 15-64}} \times 100$$

Countries with very high birth rates usually have high Age Dependency Ratio because of large proportion of children in the population.

Median Age

The age at which exactly half of the population is older and half is younger.

Birth Rate

It is also called as Crude birth rate. It is the number of live births per 1000 population in a given year.

$$\frac{\text{Number of Births}}{\text{Total Population}} \times 1000$$

General Fertility Rate

It is also called the fertility rate. It is the number of live births per 1000 women aged 15-49 in a given year.

$$\frac{\text{Number of births}}{\text{Number of women ages 15-49}} \times 1000$$

Age-Specific Fertility Rate

Fertility rates can also be calculated for specific age groups to see differences in fertility behaviour at different ages.

$$\frac{\text{Number of births to women ages 20-24}}{\text{Number of women ages 20-24}} \times 1000$$

Total Fertility Rate(TFR)

It is the sum of the fertility of all women at a given point in time. It is the total number of children a women would have if the fertility rates for a given year applied to her throughout her reproductive life. Year to year fluctuations in the TFR may reflect changes in the timing of births rather than changes in the average number of children women bear.

Gross Reproduction Rate (GRR)

It is the average number of daughters that would be born to a women or group of women during her lifetime if she passed through her childbearing years conforming to the age-specific fertility rates of a given year.

Net Reproduction Rate

It is the average number of daughters that would be born to a women or group of women if she passed through her lifetime from birth conforming to the age-specific fertility and mortality rates of a given year. This rate is less than the GRR because some women may die before completing her childbearing years.

Abortion Rate

It is the number of abortions per 1000 women of reproductive age in a year.

$$\frac{\text{Number of abortions}}{\text{Number of women ages 15-49}} \times 1000$$

Abortion Ratio

It is the number of abortions per 1000 live births in a given year.

$$\frac{\text{Number of abortions}}{\text{Number of live births}} \times 1000$$

Death Rate (Crude Death Rate)

It is the number of deaths per 1000 population in a given year.

$$\frac{\text{Number of deaths}}{\text{Total population}} \times 1000$$

Age Specific Death Rate

Death rate can be calculated for specific age groups in order to compare mortality at different ages over time. Mortality differs greatly by sex and race therefore this rate is often given separately for males and females and for different racial groups in a population.

$$\frac{\text{Number of deaths of people ages 20-24}}{\text{Total population ages 20-24}} \times 1000$$

Cause Specific Death Rates

These rates are usually expressed in deaths per 100,000 because, for most causes of deaths, the rates of occurrence are very low.

$$\frac{\text{Deaths from Cancer}}{\text{Total Population}} \times 100000$$

Infant Mortality Rate

It is the number of deaths of infants under age 1year per 1000 live births in a given year.

$$\frac{\text{Number of deaths of infants under age 1 in a year}}{\text{Total live births in that year}} \times 1000$$

Maternal Mortality Ratio

It is the number of women who die as a complications of pregnancy or childbearing in a given year per 100,000 live births in that year.

$$\frac{\text{Number of maternal deaths}}{\text{Total live births in that year}} \times 100000$$

Life Expectancy

It is an estimate of the average number of additional years a person could expect to live if the age-specific death rates for a given year prevailed for the rest of his /her life. Each person's life expectancy changes as he or she grows older and as mortality trends change. Life expectancy at birth is the most commonly cited life expectancy measure.

Incidence Rate

It is the number of persons contracting a disease during a given time period, per 1000 population at risk. This and other morbidity rates vary widely that any constant may be used i.e. per 100 or per 100000 population.

$$\frac{\text{Number of persons developing Cancer During a given period}}{\text{Population at risk}} \times 1000$$

Prevalence Rate

It is the number of persons who have a particular disease at a given point in time per 1000 population. This includes all known cases that have not resulted in death, cure or remission as well as new cases developing during the specified time.

$$\frac{\text{Number of persons with Cancer and having ages 25-50}}{\text{Total population ages 25-50}} \times 1000$$

Marriage Rate

It is the number of marriages per 1000 total population in a given year.

$$\frac{\text{Number of marriages}}{\text{Total population}} \times 1000$$

Immigration Rate

It is the number of immigrants arriving at a destination per 1000 population at that destination in a given year.

$$\frac{\text{Number of immigrants}}{\text{Total population at destination}} \times 1000$$

Emigration Rate

It is the number of emigrants departing an area of origin per 1000 population at that area of origin in a given year.

$$\frac{\text{Number of emigrants}}{\text{Total population at origin}} \times 1000$$

Population Density

It is expressed as the number of people per unit of land area. It is meaningful if given as populations per unit of arable land.

$$\frac{\text{Total population}}{\text{Total land area}} \times 1000$$

The Balancing Equation

The basic method of calculating numerical population change over time.

$$P_1+(B-D)+(I-E) = P_2$$

P_1 : The population at the earlier date

P_2 : The population at the later date

B and D are the births and the deaths between two dates respectively and I and E are immigration and emigration between the two dates respectively.

Natural Increase

It is the surplus of births over deaths in a population in a given time period. This value does not include immigration and emigration.

$$NI = B - D$$

Rate of natural increase can be calculated by NI/10.

Growth Rate

It is the rate at which a population is increasing (decreasing) in a given year due to natural increase and net migration, expressed as a percentage of the base population.

$$\frac{\text{Births-Deaths} + (-) \text{ Net migration}}{\text{Total population in that year}} \times 100$$

CHAPTER 21

COMPUTER APPLICATION

INTRODUCTION

Charles Babbage, an English scientist and Mathematician invented computer in nineteenth century. Computer is an electronic device used to perform data processing by using a set of instructions provided to it, to get the desired output in a defined format. Computer is needed because of its speed, storage capacity, accuracy and for software development. Computer consists of three main parts, i.e. Hardware, Software and Operating system. Hardware refers to the entire machinery i.e. items that can be touched. It includes input devices, output devices and secondary storage (floppy, compact disk, pen drive, tapes etc.). Software refers to the programming application. Operating system (software) [illegible] the link between hardware and software. Two types of operating system exists, single user and multi user. In single user, only one user can work at a time eg. Disk Operating System (DOS). In multiuser, many dumb terminals or computers are attached with the CPU and different users can work independently at the same time eg. Unix, Xenix etc. The computer has five basic unit,

FIG - 21.1

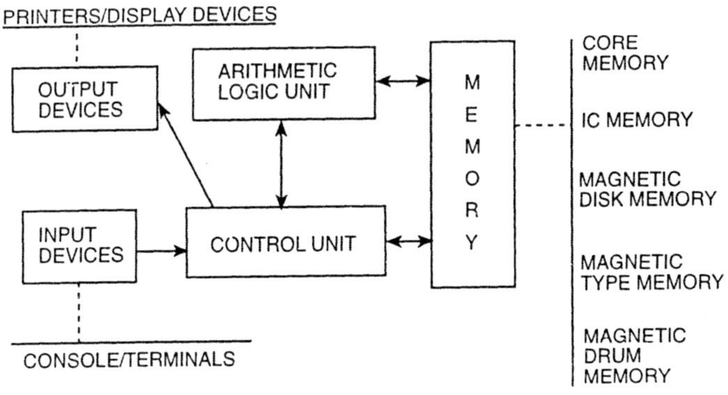

1. Input unit

   It is the unit used to communicate (feed) data or programs to the computer. There may be more than one input devices. Some of the input devices are floppy, keyboard, magnetic character reader, magnetic tapes etc.

2. Arithmetic and Logic unit

   It is the section of the computer that performs arithmetic and logical operations on the data processed by the computer.

3. Control unit

   This unit controls all the activities in the computer and directs its step by step operations.

4. Memory unit

   Memory is classified as Internal and auxiliary memory.

   Internal memory is of two types, Random Access Memory and Read Only Memory. Random access memory (RAM) is volatile type. When power goes off, all work being done in RAM vanishes, unless it is saved. In Read only memory (ROM) some utilities (programs) are saved. These programs can be only seen, no edition is allowed in it.

   Auxiliary memory is incorporated from outside. Hard Disk, Floppy, Compact disk (CD), Magnetic tapes etc. are the examples of this type of memory. Hard disk and floppy are Random access storage, takes equal access time for files at any location. Tapes are sequential access storage, takes access time according to the location of files. Hard disk, Floppy and tapes vary by their storage capacity.

5. Output unit

   The output unit receives the stored result from memory unit, converts it into a form the user needs. Output devices are Printers (Laser, Dot matrix, Line etc.), Console, floppy etc.

   Central Processing Unit (CPU) consists of Control unit, Arithmetic & Logic unit and Memory (internal). Diagrammatically, a computer can be represented as :

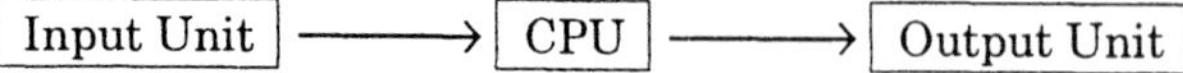

In digital computers, binary system is used. Each binary digit (1 & 0) is termed as bit. Combination of eight bit is termed as one Byte. One character is stored in one Byte. Different units used in context with storage capacity :

8 bits	=	1 Byte
1000 Bytes	=	1 Kilo Byte (2^{10} Bytes)
1000 K Bytes	=	1 Mega Byte (MB : 2^{20} Bytes)
1000 M Bytes	=	1 Gega Byte (GB : 2^{30} Bytes)

Speed : The unit of speed of a computer is mega hertz (MHz). Speed vary according to the microprocessor chip. It can be 350 MHz, 450 MHz, 800 MHz etc.

1 MHz means processing of 1 million instructions in 1 sec.

Milli sec	: 10^{-3} sec
Micro sec	: 10^{-6} sec
Nano sec	: 10^{-9} sec
Pica sec	: 10^{-12} sec

Computer is needed because of its speed, storage capacity, accuracy, software development (as per need), typing, making graphs, internet etc. Computers are widely used to develop or run the different application softwares. Application softwares are developed by using programming languages (most viable according to need). Statistical packages are available in the market. By the knowledge of FOXPRO language, scholars, students can easily develop programs for statistical analysis work.

Configuration of a Computer

Part	Description
CPU	Based on Microprocessor chip 386, 486, P-III, P-IV etc.
Speed	450 MHz, 800MHz, 1.1 GHz, 1.6 GHz etc.
RAM	8MB, 16MB, 128 MB etc.
Hard Disk	40 MB, 80 MB, 4.01 GB, 10 GB, 20 GB etc.
FDD (Floppy Disk Drive)	1.2 MB or 1.44 MB
CDROM	52X
Keyboard	Ordinary, Multimedia etc.

Display	CGA, VGA with some RAM
Monitor	Mono or Colour 14", 15", 17" (LG, Proview etc)
Mouse	Ordinary, Scroll (Logitech etc.)
Cabinet	AT, ATX etc.
Speakers	320/480 watt etc.

WINDOWS

Windows is a program that provides a graphical user interface (GUI). Program appears on screen in a rectangular form called as windows. Multiple program windows can appear on the screen at the same time and can be operated on simultaneously. Windows can run standard Disk Operating System (DOS) applications as well as Windows applications. Windows provide a standard and powerful interface for all program. Windows 98 is an advanced and most capable multimedia operating system. The internet connection wizard makes connecting to the web very simple. Own web pages can be created by using Microsoft Front page Express. Desktop is the area on the screen showing different items such as My Computer, Start button etc. The programs / Softwares used by user are displayed on the desktop. The rectangular bar that runs horizontally across the button of your screen is called as TASKBAR. It includes Start button. Taskbar and Start button are used to navigate through Windows. By clicking on the Start button, different commands like programs, documents, help and searching for items etc. can be executed. Some commands on the start menu have a right facing arrow, which means additional choices are available on a secondary menu. My Computer is used to view the contents of a drive. Double click My Computer on desktop to view the drives available on the computer. When a drive icon is double clicked, window displays the folders available on that drive. There shall be folders for Control panel, Printers and Dial Up Networking. Double click a folder to see the files within the folder. Windows Explorer displays your files in a hierarchical structure. The left side of it displays the list of the drives and folders, the right side displays the contents of a selected folder. Windows containing the program which is to be run, such as MS-Word, MS-Excel and so on are called Application Window. The Control Panel customizes the windows environment. The Control Panel is a window consisting of a collection of utilities to set your screen colours, modify the appearance of the desktop, change date and time, work for printers, modems etc.

Microsoft Word

It is a word processing product developed by Microsoft. Word 2000 has added many internet based facilities like email, designing Web pages etc. Word automatically applies the correct proofing tools like AutoCorrect, Spell Check, Grammar Check etc. MS-Word is started by double clicking the icon on desktop or by clicking start button, then placing the pointer on the PROGRAM item. A sub menu of the programs item is displayed. In this menu Microsoft Word is clicked. At the top of the Word screen Title bar appears which displays the file name being used. Menu bar is that part of the screen where all the options are available to work with the document. Menu items are those actions, which can be performed on the documents. To open a new document click on `File' then click on 'new'. A blank screen will appear. Type the contents of a file and save it by again clicking on File then clicking on 'Save as' and write the name of the file.

Microsoft Excel

MS Excel is a window based spreadsheet developed by Microsoft Corporation. It includes all features of a spreadsheet package like recalculation, graphs and functions. It also provides many statistical, financial and scientific functions. Excel can even hold graphic objects like pictures and images. In a Worksheet rows are numbered from top to bottom. The columns are labeled with letters from left to right. A cell which is the intersection of a row and a column is referred by the column name and row number combination i.e. first cell is referred to as A1 (Column A, Row 1). Excel has 65536 rows and 256 columns. The cells can contain data (numbers), text, dates, time, formulas and logical values such as true or False. To enter data, just select the cell and enter the value. To enter dates, just type the date in the format mm/dd/yy or 14-Jun-99. Four digit year can be entered directly. An '=' sign is entered before a formula. Without the '=' sign, the entry is treated as text. Let the cell A1=45, cell B1=50, in cell C1 write the formula =A1+B1, the value 95 will automatically displayed in the cell C1. By selecting the SAVE option in the FILE menu, the file is saved.

Internet

Information plays an important role in the policy making, planning and decision making process in any organizational set up. Informatics is the combination of Information Technology (IT) and Telecommunication. Computers play an important role in the information flow from the implementation level to the planners at the highest level. Internet is a computer network. It contains a large number of information which can be made available to the user on the computer. Information can be send or retrieved on any topic (Genetics, Microbiology, Environment, Statistics, Home Science etc.).

A computer network is basically, connecting computers together, to send and retrieve the information among themselves. Connections is done by using Satellite Links, Phone lines, Wires etc. The organizations which uses common information and data, can have a computer network for enhancing their efficiency.

Each computer network has a host computer, called as SERVER, which controls the complete network. If the network is composed of computers in a small area, it is known as Local Area Network (LAN). If the network is composed of computers in a wide area (locations anywhere in the world) is known as Wide Area Network (WAN).

In LAN, all the computers are located within the same department, in an office with many departments having computers connected to each other. In WAN, the computers are located in different cities, countries. The difference between a LAN and a WAN is the geographic area covered by the network.

Computer networks are being used in business, research etc. The three basic advantages of Computer network

a. Communication (electronic mail)

b. Sharing of data

c. Sharing of resources

By using a software, user can electronically communicate between computers connected to the network. This communication is commonly known as e-mail. Data and information can be shared by the users connected within the network. Sharing of resources means, computers connected to the network, can share printers, hard disk and softwares available with in the other computers.

Internet (Internet Work Systems) is described as network of

networks. The networks share a communication protocol, called as Transmission Control Protocol / Internet Protocol (TCP / IP). Computers within the network are referred to as nodes. These nodes communicate with each other by transferring data packets. Internet Explorer was developed in 1995 by Microsoft Corporation, USA. The World Wide Web (WWW) is the most advanced information system deployed on the Internet. There are many network systems readily accessible through internet. For science and research, Internet is an essential tool. World most advanced research facilities can be accessed through internet. Educationists can share ideas across vast distances.

The main goal of the Internet Society (ISOC), an organization of internet users, is to promote global information exchange through the internet. Different sections of this organization have the responsibility of technically managing and directing the internet affairs and solving technical problems facing the internet.

The minimum requirement to get the internet connections are

1. A Personal Computer (high speed)
2. A Modem (Modulator and demodulator)
3. A telephone connection

A personal computer is such that a modem is connected and communication software can run on it. A modem lets two computer communicate over a standard telephone line. Modem modulates the computer digital signal to analog signals, send it over the telephone line and by receiving, demodulates the signals back to digital form, which computer understands.

The part of the address before the symbol @ is known as user identification (user id) and the rest is called domain. This is known a Domain Naming System (DNS) which provides a method of uniquely identifying different organizations, computer systems and individuals on the internet. Using the addressing scheme, the electronic mail or other files are transmitted to the intended recipient on the internet.

Software tools required to browse the internet

Internet is a bag of different software tools, each of which is used to retrieve the information. Some of the softwares are :

1. File Transfer Protocol (FTP), allows access to million of computer files stored world wide.

2. Archie, helps to locate those FTP files.
3. Communication between hyperlinks is transparent , the name given to the underlying communication protocol used by Web Servers is Hypertext Transport Protocol (HTTP). Hypertext documents are written in a standard markup language known as Hypertext Markup Language (HTML).
4. Gopher, a menu based file and service search and retrieval system.
5. Internet Relay Chart (IRC) : Used to have an online interactive discussion. It enables group discussion also.
6. World Wide Web (WWW) : It is a collection of documents, graphics, video and other files scattered throughout the internet and linked together using hypertext method. A program called Web Browser is used to run the web. Commonly used web browser is MOSAIC.

Colour Graphics

An extremely useful and interesting application of terminals is **Graphics**. Here the terminal is capable of displaying not only alphanumeric characters but also pictures, usually in colour. Thus it can show graphs, drawings, charts, maps etc. The pictures can be static, show movements or change like a video game. A graph showing day by day reducing blood pressure of a patient conveys much more that a table of figure. Designs can be changed directly on screen by using a LIGHT PEN attached to the terminal. The Light Pen is a small tube containing a photoelectric cell.

Voice Response and Speech Recognition

Getting a computer to talk to us is easier than making them recognize our speech. VOICE RESPONSE SYSTEMS are available. An American toy teaches children to spell and pronounce different words. Voice response is very useful in situations where the human operator has many things to do at the same time.

Web Services

Remember the time when things like a wheel, typewriter, engine etc. were considered man's greatest inventions of all times and it was thought that nothing could surpass or match the kind of revolution they brought about. Time changed and the emergence of 'INTERNET' shattered all such myths. The Net brought about new dimensions of revolution in the way humans interacted with each other and shared information over distances and in turn redefined the whole paradigm of communication.

Amongst the various ways in which the 'Net' has now become a part of our lives lies 'WWW', or the World Wide Web which has effectively rendered the concept of International Boundaries and physical distances meaningless. Web presence today has become a vital element for an organization striving to fulfill its objectives in an efficient manner. And equally important, if not more, in the mantra of success is the role of the web service provider. Setting up a powerful web presence is a voyage of discovery.

WEB SERVICE BASICS

The simplest definition of a Web service is an application that provides a Web API. The Web API exposes the functionality of the application to other applications. The Web API relies on Web services technology to manage communications. Web services technology is pervasive, vendor-independent, language-neutral, and very low-cost.

The purpose of a Web API is to enable application integration. More specifically, a Web API lets you integrate heterogeneous applications. You can use Web services to achieve many different goals. You can use them to implement internal point-to-point application integration projects. You can use them to consolidate your development efforts and reduce redundant applications. You can use them to implement a general purpose integration bus for your internal application systems. And you can use them to make it easier for your partners and your customers to do business with you. Web services do not represent a new business model. Instead Web services are a technology that you can use to build systems to support a business model. IT departments are being asked to do more with less. There's less money in the budget to buy software, and there are fewer people to do the work. Nearly every application development project involves some level of application integration. It just makes sense to reduce the cost and simplify the process of doing integration. Web services are an obvious choice.

Videoconferencing

Videoconferencing is changing the way companies do business. It is bringing decision-makers together, face-to-face, wherever they are, across the country around the globe. Experts from remote locations can interact with each other time. It is bringing education and training to corporations and to students. A Videoconferencing opens the lines in every area-business, government. institutions and healthcare facilities.

With over a decade of experience in Videoconferencing Technology, National Informatics Center's technical expertise is unmatched in the country. NIC is currently providing videoconferencing service from 490 locations in India including all North-eastern state capitals over its high speed satellite based network called "NICNET". This is the largest videoconferencing network in India, spread across length and width of the country. The Advantage of using satellite based communications is that it can deliver high speed data and provide videoconferencing at remote locations, which were earlier not easily access.

There are Multipoint Conference Server (MCS), which facilitates several sites to participate in a live conference with audio-video and document sharing. MCS is the central point of connectivity for endpoints. It enables the operations very effectively. MCS supports both "Voice Activated" and "Chairman Control" multi point conferencing.

A videoconferencing facility of many elements. Firstly, there is the or the conferencing system, which comes in various types, depending on its application. All conferencing systems use CODEC, which stands for coder. Codec is a device, which converts and compresses an analog audio-video digital data and then sends it over a digital network. The decoder reverses Process at the receiving end. All videoconferencing systems work in full dup i.e. encoding and decoding of audio-video is done simultaneously in both direction. One can use a number of networks for conducting videoconferencing over Wide Area Networks (WAN) such as ISDN lines of satellite based links. It is possible to bandwidth of 128 Kbps for good quality conference. However data rate may be needed for near TV quality video.

There is a SCPC DAMA Network Management System started with voice, videoconferencing and high speed Internet access services in integrated manner using a single VSAT. Using this technology, any DAMA lo simply using a handset can initiate a voice, video or data call, without the n intervention of Hub operator. Connections are made in mesh topology on to-point basis between any nodes in the network using on demand SCPC carrier.

The key feature of SCPC, DAMA is that bandwidth is provided to the remote only when it is required. This helps in better utilization of satellite bandwidth amongst various VSAT's in a closed user network. SCPC, DAMA, NMS is like a telephone exchange in the sky, which works on the switching concept. It sets up Voice circuits at 8 Kbps, Videoconferencing in 384 Kbps and asymmetric data circuits up to 2 Mbps within 5 seconds of per application in an automatic manner.

A Videoconferencing meeting is usually brief and more focused than a face meeting. Benefits available to business through ability to meet and work over a distance, are extensive. It enable top management to communicate and effectively with employees sitting at multiple locations. Videoconferencing to reduce travel costs, improves use of executive time and speeds up decision making.

Video and data conferencing enables virtual project management by getting geographically dispersed peer groups at short notice. It provides an effect of delivering cost-efficient training to individuals without the need to constant travel to central locations. In order to bring about cultural change, efforts are being made in educating users to see videoconferencing as an alternative conventional meeting.

Geographical Information System (GIS)

Geographical Information System (GIS) In emerging technology paradigm, "Geographical Information System (GIS)" has emerged as powerful tool which has potential to organize complex spatial environment with tabular relationships. The emphasis is on developing digital spatial database.

In emerging technology paradigm, "Geographical Information System (GIS)" has emerged as powerful tool which has potential to organize complex spatial environment with tabular relationships. The emphasis is on developing digital spatial database, using the data sets derived from precise navigation and imaging satellites, aircrafts, digitization of maps and transactional databases. The power and potential of GIS is limited only by ones imagination.

However to exploit the technology to benefit the planning process there is need to initiate aprocess for integration of data, based on Interoperable open standards, specifications & formats.

The enormous demand for the storage, analysis and display of complex and voluminous data has led, in recent years, to the use of Geographic Information Systems for effective data handling and also for analyzing and geographically transferring the information around the world. NIC offers its users, GISNIC, a software designed to provide a complete state-of-the-art desktop GIs solution for retrieval, projection, transformation and analysis of both spatial and non-spatial data, so that the User is able to manipulate and manage coordinate (locational) and attribute (thematic) data and produce thematic maps as well as tabular reports.

Through its GISNIC software, NIC offers to undertake the tasks to generate and plot various types of thematic maps (Flow Lines maps, Graduated Symbol maps, Choropleth maps, Pie charts and Bar charts). The various tasks related to geographic analysis such as creation of buffer zones, performing polygon overlay and manipulating tabular data, are also carried out using GISNIC.

Also, the policy framework provided by IT Task Force for India to emerge as Global Info tech Superpower in this millennium emphasizes the availability of Spatial data to GIS user community and industry and provide a direction for the liberalization to this vital sector. With the evolution of this framework, it is now possible to have Spatial Decision-Support Information Systems Network, with distributed Network-Centric Web-Enabled GIS Application Services using NICNET facilities.

FOXPRO APPLICATION

Researchers, Scientists and students working in different fields, topics collect data for their research/studies. The data collected must be stored in a database. A database is a collection of records, a record is a set of fields and a field is a set of characters.

Types of Fields

a. Numeric : Contains only numeric data

b. Character : Contains any character value
c. Logical : Logical values only Y or N, T or F
d. Date : dates
e. Memo : used for large data of text

To create a database, in foxpro

In command window type "create abc" and press "enter" key, means a data base named "abc" is to be created.

The screen looks like

Table Structure

Name	Type	Width	Dec

Insert
Delete
Ok
Cancel

Click the left side of a mouse below "Name" and type the field name you want eg. hb for haemoglobin. Press the "tab" key to enter the "Type" of data. Data can be character, numeric, date, logical and memo type etc. Since Haemoglobin (hb) is numeric value, numeric type is selected. Press the "tab" key to enter the width of the field "hb". The value of haemoglobin (hb) cannot be of three digits, but it may have a decimal. Enter "4" as width and again press "tab" key to enter decimal as "1".

In numeric data with decimals, width becomes total digits including "." eg. 11.2 means total Width = 4 and Decimal (Dec) as "1". The width of a field should be according to its values.

Again press "tab" key if you want to enter another fieldname. Eg. "chol" for cholestrol, enter its type, width and dec. As many as needed, fields can be added similarly.

After completing the structure of the database, put one finger on "Ctrl" key and press "w" key by another finger (^w) to save the database. Foxpro will ask for "input data records now", type "y" and data entry screen will come. Fill all the fields for each records. The record numbers will automatically appears on the screen. The dbase file has an extension of ".dbf" means your file "abc" after entering records and saving it will become abc.dbf. <> sign indicates to press the enter key.

Using a file

A database file is invoked with the USE command in following way

USE ptics

USE ptics index ptics

Closing a file

A database file is closed by using commands

- CLOSE DATA BASES
- CLEAR ALL

DISPLAY STRUCTURE

ptics is a database in which field names are pcode for patient's code, pname for patient's name, page for patient's age, pcat for patient's category and pbg for the blood group of patient's is stored. Structure of a database file can be seen on screen by using command

- USE PTICS
- DISP STRU /LIST STRU

Field	*Field name*	*Type*	*Width*	*Dec*
1	pcode	Character	5	
2	pname	Character	20	
3	page	Numeric	3	
4	pcat	Character	3	
5	pbg	Character	3	

Modifying the structure

Suppose a field is to be added/deleted in a data base, in command window,

- use "[data base name]" eg. use abc < >
- Modify structure < >(only four letters can also be used : modi stru)

Reach to the field before it you want new field, by down arrow key. Click on "insert", enter its name, type, width and dec as mentioned above. You cannot enter data of the new field now.

Similarly, if you want to delete a field, just reach to that field by arrow key and click on "delete". After you have finished modifications press ^w to save it.

INDEX

The INDEX ON command is used

INDEX ON FIELD

INDEX ON FIELD1+FIELD2+FIELD3 TO F123

INDEX ON SUBSTR(FIELD1,1,6)+SUBSTR(FIELD2,1,3) TO F12

- An index key may be single or a combination of fields.
- If more than one type of field is included in the index key, all must be converted to character type using STR function for numeric fields or DTOC for date fields.
- Once an INDEX ON command has been executed, that index is in use and other indexes which were invoked earlier are not in use.

Moving around files

dbase has a record pointer which points to the current record in the database file. The current record is the record which is output when a DISPLAY command is issued. When a dbase file is used, the record pointer is automatically positioned at the first record in the file. Records are located physically in the file in order in which they are placed there. The first record entered is #1, the second is #2 and so on.

When a database is indexed on some field, which is essential for fast processing, the record numbers i.e. recno() of the records does not change but the records are repositioned according to index field. Let a database named xyz, is having fields as name, salary, dept. The first record entered is of Manoj, second is of Atul, third is of Rakesh etc.

#1 Manoj

#2 Atul

#3 Rakesh

To index a database, in command window,

- use xyz < >

- index on name to xyz
- go top

If file is indexed on name, after repositioning of records, database becomes

#2 Atul

#1 Manoj

#3 Rakesh

Index order of records is known as logical order. Indexing can also be done by adding two or more fields but for this TYPE of fields should be same. Let a database is to be indexed on name i.e. CHARACTER TYPE and date of joining i.e. DATE type. DATE type can be converted to character type by using DTOC function and the database can be indexed as

- USE company
- Index on name+dtoc(date)

Listing records

- USE abc
- Index on RECNO() to abc
- LIST (List all the records)

The file 'abc' will be indexed by record numbers. LIST command will list all the records. Records will go through the screen and only last few records can be seen.

- LIST NEXT 10

By this command, 10 records can be seen.

Counting number of records

Number of records can be counted for any specification by using FOR clause

- USE XYZ
- COUNT FOR hb<=5.0

Displaying the records

All records whose value of hb (haemoglobin) is <5.0 can be displayed on the screen

- DISPLAY FOR hb<=5.0

Deleting the records

Syntax of record number is recno()

Let the record number 5 of a database is to be deleted. In command window, type 5, press enter, type delete press enter. The delete command merely flags a record for deletion with an asterisk. When a deleted record is displayed, an asterisk appears after the record number. Let the wrong recno() is deleted, the RECALL command simply removes the deletion flag. If it is sure that recno() = 5 is to be deleted, give PACK command. Pack command actually deletes the records which are flagged for deletion and cannot be recovered.

- Use the file name, let it be "use abc" < >
- Check the record number, let it be 4
- Type "delete for recno() = 4" < >
- Type "pack" < >

If all records are to be deleted of a database,

Eg. all records of xyz are to be deleted, in command window,

- Use xyz < >
- Zap < >

It will ask "are you sure(y/n)" type "y"

Editing

Editing in a record can be done by using edit command.

- Use xyz < >
- Edit 5 < >

The record 5 is displayed on the screen, make changes in the record and press ^w to save the changes.

Browse

All records are displayed on the screen horizontally, go to particular record by using arrow keys and make changes, press ^ w to save the changed records.

Append

If records are to be appended in a database, first use the database by

- Use xyz < >
- Append < >

The blank screen of all fields will appear, enter all the fields, when finished press ^w to save the data base.

Go Top/Go Bottom

This command is used to assign the pointer to the first /last record of a database. Go top command must be used after indexing the database, so that processing starts from the first record.

Date Input and Output

The SET DATE command determines how dates are displayed, but does not actually affect how they are stored.

set date BRIT (ish)	dd/mm/yy
set date amer (ican)	mm/dd/yy
set date ANSI	yy/mm/dd

If first is used, all the dates will be displayed as British type.

SET TALK OFF/ON

If it is OFF, whatever the processing being done i.e. different type of calculation, is not displayed on the screen.

SET SAFE OFF/ON

If it is OFF, foxpro will not ask "abc.dbf is already indexed, do you want to overwrite it".

SET CENTURY ON/OFF

If it is ON, year is displayed in 4 digits.

SET PRINT ON

The results/formats which are to printed on printer, SET PRINT ON command is to be used before the first appearance of ? in the program. If it is not used, the results will come on the screen.

SET ALTERNATE TO

When the results or output of any program is to be saved in a file SET ALTERNATE TO <file name> command is used. Filename is to be given in which results are saved. 'set alternate to' or 'set alternate off' command is to be given at the end.

```
set alternate to rep.txt
set alternate on
set safe off
...............
............
statements
............
set alternate to
```

Type Conversion

The following functions allow for conversions between variable types :

Numeric field is right justified. If width of a field is 5, the value 234 will be stored as

spaces	1	2	3	4	5
value			2	3	4

means leaving first two spaces as blank. The character field is left justified. The value 234 will be stored as

spaces	1	2	3	4	5
value	2	3	4		

means leaving last spaces as blank.

FUNCTION	FROM	TO
STR	Numeric	Character
VAL	Character	Numeric
DTOC	Date	Character
CTOD	Character	Date

Type conversions are necessary

1. When an output is required for two or more variables with a ? or SAY statement, both must be of same type.

   If a database named 'abc' has three fields as name (char), salary (numeric) and dd1 (date), if print command is to be given.

```
use abc
go top
do whil .not. eof()
?spa(3)+name+str(salary) [all characters]
skip
enddo
```

2. When indexing is done on the several fields of different types, all must be converted to character type.
3. DTOC function converts DATE memory variable to a character string.

Indexing of database by using all fields

- use abc
- index on name + str(salary)+dtoc(dd1)

Mathematical Functions

FUNCTIONS	MEANING
ABS	Absolute value
EXP	Exponential
INT	Integer
LOG	Logarithm
MAX	Maximum of two numbers
MIN	Minimum of two numbers
MOD	Modulus
SQRT	Square root

clear

This statement clears the screen.

Replace

Input of the value of variables or results obtained by calculations can be replaced to the database by using REPLACE command.

Replace nm(field) with name(program variable),sal (field) with salary (program variable).

Modify Command

To write a program in foxpro, in command window

Modify command [raj] < >

This will create a blank screen in which program is to be typed. Raj is the name of program, it is optional [], any name can be used.

@, SAY, GET, PICTURE

These statements are used when an input is done through a program or for getting an output. The editor screen of foxpro contains 25 rows and 80 columns. Positions are defined by using @ function. SAY statements when combined with GET statements can be used to design powerful input screens. PICTURE statement is used for defining type of variable and its width. All the variables must be defined before using SAY, GET statements. The program variables must be different from the database variables.

In command window,

Clear < >

@5,10 say " NAME" < >

at 5th row and 10th column NAME will be displayed.

Let a program (exp) is to be made for entering records in a database (xyz) whose field names are name, salary, age, DOJ.

In command window,

Modi(fy) **comm**(and) **xyz** < > [only four letters of command can be used].

The blank screen will appear, start writing a program

```
Set talk off
Set date brit
Set century on
op="Y"
do whil uppe(op) # "N"
Stor spac(15) to nm
Stor 0 to sal, ag
Dd1=ctod("//    ")
Clea
```

```
@5,5 say "NAME"
@5,14 get nm
@5,32 say "SALARY"
@5,41 get sal pict "99999.99"
@7,5 say "AGE"
@7,14 get ag pict "99"
@7,32 say "Date of Joining"
@7,41 get dd1
read
use xyz
index on name to xyz
replace name with nm,salary with sal,age with ag, doj with dd1
@20,5 say "do you want to enter more records"
@20,41 get op
read
if upper(op) = "Y"
loop
else
retu
endif
endd
```

1. set statements
2. initialization of memory variables
3. screen for input (values of memory variables)
4. replacement of record in the database
5. Question for entering another record (y/n)

If the value of op="y", the pointer will again go to the statement just after do while statement, again initializes memory variables and completes the entering of another record. From do while statement upto read statement (after get op), all statements will continue to execute (if op="y") unless the value of op="n". Replace command is used for replacing the value of database fields by program memory variables.

TEXT .... ENDTEXT

The TEXT ...ENDTEXT segment displays the actual menu choices. The user's choice is stored in the memory variable defined as ch (get ch). The variable ul gives a 80 character line using "-". The PICTURE statement ensures that only a single numeral will be accepted, RANGE option gives the range for the variable ch i.e. 1 to 5.

```
ch=0
ul=repl("-",80)
DO WHIL ch # 5
@5,5 say "CHROMOSOMAL ANOMALIES INFORMATION SYSTEM"
@6,5 say ul
TEXT
    1.  ADD NEW RECORDS
    2.  REPORTS
    3.  EDIT
    4.  DELETE
    5.  EXIT
ENDTEXT
@22,5 SAY "ENTER CHOICE (1-5)" GET ch PICT "9" RANG 1,5
READ
```

DO CASE..... ENDCASE

A DO CASE... ENDCASE clause tells a program what to do based on any one of several mutually exclusive possibilities. Programs are executed depending on the value of ch i.e. If ch=1, program NIS is executed. Since DO WHILE statement is used at the beginning, ENDDO must be given after endcase.

```
DO CASE
    CASE CH='1'
        DO NIS
    CASE CH='2'
        DO REP
    CASE CH='3'
        DO MEDIT
```

```
        CASE CH='4'
            DO MDEL
    ENDCASE
    ENDDO
```

DO WHILE <condition> .... ENDDO

This statement checks for the condition and the statements between do while and enddo will be executed, if the condition is true.

```
Int=1
Do whil int <= 10
?int,int*int
int=int+1
enddo
```

first int is defined as a variable whose value is 1. The condition of do while statement is int <= 10 i.e. continue to execute the statements between **do while** and **enddo** unless int becomes 10. The program will run for 10 times and prints int, int*int as

```
 1     1
 2     4
 3     9
 4    16
 5    25
 6    36
 7    49
 8    64
 9    81
10   100
```

DO WHILE .NOT. EOF() [end of file]

If all records of a database are to be used for some analysis, "skip" statement is used before enddo statement for skipping to the next record. GO TOP must be used before DO WHILE .NOT. EOF(). All the statements between 'do while' and 'enddo' will be executed for the first record, all the records are processed in the similar way till the last record is processed, by using "skip" statement.

Let Standard Deviation of the variable DO(Dissolved Oxygen) is to be calculated. Data can be stored by giving different field names to different chemical parameters in one database. Let it be 'chemical'. n1 be the total number of records.

```
SET TALK OFF
SET SAFE OFF
USE CHEMICAL
INDEX ON RECNO() to CHEMICAL
SUM DO to s1
M1=s1/n1
GO TOP
SS=0.0
DO WHIL .NOT. EOF()
A1=DO-M1
A11=A1*A1
 SS=SS+A11
SKIP
ENDD
VAR=ss/n1
SD=sqrt(VAR)
?"Variance=",VAR
?"Standard Deviation=",SD
```

IF <condition>......... ENDIF

This statement checks for the condition and the statements between if and endif will be executed, if the condition is true.

```
IF sal<=5000
Incometax=0.0
endi
```

IF <condition>......ELSE......ENDIF

This statement checks for the condition and the statements between if and else will be executed, if the condition is true. If the condition is not true, it will execute the statements between else and endif.

```
TTAB=2.15
```

```
IF TCAL>TTAB
?"SIGNIFICANT DIFFERENCE"
ELSE
?"INSIGNIFICANT DIFFERENCE"
ENDIF
```

Multiple File Handling

Database files with one common indexed field can be used for programming. When multiple files are used, they are opened in different areas which are accessed through SELECT command. The files are designated by 1, 2 etc. or by A, B etc. Let there are two databases ptics and gene. Both the databases are indexed on field pcode. gene is a database in which fields are pcode for patient's code, ano1 for anomaly 1, chrno1 for chromosome number, ano2 for anomaly 2, chrno2 for chromosome number. Both the databases are used to get the report of chromosomal anomalies.

```
select A
use ptics
index on pcode to ptics
go top
sele B
use gene
index on pcode to gene
go top
sele A
do whil .not. eof()
if pcode=b->pcode
?pcode,pname,page,pcat,pbg,b->ano1,b->chrno1,b->ano2,b-
   >chrno2
?
endif
skip
sele b
skip
enddo
```

SET RELATION TO

The command which supports linking between two databases based on a common key.

```
select A
use ptics index ptics
go top
select B
use gene index gene
go top
sele A
set relation to pcode into gene
do whil .not. eof()
?pcode,name,b->anol
skip
enddo
```

FIND

If certain record is to be searched on the basis of value of indexed field. Let a database is indexed on lname (last name)

```
FIND goswami
```

would be used to find the first occurrence of goswami in the file. SKIP command is used if successive goswami is to be searched.

SEEK

Looks up the contents of a memory variable in an indexed database file.

```
use xyz
Index on doj to xyz
go top
dt1=ctod(" / / ")
@5,5 say "Date of Joining"
@5,14 get dt1
read
seek dt1
if found()
```

```
?recno(),name,desig
endif
```

IF FOUND()

This command is used with SEEK to execute the statements accordingly. ELSE can also be used with it. Let a database CHEMICAL in which the value of pH is wrongly entered as 0.7 in place of 7.7. The database is to be indexed on the field pH because the value of pH is to be searched.

```
use chemical
Index on ph to chemical
go top
v1=0.7
v2=7.7
do whil .not. eof()
seek v1
if found()
repl ph with v2
skip
else
skip
enddo
```

PROCEDURE FILE

Small routines/programs with their names can be written in one file called as PROCEDURE file. These programs have a RETURN statement at the end to give the results to the program from it is executed. These programs are executed by using DO 'program name' in the main file. When a SET PROCEDURE TO command is encountered, FOX reads through the procedure file and sets up a table in RAM which contains a list of the procedures and their locations contained in the file. Whenever a DO command is encountered, FOX checks through this table to see if the argument of DO command is the name of a procedure in the procedure file. To be used effectively, procedure files must become very large. They result in only a marginal speed increase. Public variables are not erased when command file terminates. SET PROCEDURE TO <file name>

is to be given at top of the MAIN program. The parameters command is used to assign variable names that are local to procedure. The parameters command must be the first executable command in the procedure.

MAIN PROGRAM

```
SET PROCEDURE TO PROCE.LIB
Statements
........
.........
statements
SET PROCEDURE TO
```

PROCE.LIB

```
procedure aa
statements
.......
.........
return
----------------------------------
procedure bb
statements
..............
...........
return
-----------------------------------
procedure area
parameters len,width,area
area = len*width
retu
----------------------
```

Let a database named “salary” having fields as “name” & “basic”, DA should be given as

Basic salary	DA
<= 5000	15%

5000-10000 10%

10000-20000 5%

The program used to calculate DA and total salary for all records

```
set talk off
set safe off
use salary
index on recno() to salary
go top
do while .not. eof()
if basic <= 5000
da=0.15*basic
total=basic+da
?name,basic,da,total
skip
endif
if basic >5000 .and. basic <=10000
da=0.1*basic
total=basic+da
?name,basic,da,total
else
da=0.05*basic
total=basic+da
?name,basic,da,total
endif
skip
enddo
```

Program for mean and standard deviation

Let a database named "legal" having a field as "p1", total records are 236, the mean and standard deviation of "p1" can be obtained by the program

```
set talk off
set safe off
use legal
```

```
index on recno() to legal
sum p1 to s1
m1=s1/236
go top
sss=0
do while .not. eof()
dev=p1-m1
ss=dev*dev
sss=sss+ss
skip
endd
var=sss/236
stv=sqrt(var)
?"mean=",m1
?"stdv=",stv
```

Program for correlation coefficient and its significance

Let a database named "w4" having fields as "n12" and "pt", the correlation coefficient between n12 and pt can be obtained by the program

```
CLEA
SET TALK OFF
SET SAFE OFF
USE w4
INDEX ON RECNO() TO w4
GO TOP
COUN TO N1 (when total records are not known)
GO TOP
S1=0.0
S2=0.0
DO WHILE .NOT. EOF()
S1=S1+n12
S2=S2+pt
SKIP
ENDDO
```

```
M1=S1/n1
M2=S2/n1
?"n12",M1,"pt",M2
S3=0.0
S4=0.0
S5=0.0
S6=0.0
GO TOP
DO WHILE .NOT. EOF()
A1=n12-M1
A2=pt-M2
AA=A1*A2
S3=S3+AA
AA1=A1*A1
AA2=A2*A2
S4=S4+AA1
S5=S5+AA2
SKIP
ENDDO
COV=S3/n1
VAR1=S4/n1
VAR2=S5/n1
ST1=SQRT(VAR1)
ST2=SQRT(VAR2)
?"stdev : n12",st1,"pt",st2
DENO=ST1*ST2
COR=COV/DENO
?"correlation coefficient",COR
COR1=COR*COR
CORR=(1-COR1)
DEN=SQRT(CORR)
NN=n1-2
NN1=SQRT(NN)
NUM=COR*NN1
```

```
TCAL=NUM/DEN
?"tcalculated",TCAL
```

Program for Analysis of Variance (One Way)

```
set alternate to repo.txt
set alternate on
set safe off
clear
set talk off
set safe off
use tds
index on recno() to tds
go top
*msg=" 1000 grain weight(fp)"
*?spac(2)+msg
?" T1      T2        T3        T4"
do whil .not. eof()
?t1,t2,t3,t4
skip
enddo
sum t1 to st1
sum t2 to st2
sum t3 to st3
sum t4 to st4
m=3
n=4
mn=m*n
gt=st1+st2+st3+st4
cf=(gt*gt)/mn
?"gt=",gt
?"cf=",cf
go top
ss=0.0
m1=st1/m
```

```
m2=st2/m
m3=st3/m
m4=st4/m
do while .not. eof()
k1=0.0
k1=(t1*t1)+(t2*t2)+(t3*t3)+(t4*t4)
ss=ss+k1
skip
enddo
?"rss=",ss
tss=ss-cf
?"tss=",tss
k2=(st1*st1)+(st2*st2)+(st3*st3)+(st4*st4)
sst=(k2/m)-cf
?"sst=",sst
go top
sss=0.0
sse=tss-sst
?"sse=",sse
nn=n-1
mm=m-1
nm=(mn-1) - (n-1)
mst=sst/nn
mse=sse/nm
ft=mst/mse
?"source    df     ss    mss     f"
?"treatments"+spac(1),nn,spac(1),sst,spac(2),mst,spac(1),ft
?
?"error"+spac(6),nm,spac(1),sse,spac(1),mse
?"--------------------------------------------------------------------------------"
?"total"+spac(8),str((m*n)-1),tss
terr=2.10
j1=sqrt[(2*mse)/m]
cd=terr*j1
```

```
?"cd=",cd
l12=m1-m2
l13=m1-m3
l14=m1-m4
l23=m2-m3
l24=m2-m4
l34=m3-m4
?"l12=",l12,"l13=",l13,"l14=",l14
?"l23=",l23,"l24=",l24,"l34=",l34
set alternate to
```

Software for Calculating Genetic Load of a Population

Create a database 'GL' by using field names IL (Inbreeding Level), WS(Woman Studied), CB (Children Born), SB (Still birth/Abortion), BIRTHR (Birth rate),STILLBR (Still birth rate),VAL, GLOAD(Genetic Load). Enter data for first four fields only. Structure of database is defined below.

Field name	*Type*	*Width*	*Decimal*
IL	Numeric	6	4
WS	Numeric	5	
CB	Numeric	5	
SB	Numeric	3	
BIRTHR	Numeric	5	3
STILLBR	Numeric	5	3
VAL	Numeric	6	4
GLOAD	Numeric	6	4

```
SET SAFE OFF
SET TALK OFF
USE GL
INDEX ON RECNO() TO GL
GO TOP
DO WHILE .NOT. EOF()
MBR=CB/WS
SBR=SB/WS
```

```
K1=MBR*IL
GL = SBR+K1
REPL BIRTHR WITH MBR,STILLBR WITH SBR,VAL WITH
K1,GLOAD WITH GL
Stor 0.0 to K1,GL
SKIP
ENDDO
GO TOP
?"IL    WS    CB    SB    MBR    SBR  VAL   GLOAD"
Do WHIL .NOT. EOF()
?IL,WS,CB,SB,MBR,SBR,VAL,GLOAD
SKIP
ENDDO
```

IL	*WS*	*CB*	*SB*	*MBR*	*SBR*	*VAL*	*GLOAD*
0.0310	1273	4322	55	3.3951	0.0432	0.1052	0.1485
0.0620	970	4774	165	4.9216	0.1701	0.3051	0.4752
0.1250	685	2802	130	4.0905	0.1898	0.5113	0.7011
0.2500	624	1630	162	2.6122	0.2596	0.6530	0.9127
0.0000	570	1789	32	3.1386	0.0561	0.0000	0.0561

To change a dbf file to excel worksheet

USE MASTF

COPY TO ABC SDF (for text file)

Go To EXCEL

EXCEL

DATA

GET EXTERNAL DATA

CHOSE THE FILE NAME

IMPORT

FIXED WITH

In preview of file

Drag according to spaces of each field

NEXT

FINISH

To change an ADOBE PAGEMAKER FILE to MSWORD

ABC.PM4

Click on first letter

^E (converts file in edit mode)

^A (select full file)

^C (copy the file)

Open a new document in MSWORD

^V (paste the file)

!	Converts character to uppercase in SAY.. GET commands
#	Not equal to
$	Substring function used for finding a character string embedded within a larger character string. LIST FOR "OKHLA" $ADD1
&	Used as a prefix on a name to declare that name as macro function instead of a literal.
()	Used for logical and mathematical grouping.
*	Multiplies two numbers
**	Exponent symbol. ?2**3=8(cube of 2)
^	Exponent symbol. ?8^1/3=2(cube root of 8)
+	Adds two numbers
-	Subtracts two numbers
/	Divides two numbers
<	Less than
<=	Less than or equal to
>	Greater than
>=	Greater than or equal to
=	Equal to
?	Moves to the beginning of a new line and displays the result

??	Displays the contents of a field, memory variable or expression at the current cursor position.
@	Displays information in specified format on screen or printer. @5,5 Say "HELLO"
ABS	Returns absolute value of a number.
ALL	Refers to all records in a database. DISPLAY ALL, DELETE ALL
APPEND	Adds new records of data to the end of the currently open database.
APPEND BLANK	Adds a new record to the bottom of a database, with all fields blank.
APPEND FROM	Reads the records from another database and adds them to the bottom of the database in use.
ASC	Displays the ASCII value of a character. ? ASC("B") displays 66
BOF()	Function that determines whether the beginning of the file has been reached.
BROWSE	Displays a screen full of the database and allows to edit(change values) in it.
/C	Used with SORT command to ignore upper/lower case.
CANCEL	Aborts command file execution.
CDOW()	Displays the day of the week as a character (Monday etc) for a date field or memory variable.
CHR()	Displays the ASCII character for a number. ?chr(7) rings the bell.
CLEAR	Clears the screen and repositions the cursor to the upper left corner
CLEAR ALL	Close all databases, index, format and relational databases. Frees all memory used by memory variable.
CLEAR GETS	Releases GET variables from READ access.

CLEAR MEMORY	Erases all current memory variables.
CLOSE	Closes open files, of either alternate database, format, index or procedure type.
CMONTH()	Displays the month for a date field or a memory variable as a character.
COL()	Returns the current column position of the cursor.
CONTINUE	Used with LOCATE command to find the next record with a particular characteristic.
COPY	Copies the content of one database into another database. Similarly structure of a database and .prg files can also be copied.
COUNT	Counts for number of records in a database with some specification.
CREATE	Allows to create a database and define the structure.
CREATE REPORT	Creates a custom report format.
CREATE QUERY	Creates a query form and allows user to fill the query.
CTOD()	Converts a data stored as a character string ("14/06/64") to a date data type.
/D	Used with SORT to sort in descending order.
DATE()	Displays internal date.
DBF()	Returns the name of the database file currently in use.
DELETE	Marks a record for deletion
DELETED()	Evaluates to TRUE if record is marked for deletion. [LIST FOR DELETED()]
DIR	Shows files on disk.
DISPLAY	Shows information about a database or its content.
DISPLAY HISTORY	Displays last commands typed

DISPLAY MEMORY	Displays the name, type, size and status of all current memory variables.
DISPLAY STATUS	Displays the current status of databases and index files in use.
DO	Runs a command file or procedure
DO CASE	Sets up a clause of mutually exclusive options in a command file. Terminated by ENDCASE command
DO WHILE	Used with ENDDO to set up a loop in a command file. [do while .not. eof()]
DTOC()	Converts a date field or memory variable to a character data type.
EDIT	Displays existing record to change the value of fields. [edit 10]
EJECT	Advances paper in printer to top of new page.
ELSE	Performs a set of commands if the specification given is not true in IF ..... ENDIF statement.
ENDDO	Used with DO WHILE command to mark the bottom of the loop.
ENDIF	Marks the end of an IF clause in a command file.
EOF()	Function that returns True if the end of the database file has been reached.
ERASE	Deletes the specific file from the directory.
ERROR()	Returns a number indicating the error caught by an ON ERROR command
EXIT	Escapes from a DO WHILE loop without terminating execution of the command file. Control is transferred to the statement just after ENDDO.
EXP()	Natural exponent of a number.
FIELD()	Returns name of a field in a database file. [?field(4)] displays the name of field number 4 in the currently open database.

FIND	Looks up information rapidly in an indexed database.
FOUND()	The found function is true(.T.) when a FIND, SEEK, LOCATE or CONTINUE commands finds the requested record.
GET	Used with the READ command to accept field and memory variable data from the screen.
GO BOTTOM	Control goes to the last record of a database.
GO TOP	Go to the first record of a database.
HELP	Provides help on the screen for a command or function.
IF	Determines whether to perform commands in a command file based on some criteria.
IIF()	Abbreviated version of the IF command using the syntax IIF<this is true>, <do this> otherwise <do this>
INDEX	Creates an index file on some field or use an existing index to display data in sorted order.[use abc index names]
INPUT	Displays a prompt on the screen and waits for a response terminated by pressing the return key. Used with numeric data.
INSERT	Puts a new record into the database at the current record location.
ISALPHA()	Determines whether the first letter of a variable is a letter.
ISCOLOR()	Returns .T. if color monitor is n use.
ISLOWER()	Determines whether the first letter of a character string is a lower case.
ISUPPER()	Determines whether the first letter of a character string is a upper case.
LEN()	Returns the length of a string.
LIST	Show the records of a database.

LIST FOR	List records that have some characteristics common.[List for sal>10000]
LOCATE	Finds a record with particular characteristic. [Locate for name="BHAVYA"]
LOG()	Calculates the natural logarithm of a number.
LOOP	Skips all commands between itself and the ENDDO command in a DO WHILE loop.
LOWER()	Converts uppercase letters to lower case.
LTRIM()	Removes leading blanks from character string.
M->	Specifies a memory variable. Useful when a field and memory variable share the same name. [?M->lname]
MAX()	Returns the higher number of two numbers.
MIN()	Returns the lower number of two numbers.
MOD()	Returns the modulus (remainder) of two numbers.
MODIFY	Used to create or change a command file.
MONTH()	Returns the month of a date field or variable as a number.
OFF	Leaves record numbers out of displays. [LIST OFF]. Also turns off parameters [SET PRINT OFF]
ON	Set parameters into ON mode.
PACK()	Permanently deletes records marked for deletion.
PICTURE	Used with the GET command to accept values in specified format.
PRIVATE	Specifies memory variables that are automatically erased when a command file terminates.
PROCEDURE	An advanced programming technique whereby tasks are broken down into flexible routines accessed throughout a system.

PROW()	Displays the current row position of the printer head.
PUBLIC	Specifies memory variables that are not to be erased when the command file terminates.
QUIT	Closes all files and exists.
RANGE	Specifies a range of acceptable values with @... SAY... GET and READ commands.
READ	Used with @... SAY... GET statements to read the value of field from screen.
RECALL	Brings back a record marked for deletion. If the record is permanently deleted by using PACK command, it will not be recalled.
RECOUNT()	Displays the number of records in the open database file.
RECNO()	Returns the current record number. It can also be used with DO WHILE statement. [DO WHILE RECNO()<=55]
RECORD	Refers to a single record. [DELETE RECORD 6]
RECSIZE()	Returns the number of bytes in each record in a database.
REINDEX	Recreates all active index files.
RELEASE	Erase current memory variables to free memory space for other use.
RENAME	Changes the name of a disk file. [RENAME cor.prg to CORRE.prg]
REPLACE	Changes the current contents of a field with new data. Can also be used in global changes [REPLACE ALL LNAME with 'SMITH' FOR LNAME ='Smith']
REPLICATE()	Replicates a character in a variable. [UL=REPLICATE "-",80]
REPORT	Allows you to either create a report format. [MODIFY REPORT]

RESTORE	Recalls memory variables that were saved to disk with SAVE command back into RAM. [RESTORE from exp]
RESUME	Continues running a program that has been temporarily suspended for the purposes of debugging.
RETURN	Returns controls from a command file to the command window or to call the command file.
RETURN TO MASTER	Returns control from a subprogram back to the first run program.
RIGHT	Takes characters from the right side of a character string. [?RIGHT ("ABCDE,3")] displays CDE
ROUND()	Rounds a number to a specified number of decimal places.
ROW()	Returns the current row position of the cursor on screen.
RTRIM()	Trim the blanks on right side of a field.
SAY	Used with @ to position output on the screen or printer.
SDF	Standard Data Format
SEEK	Looks up the contents of a memory variable in an indexed database file.
SELECT	Assigns databases in use to any one of the databases defined.
SET ALTERNATE ON	Transfers all screen activity (except @ SAY commands) to a text file. Default is OFF
SET BELL ON	Bell sounds when a field is filled. Default is OFF.
SET CENTURY ON	Displays the century in date. OFF hides the century.
SET COLOR	Changes the color of the screen foreground, background or borders.
SET CONFIRM	Determines whether pressing the return key is necessary after filling a screen prompt.

SET DATE	Determines the format to display date. [set date british]
SET DEBUG	Determines whether the SET ECHO command directs output to the Printer or the screen. With SET DEBUG ON and SET ECHO ON directs echo output to printer while execution goes to screen.
SET DECIMAL	Sets the minimum numbers of decimals displayed in the results of mathematical calculation. [SET DECIMAL TO 3]
SET DELETED	Set deleted ON hides deleted records.
SET DEVICE	Determines whether @... SAY commands display data on the screen or on the printer. [set device to printer]
SET ECHO	Debugging aid to display each line of a command file as it is being processed. [SET ECHO ON]
SET ESCAPE	Determines whether a command file terminates when ESC key is pressed.
SET EXACT ON	The values are compared with an exact match. SET EXACT OFF will match JOHN with JOHNSON.
SET FILTER	Limits display of data to those records that match a criterion. [SET FILTER TO NAME="AMIT"]
SET FIXED	Set the number of decimal places that will appear with all numeric displays.
SET MARGIN	Adjusts the left margin for printer displays.
SET MEMOWIDTH	Determines the width of a memo field.
SET PRINT	Determines whether displays will be echoed to the printer. SET PRINT ON causes all screen displays to be printed. SET PRINT OFF returns to normal mode.
SET PROCEDURE	Advanced programming technique whereby subprograms are combined into a single file and assigned procedure names. [SET PROCEDURE TO XYZ]

SET RELATION	SETS up relationship between two data files in use, based on a field they have in common. [SET RELATION TO NAME TO MASTER]
SET SAFETY	Determines whether the message `file name already exists-overwrite(y/n)' appears when a file is about to be overwritten. [SET SAFE OFF disables]
SET STATUS ON/OFF	Turns the status bar at the bottom of the screen ON/OFF
SET STEP	Debugging aid used to limit command file execution to a single line at a time. [SET ECHO ON]
SET TALK	SET TALK OFF does not show messages / processing /calculations on the screen.
SKIP	Skips to the next record in the database.
SORT	Rearrange records in a database into sorted order. [SORT on age to file1]
SPACE()	Generates a string of blanks. [store space(20) to name] Store 20 blanks for the memory variable `name'.
SQRT()	Displays the square root of a number.
STORE	Assigns a value to a memory variable.
STR()	Converts a number to a string. Useful when indexing with character and numeric variables.[INDEX on NAME+STR(SALARY) to abc]
STRUCTURE	Refers to the structure of a database.
SUBSTR()	Isolates a portion of the string [?substr("XYZ",1,2)] displays XY a substring starting at first character, 2 characters long.
SUM	Add column of a field and displays the total.
SUSPEND	Halts execution of a command file and returns control to command window.
TIME()	Displays current system time.
TRIM()	Removes trailing blanks from a character string.

LOGARITHMS OF NUMBERS

If 'a' is a positive real number, other than 1 and $a^m=x$, then m is called the logarithm of x to the base a, written as $\log_a x$. The logarithm (base=10) of a number (X in the table) is the power to which 10 must be raised to produce X. When base is not mentioned, it will be taken as 10. Logarithms to the base 10 are known as common logarithms. A logarithm is composed of two parts, the characteristic and mantissa.

$$10^2 = 100 \Rightarrow \log_{10}100 = 2$$

$$5^3 = 125 \Rightarrow \log_5 125 = 3$$

The characteristic is always an integer and is determined as :

If X =>1, the characteristic is positive and its value is one less than the number of digits in X which are to the left of the decimal point.

X	*characteristic*
3456	3
345.6	2
34.56	1
3.456	0

If X <1, the characteristic is negative and its value is one more than the number of zeros between the decimal point and the first significant digit of the number

X	*characteristic*
0.3456	-1
0.03456	-2
0.003456	-3
0.0003456	-4

The mantissa is obtained from the log table. The mantissa is the same for any given combination of digits no matter where the decimal point is placed. Thus for all eight X's listed the mantissa is 0.5386.

Combining the characteristic and mantissa gives the logarithm.

For eight values of X

X	*logarithm*
3456	3.5386
345.6	2.5386
34.56	1.5386
1.456	0.5386
0.3456	-1.5386
0.03456	-2.5386
0.003456	-3.5386

Antilogarithms

When the characteristic of the logarithms is positive, decimal point is inserted after the (n+1)th digit, where n is the characteristic. If characteristic is negative, decimal point is inserted such that first significant digit is at the nth place, where n is the characteristic.

Antilogarithm is calculated for mantissa and decimal point is inserted according to the value of characteristic.

Antilog (2.4567) => 2 as characteristic and antilog (.4567) = 2863

Since characteristic is positive, decimal point is inserted after (2+1=3) places,

Thus antilog (2.4567) = 286.3

Antilog (-1.4567) => -1 as characteristic and antilog(.4567) = 2863

Since characteristic is negative, decimal point is inserted so that first significant digit is at first place.

Thus antilog (-1.4567) = 0.2863

The common used formula for logarithms are as follows :

(1) Log (a/b) = log a – log b

i.e. log (25/32) = log 25 – log 32

= 1.3979 – 1.5051

= - 0.1072

(25/32) = antilog (-0.1072)

= antilog (-1.8928)

= 0.7812

(2) Log (a∗b) = log a + log b

$$\begin{aligned}
\text{Log}\,(25*32) &= \log(25) + \log(32)\\
&= 1.3979 + 1.5051\\
&= 2.9030\\
(25*32) &= \text{antilog}\,(2.9030)\\
&= \text{antilog}\,(.9030) = 7998 \text{ and characteristic} = 2\\
&= 799.8 \Rightarrow 800
\end{aligned}$$

(3) $\text{Log}\ a^{b} = b \log(a)$

$$\begin{aligned}
\text{Log}\ 15^{2} &= 2\log(15)\\
&= 2*1.1761\\
&= 2.3522\\
15^{2} &= \text{antilog}(2.3522)\\
&= 225.0
\end{aligned}$$

(4) $\text{Log}_{x}\, x = 1$

(5) $\text{Log}_{a}\, x = 1/(\log_{x} a)$

GENERAL

- Squares of the numbers formed by digit 1

  $11^{2} = 121$

  $111^{2} = 12321$

  $1111^{2} = 1234321$

- Squares of numbers ending with 5

  15^2 = 1X2 25 = 225

  35^2 = 3X4 25 = 1225

  105^2 = 10X11 25 = 11025

- The above logic is applicable not only to the squaring of a number ending in 5 but also to the multiplication of two numbers whose last digits together total 10 and whose previous part is exactly same.

  27X23 = 2X3 21 = 621

  96X94 = 9X10 24 = 9024

- The 11rule

  To multiply any two digit number by 11

  54 X 11

Separate two digits 5---4, add total of 5&4 i.e. 9, put resulting 9 in between 5 & 4. Thus 54X11 = 594

If the result of addition is greater than 9, put the 'one's digit' at '---' and carry the tens digit from the addition.

57X11 = 5---7

5+7=12

one's digit of 12 is 2, put 2 at '---' and add tens digit i.e. 1 to 5

thus 57X11 = (5+1) 2 7 = 627

- Multiplying a 2, 3, 4 or 5 digit number by 100001

  2 digit number : 24X100001

  = first two digits, then three zeros then again two digits

  thus 24X100001 = 24 000 24

- 3 digit number

  = first three digits, then two zeros, then three digits

  321X100001 = 321 00 321

- 4 digit number

  = first four digits, then one zero, then four digits

  1245X100001 = 1245 0 1245

- 5 digit number

  = first five digit number, then five digit number

  12345X100001 = 12345 12345

- 728X101

  = 7+8 = 15

  72+1=73

  28 then =7 3 5 2 8

- Any three digit number multiply it by 7X11X13=1001

  321X7X11X13 = 321321

- Squares of numbers between 40 to 50.

  1. Find out how far is the number from 50, square the difference to get the last two digit.
  2. Subtract the difference from 25 to get first two digit.

  43^2 = difference between 50 and 43 =7 ; square of 7 = 49

last two digit is 49.

25-7 = 18 thus first two digits are 18

finally 43^2 = 18 49

- a% of b = (a X b)/100
- What % of b is a, it is (bX100)/a
- a% of b = b% of a
- If a is x% of b then b is (10^4/x)% of a
- Successive discounts of p% and q% is equal to p+q-(pq/100)%
- Two trains each of length l meters are moving on parallel track with a speed of u km/hr and v km/hr respectively in opposite direction then time taken by them to pass each other

  = 2l/1000(u+v)

- If m1 men can complete a work in t1 days, in how many days m2 men can complete the same work

  Total work done should be equal

  => m1Xt1 = m2Xt2

  Thus, t2 = (m1Xt1)/m2

- If m1,m2 and m3 men can complete a piece of work in t1, t2 and t3 days respectively then working together they will complete the work in T days

$$T = \frac{t1Xt2Xt3}{(t2Xt3)+(t1Xt3)+(t1Xt2)}$$

  1/T = 1/t1 +1/t2 + 1/t3

- 8 men or 14 women can complete a piece of work in 30 days. How many days would 12 men and 4 women need to complete the same work

  m1=8 ; t1=30

  m2=12+4 ; t2=?

  m1Xt1 = m2Xt2

  30X8 = 16Xt2 => t2 = (30X8)/16 = 15days

  M(men)XT(hours)XD(days) = constant

- The average monthly salary of n employees is Rs r. If salary of manager is included, the average becomes y. The salary of manager will be [y X (n+1)] – (rXn)
- If a shopkeeper allows a x% discount on an article. He also wants p% profit, the selling price of the article will be

$$\frac{100 \text{ X } (p+100)}{(100-x)}$$

- Certain money becomes x in n years and y in (n+1) years at compound interest

  Rate of interest = [(y-x)X100]/x
- Two chairs are sold for Rs x, one at a gain of y% and another at a loss of y% then the net loss will be $Y^2/100\%$
- If A goes to his office at a speed of U km/hr and returns back at a speed of Vkm/hr, then the average speed = (2 UV)/(U+V)
- The quadratic equation in x such that the arithmetic mean of roots is m and geometric mean is n is

$$X^2\text{-}2mx+n^2$$

- In a triangle Tan A + Tan B + Tan C = TanA.TanB.TanC
- Three medians of an equilateral triangle are equal.

Suggested Reading

a. Fundamentals of Mathematical Statistics by S.C. Gupta and V.K. Kapoor

b. Fundamentals of Applied Statistics by S.C. Gupta and V.K. Kapoor

c. Statistical methods for Agricultural Workers by V.G. Panse and P.V. Sukhatme

d. Statistics for Business and Economics IV Edition by James T McClave and P. George Benson

e. Practical Cytology – Applied Genetics and Biostatistics by H.K. Goswami and Rajeev Goswami

APPENDIX-I

Logarithms

	0	1	2	3	4	5	6	7	8	9	1	2	3	4	5	6	7	8	9
10	0000	0043	0086	0128	0170						5	9	13	17	21	26	30	34	38
						0212	0253	0294	0334	0374	4	8	12	16	20	24	28	32	36
11	0414	0453	0492	0531	0569						4	8	12	16	20	23	27	31	35
						0607	0645	0682	0719	0755	4	7	11	15	18	22	26	29	33
12	0792	0828	0864	0899	0934						3	7	11	14	18	21	25	28	32
						0969	1004	1038	1072	1106	3	7	10	14	17	20	24	27	31
13	1139	1173	1206	1239	1271						3	6	10	13	16	19	23	26	29
						1303	1335	1367	1399	1430	3	7	10	13	16	19	22	25	29
14	1461	1492	1523	1553	1584						3	6	9	12	15	19	22	25	28
						1614	1644	1673	1703	1732	3	6	9	12	14	17	20	23	26
15	1761	1790	1818	1847	1875						3	6	9	11	14	17	20	23	26
						1903	1931	1959	1987	2014	3	6	8	11	14	17	19	22	25
16	2041	2068	2095	2122	2148						3	6	8	11	14	16	19	22	24
						2175	2201	2227	2253	2279	3	5	8	10	13	16	18	21	23
17	2304	2330	2355	2380	2405						3	5	8	10	13	15	18	20	23
						2430	2455	2480	2504	2529	3	5	8	10	12	15	17	20	22
18	2553	2577	2601	2625	2648						2	5	7	9	12	14	17	19	21
						2672	2695	2718	2742	2765	2	4	7	9	11	14	16	18	21
19	2788	2810	2833	2856	2878						2	4	7	9	11	13	16	18	20
						2900	2923	2945	2967	2989	2	4	6	8	11	13	15	17	19

20	3010	3032	3054	3075	3096	3118	3139	3160	3181	3201	2	4	6	8	11	13	15	17	19
21	3222	3243	3263	3284	3304	3324	3345	3365	3385	3404	2	4	6	8	10	12	14	16	18
22	3424	3444	3464	3483	3502	3522	3541	3560	3579	3598	2	4	6	8	10	12	14	15	17
23	3617	3636	3655	3674	3692	3711	3729	3747	3766	3784	2	4	6	7	9	11	13	15	17
24	3802	3820	3838	3856	3874	3892	3909	3927	3945	3962	2	4	5	7	9	11	12	14	16
25	3979	3997	4014	4031	4048	4065	4082	4099	4116	4133	2	3	5	7	9	10	12	14	15
26	4150	4166	4183	4200	4216	4232	4249	4265	4281	4298	2	3	5	7	8	10	11	13	15
27	4314	4330	4346	4362	4378	4393	4409	4425	4440	4456	2	3	5	6	8	9	11	13	14
28	4472	4487	4502	4518	4533	4548	4564	4579	4594	4609	2	3	5	6	8	9	11	12	14
29	4624	4639	4654	4669	4683	4698	4713	4728	4742	4757	1	3	4	6	7	9	10	12	13
30	4771	4786	4800	4814	4829	4843	4857	4871	4886	4900	1	3	4	6	7	9	10	11	13
31	4914	4928	4942	4955	4969	4983	4997	5011	5024	5038	1	3	4	6	7	8	10	11	12
32	5051	5065	5079	5092	5105	5119	5132	5145	5159	5172	1	3	4	5	7	8	9	11	12
33	5185	5198	5211	5224	5237	5250	5263	5276	5289	5302	1	3	4	5	6	8	9	10	12
34	5315	5328	5340	5353	5366	5378	5391	5403	5416	5428	1	2	4	5	6	8	9	10	11
35	5441	5453	5465	5478	5490	5502	5514	5527	5539	5551	1	2	4	5	6	7	9	10	11
36	5563	5575	5587	5599	5611	5623	5635	5647	5658	5670	1	2	3	5	6	7	8	10	11
37	5682	5694	5705	5717	5729	5740	5752	5763	5775	5786	1	2	3	5	6	7	8	9	10
38	5798	5809	5821	5832	5843	5855	5866	5877	5888	5899	1	2	3	5	6	7	8	9	10
39	5911	5932	5933	5944	5955	5966	5977	5988	5999	6010	1	2	3	4	5	7	8	9	10

40	6021	6031	6042	6053	6064	6075	6085	6096	6107	6117	1	2	3	4	5	6	8	9	10
41	6128	6138	6149	6160	6170	6180	6191	6201	6212	6222	1	2	3	4	5	6	7	8	9
42	6232	6243	6253	6263	6274	6284	6294	6304	6314	6325	1	2	3	4	5	6	7	8	9
43	6335	6345	6355	6365	6375	6385	6395	6405	6415	6425	1	2	3	4	5	6	7	8	9
44	6435	6444	6454	6464	6474	6484	6493	6503	6513	6522	1	2	3	4	5	6	7	8	9
45	6532	6542	6551	6561	6571	6580	6590	6599	6609	6618	1	2	3	4	5	6	7	8	9
46	6628	6637	6646	6656	6665	6675	6684	6693	6702	6712	1	2	3	4	5	6	7	7	8
47	6721	6730	6739	6749	6758	6767	6776	6785	6794	6803	1	2	3	4	5	5	6	7	8
48	6812	6821	6830	6839	6848	6857	6866	6875	6884	6893	1	2	3	4	4	5	6	7	8
49	6902	6911	6920	6928	6937	6946	6955	6964	6972	6981	1	2	3	4	4	5	6	7	8
50	6990	6998	7007	7016	7024	7033	7042	7050	7059	7067	1	2	3	3	4	5	6	7	8
51	7076	7084	7093	7101	7110	7118	7126	7135	7143	7152	1	2	3	3	4	5	6	7	8
52	7160	7168	7177	7185	7193	7202	7210	7218	7226	7235	1	2	2	3	4	5	6	7	7
53	7243	7251	7259	7267	7275	7284	7292	7300	7308	7316	1	2	2	3	4	5	6	6	7
54	7324	7332	7340	7348	7356	7364	7372	7380	7388	7396	1	2	2	3	4	5	6	6	7
55	7404	7412	7419	7427	7435	7443	7451	7459	7466	7474	1	2	2	3	4	5	5	6	7
56	7482	7490	7497	7505	7513	7520	7528	7536	7543	751	1	2	2	3	4	5	5	6	7
57	7559	7566	7574	7582	7589	7597	7604	7612	7619	7627	1	2	2	3	4	5	5	6	7
58	7634	7642	7649	7657	7664	7672	7679	7686	7694	7701	1	1	2	3	4	4	5	6	7
59	7709	7716	7723	7731	7738	7745	7752	7760	7767	7774	1	1	2	3	4	4	5	6	7

60	7782	7789	7796	7803	7810	7818	7825	7832	7839	7846	1	1	2	3	4	4	5	6	6
61	7853	7860	7868	7875	7882	7889	7896	7903	7910	7917	1	1	2	3	4	4	5	6	6
86	9345	9350	9355	9360	9365	9370	9375	9380	9385	9390	1	1	2	2	3	3	4	4	5
87	9395	9400	9405	9410	9415	9420	9425	9430	9435	9440	0	1	1	2	2	3	3	4	4
88	9445	9450	9455	9460	9465	9469	9474	9479	9484	9489	0	1	1	2	2	3	3	4	4
89	9494	9499	9504	9509	9513	9518	9523	9528	9533	9538	0	1	1	2	2	3	3	4	4
90	9542	9547	9552	9557	9562	9566	9571	9576	9581	9586	0	1	1	2	2	3	3	4	4
91	9590	9595	9600	9605	9609	9614	9619	9624	9628	9633	0	1	1	2	2	3	3	4	4
92	9638	9643	9647	9652	9657	9661	9666	9671	9675	9680	0	1	1	2	2	3	3	4	4
93	9685	9689	9694	9699	9703	9708	9713	9717	9722	9727	0	1	1	2	2	3	3	4	4
94	9731	9736	9741	9745	9750	9754	9759	9763	9768	9773	0	1	1	2	2	3	3	4	4
95	9777	9782	9786	9791	9795	9800	9805	9809	9814	9818	0	1	1	2	2	3	3	4	4
96	9823	9827	9832	9836	9841	9845	9850	9854	9859	9863	0	1	1	2	2	3	3	4	4
97	9868	9872	9877	9881	9886	9890	9894	9899	9903	9908	0	1	1	2	2	3	3	4	4
98	9912	9917	9921	9926	9930	9934	9939	9943	9948	9952	0	1	1	2	2	3	3	4	4
99	9956	9961	9965	9969	9974	9978	9983	9987	9991	9996	0	1	1	2	2	3	3	3	4

APPENDIX-II

Antilogarithms

.00	1000	1002	1005	1007	1009	1012	1014	1016	1019	1021	0 0 1	1 1 1	2 2 2
.01	1023	1026	1028	1030	1033	1035	1038	1040	1042	1045	0 0 1	1 1 1	2 2 2
.02	1047	1050	1052	1054	1057	1059	1062	1064	1067	1069	0 0 1	1 1 1	2 2 2
.03	1072	1074	1076	1079	1081	1084	1086	1089	1091	1094	0 0 1	1 1 1	2 2 2
.04	1096	1099	1102	1104	1107	1109	1112	1114	1117	1119	0 1 1	1 1 2	2 2 2
.05	1122	1125	1127	1130	1132	1135	1138	1140	1143	1146	0 1 1	1 1 2	2 2 2
.06	1148	1151	1153	1156	1159	1161	1164	1167	1169	1172	0 1 1	1 1 2	2 2 2
.07	1175	1178	1180	1183	1186	1189	1191	1194	1197	1199	0 1 1	1 1 2	2 2 2
.08	1202	1205	1208	1211	1213	1216	1219	1222	1225	1227	0 1 1	1 1 2	2 2 3
.09	1230	1233	1236	1239	1242	1245	1247	1250	1253	1256	0 1 1	1 1 2	2 2 3
.10	1259	1262	1265	1268	1271	1274	1276	1279	1282	1285	0 1 1	1 1 2	2 2 3
.11	1288	1291	1294	1297	1300	1303	1306	1309	1312	1315	0 1 1	1 2 2	2 2 3
.12	1318	1321	1324	1327	1330	1334	1337	1340	1343	1346	0 1 1	1 2 2	2 2 3
.13	1349	1352	1355	1358	1361	1365	1368	1371	1374	1377	0 1 1	1 2 2	2 3 3
.14	1380	1384	1387	1390	1393	1396	1400	1403	1406	1409	0 1 1	1 2 2	2 3 3
.15	1410	1416	1419	1422	1426	1429	1432	1435	1439	1442	0 1 1	1 2 2	2 3 3
.16	1445	1449	1452	1455	1459	1462	1466	1469	1472	1476	0 1 1	1 2 2	2 3 3
.17	1479	1483	1486	1489	1493	1496	1500	1503	1507	1510	0 1 1	1 2 2	2 3 3

.18	1514	1517	1521	1524	1528	1531	1535	1538	1542	1545	0	1	1	1	2	2	2	3	3
.19	1549	1552	1556	1560	1563	1567	1570	1574	1578	1581	0	1	1	1	2	2	3	3	3
.20	1585	1589	1592	1596	1600	1603	1607	1611	1614	1618	0	1	1	1	2	2	3	3	3
.21	1622	1626	1629	1633	1637	1641	1644	1648	1652	1656	0	1	1	2	2	2	3	3	3
.22	1660	1663	1667	1671	1675	1679	1683	1687	1690	1694	0	1	1	2	2	2	3	3	3
.23	1698	1702	1706	1710	1714	1718	1722	1726	1730	1734	0	1	1	2	2	2	3	3	4
.24	1738	1742	1746	1750	1754	1758	1762	1766	1770	1774	0	1	1	2	2	2	3	3	4
.25	1778	1782	1786	1791	1795	1799	1803	1807	1811	1816	0	1	1	2	2	2	3	3	4
.26	1820	1824	1828	1832	1837	1841	1845	1849	1854	1858	0	1	1	2	2	3	3	3	4
.27	1862	1866	1871	1875	1879	1884	1888	1892	1897	1901	0	1	1	2	2	3	3	3	4
.28	1905	1910	1914	1919	1923	1928	1932	1936	1941	1945	0	1	1	2	2	3	3	4	4
.29	1950	1954	1959	1963	1968	1972	1977	1982	1986	1991	0	1	1	2	2	3	3	4	4
.30	1995	2000	2004	2009	2014	2018	2023	2028	2032	2037	0	1	1	2	2	3	3	4	4
.31	2042	2046	2051	2056	2061	2065	2070	2075	2080	2084	0	1	1	2	2	3	3	4	4
.32	2089	2094	2099	2104	2109	2113	2118	2123	2128	2133	0	1	1	2	2	3	3	4	4
.33	2138	2143	2148	2153	2158	2163	2168	2173	2178	2183	0	1	1	2	2	3	3	4	4
.34	2188	2193	2198	2203	2208	2213	2218	2223	2228	2234	1	1	2	2	3	3	4	4	5
.35	2239	2244	2249	2254	2259	2265	2270	2275	2280	2286	1	1	2	2	3	3	4	4	5
.36	2291	2296	2301	2307	2312	2317	2323	2328	2333	2339	1	1	2	2	3	3	4	4	5
.37	2344	2350	2355	2360	2366	2371	2377	2382	2388	2393	1	1	2	2	3	3	4	4	5

.38	2399	2404	2410	2415	2421	2427	2432	2438	2443	2449	1	1	2	2	3	3	4	4	5
.39	2455	2460	2466	2472	2477	2483	2489	2495	2500	2506	1	1	2	2	3	3	4	5	5
.40	2512	2518	2523	2529	2535	2541	2547	2553	2559	2564	1	1	2	2	3	4	4	5	5
.41	2570	2576	2582	2588	2594	2600	2606	2612	2618	2624	1	1	2	2	3	4	4	5	5
.42	2630	2636	2642	2649	2655	2661	2667	2673	2679	2685	1	1	2	2	3	4	4	5	6
.43	2692	2698	2704	2710	2716	2723	2729	2735	2742	2748	1	1	2	3	3	4	4	5	6
.44	2754	2761	2767	2773	2780	2786	2793	2799	2805	2812	1	1	2	3	3	4	4	5	6
.45	2818	2825	2831	2838	2844	2851	2858	2864	2871	2877	1	1	2	3	3	4	4	5	6
.46	2884	2891	2897	2904	2911	2917	2924	2931	2938	2944	1	1	2	3	3	4	5	5	6
.47	2951	2958	2965	2972	2979	2985	2992	2999	3006	3013	1	1	2	3	3	4	5	5	6
.48	3020	3027	3034	3041	3048	3055	3062	3069	3076	3083	1	1	2	3	4	4	5	6	6
.49	3090	3097	3105	3112	3119	3126	3133	3141	3148	3155	1	1	2	3	4	4	5	6	6
.50	3162	3170	3177	3184	3192	3199	3206	3214	3221	3228	1	1	2	3	4	4	5	6	7
.51	3236	3243	3251	3258	3266	3273	3281	3289	3296	3304	1	2	2	3	4	5	5	6	7
.52	3311	3319	3327	3334	3342	3350	3357	3365	3373	3381	1	2	2	3	4	5	5	6	7
.53	3388	3396	3404	3412	3420	3428	3436	3443	3451	3459	1	2	2	3	4	5	6	6	7
.54	3467	3475	3483	3491	3499	3508	3516	3524	3532	3540	1	2	2	3	4	5	6	6	7
.55	3548	3556	3565	3573	3581	3589	3597	3606	3614	3622	1	2	2	3	4	5	6	7	7
.56	3631	3639	3648	3656	3664	3673	3681	3690	3698	3707	1	2	3	3	4	5	6	7	8
.57	3715	3724	3733	3741	3750	3758	3767	3776	3784	3793	1	2	3	3	4	5	6	7	8

.58	3802	3811	3819	3828	3837	3846	3855	3864	3873	3882	1	2	3	4	4	5	6	7	8
.59	3893	3899	3908	3917	3926	3936	3945	3954	3963	3972	1	2	3	4	5	5	6	7	8
.60	3981	3990	3999	4009	4018	4027	4036	4046	4055	4064	1	2	3	4	5	6	6	7	8
.61	4074	4083	4093	4102	4111	4121	4130	4140	4150	4159	1	2	3	4	5	6	7	8	9
.62	4169	4178	4188	4198	4207	4217	4227	4236	4246	4256	1	2	3	4	5	6	7	8	9
.63	4266	4276	4285	4295	4305	4315	4325	4335	4345	4355	1	2	3	4	5	6	7	8	9
.64	4365	4375	4385	4395	4406	4416	4426	4436	4446	4457	1	2	3	4	5	6	7	8	9
.65	4467	4477	4487	4498	4508	4519	4529	4539	4550	4560	1	2	3	4	5	6	7	8	9
.66	4571	4581	4592	4603	4613	4624	4634	4645	4656	4667	1	2	3	4	5	6	7	9	10
.67	4677	4688	4699	4710	4721	4732	4742	4753	4764	4775	1	2	3	4	5	7	8	9	10
.68	4786	4797	4808	4819	4831	4842	4853	4864	4875	4887	1	2	3	4	6	7	8	9	10
.69	4893	4909	4920	4932	4943	4955	4966	4977	4989	5000	1	2	3	5	6	7	8	9	10
.70	5012	5023	5035	5047	5058	5070	5082	5093	5105	5117	1	2	4	5	6	7	8	9	11
.71	5129	5140	5152	5164	5176	5183	5200	5212	5224	5236	1	2	4	5	6	7	8	10	11
.72	5248	5260	5272	5284	5297	5309	5321	5333	5346	5358	1	2	4	5	6	7	9	10	11
.73	5370	5383	5395	5408	5420	5433	5445	5458	5470	5483	1	3	4	5	6	8	9	10	11
.74	5495	5508	5521	5534	5546	5559	5572	5585	5598	5610	1	3	4	5	6	8	9	10	12
.75	5623	5636	5649	5662	5675	5689	5702	5715	5728	5741	1	3	4	5	7	8	9	10	12
.76	5754	5768	5781	5794	5808	5821	5834	5848	5861	5875	1	3	4	5	7	8	9	11	12
.77	5888	5902	5916	5929	5943	5957	5970	5984	5998	6012	1	3	4	5	7	8	10	11	12

.78	6026	6039	6053	6067	6081	6095	6109	6124	6138	6152	1 3 4	6 7 8	10 11 13
.79	6166	6180	6194	6209	6223	6237	6252	6266	6281	6295	1 3 4	6 7 9	10 11 13
.80	6310	6324	6339	6353	6368	6383	6397	6412	6427	6442	1 3 4	6 7 9	10 12 13
.81	6457	6471	6486	6501	6516	6531	6546	6561	6577	6592	2 3 5	6 8 9	11 12 14
.82	6607	6622	6637	6653	6668	6683	6699	6714	6730	6745	2 3 5	6 8 9	11 12 14
.83	6761	6776	6792	6808	6823	6839	6855	6871	6887	6902	2 3 5	6 8 9	11 13 14
.84	6918	6934	6950	6966	6982	6998	7015	7031	7047	7063	2 3 5	6 8 10	11 13 15
.85	7079	7096	7112	7129	7145	7161	7178	7194	7211	7228	2 3 5	7 8 10	12 13 15
.86	7244	7261	7278	7295	7311	7328	7345	7362	7379	7396	2 3 5	7 8 10	12 13 15
.87	7413	7430	7447	7464	7482	7499	7516	7534	7551	7568	2 3 5	7 9 10	12 14 16
.88	7586	7603	7621	7638	7656	7674	7691	7709	7727	7745	2 4 5	7 9 11	12 14 16
.89	7762	7780	7798	7816	7834	7852	7870	7889	7907	7925	2 4 5	7 9 11	13 14 16
.90	7943	7962	7980	7998	8017	8035	8054	8072	8091	8110	2 4 6	7 9 11	13 15 17
.91	8128	8147	8166	8185	8204	8222	8241	8260	8279	8299	2 4 6	8 9 11	13 15 17
.92	8318	8337	8356	8375	8395	8414	8433	8453	8472	8492	2 4 6	8 10 12	14 15 17
.93	8511	8531	8551	8570	8590	8610	8630	8650	8670	8690	2 4 6	8 10 12	14 16 18
.94	8710	8730	8750	8770	8790	8810	8831	8851	8872	8892	2 4 6	8 10 12	14 16 18
.95	8913	8933	8954	8974	8995	9016	9036	9057	9078	9099	2 4 6	8 10 12	15 17 19
.96	9120	9141	9162	9183	9204	9226	9247	9268	9290	9311	2 4 6	8 11 13	15 17 19
.97	9333	9354	9376	9397	9419	9441	9462	9484	9506	9528	2 4 7	9 11 13	15 17 20
.98	9550	9572	9594	9616	9638	9661	9683	9705	9727	9750	2 4 7	9 11 13	16 18 20
.99	9772	9795	9817	9840	9863	9886	9908	9931	9954	9977	2 5 7	9 11 13	16 18 20

APPENDIX-III

Normal Curve Areas

Z→ ↓	.00	.01	.02	.03	.04	.05	.06	.07	.08	.09
.0	.0000	.0040	.0080	.0120	.0160	.0199	.0239	.0279	.0319	.0359
.1	.0398	.0438	.0478	.0517	.0557	.0596	.0636	.0675	.0714	.0753
.2	.0793	.0832	.0871	.0910	.0948	.0987	.1026	.1064	.1103	.1141
.3	.1179	.1217	.1255	.1293	.1331	.1368	.1406	.1443	.1480	.1517
.4	.1554	.1591	.1628	.1664	.1700	.1736	.1772	.1808	.1844	.1879
.5	.1915	.1950	.1985	.2019	.2054	.2088	.2123	.2157	.2190	.2224
.6	.2257	.2291	.2324	.2357	.2389	.2422	.2454	.2486	.2517	.2549
.7	.2580	.2611	.2642	.2673	.2704	.2734	.2764	.2794	.2823	.2852
.8	.2881	.2910	.2939	.2967	.2995	.3023	.3051	.3078	.3106	.3133
.9	.3159	.3186	.3212	.3238	.3264	.3289	.3315	.3340	.3365	.3389
1.0	.3413	.3438	.3461	.3485	.3508	.3531	.3554	.3577	.3599	.3621
1.1	.3643	.3665	.3686	.3708	.3729	.3749	.3770	.3790	.3810	.3830
1.2	.3849	.3869	.3888	.3907	.3925	.3944	.3962	.3980	.3997	.4015
1.3	.4032	.4049	.4066	.4082	.4099	.4115	.4131	.4147	.4162	.4177
1.4	.4192	.4207	.4222	.4236	.4251	.4265	.4279	.4292	.4306	.4319
1.5	.4332	.4345	.4357	.4370	.4382	.4394	.4406	.4418	.4429	.4441

1.6	.4452	.4463	.4474	.4484	.4495	.4505	.4515	.4525	.4535	.4545
1.7	.4554	.4564	.4573	.4582	.4591	.4599	.4608	.4616	.4625	.4633
1.8	.4641	.4649	.4656	.4664	.4671	.4678	.4686	.4693	.4699	.4706
1.9	.4713	.4719	.4726	.4732	.4738	.4744	.4750	.4756	.4761	.4767
2.0	.4772	.4778	.4783	.4788	.4793	.4798	.4803	.4808	.4812	.4817
2.1	.4821	.4826	.4830	.4834	.4838	.4842	.4846	.4850	.4854	.4857
2.2	.4861	.4864	.4868	.4871	.4875	.4878	.4881	.4884	.4887	.4890
2.3	.4893	.4896	.4898	.4901	.4904	.4906	.4909	.4911	.4913	.4916
2.4	.4918	.4920	.4922	.4925	.4927	.4929	.4931	.4932	.4934	.4936
2.5	.4938	.4940	.4941	.4943	.4945	.4946	.4948	.4949	.4951	.4952
2.6	.4953	.4955	.4956	.4957	.4959	.4960	.4961	.4962	.4963	.4964
2.7	.4965	.4966	.4967	.4968	.4969	.4970	.4971	.4972	.4973	.4974
2.8	.4974	.4975	.4976	.4977	.4977	.4978	.4979	.4979	.4980	.4981
2.9	.4981	.4982	.4982	.4983	.4984	.4984	.4985	.4985	.4986	.4986
3.0	.4987	.4987	.4987	.4988	.4988	.4989	.4989	.4989	.4990	.4990

Source : Abridged from Table I of A. Hald, Statistical Tables and Formulas (New York : John Wiley & Sons, Inc.), 1952. Reproduced by permission of A. Hald and the publisher, John Wiley & Sons, Inc.

APPENDIX-IV

Critical Values of t

N	Level of Significance(P)						
	0.2	0.025	0.1	0.05	0.01	0.005	0.001
1	3.078	25.452	6.314	12.706	63.657	127.320	636.619
2	1.886	6.205	2.920	4.303	9.925	14.089	31.598
3	1.638	4.176	2.353	3.182	5.841	7.453	12.941
4	1.533	3.495	2.132	2.776	4.604	5.598	8.610
5	1.476	3.163	2.015	2.571	4.032	4.773	6.859
6	1.440	2.969	1.943	2.447	3.707	4.317	5.959
7	1.415	2.841	1.895	2.365	3.499	4.029	5.405
8	1.397	2.752	1.860	2.306	3.355	3.832	5.041
9	1.383	2.685	1.833	2.262	3.250	3.690	4.781
10	1.372	2.634	1.812	2.228	3.169	3.581	4.587
11	1.363	2.593	1.796	2.201	3.106	3.497	4.437
12	1.356	2.560	1.782	2.179	3.055	3.428	4.318
13	1.350	2.533	1.771	2.160	3.012	3.372	4.221
14	1.345	2.510	1.761	2.145	2.977	3.326	4.140
15	1.341	2.490	1.753	2.131	2.947	3.286	4.073
16	1.337	2.473	1.746	2.120	2.921	3.252	4.015
17	1.333	2.458	1.740	2.110	2.898	3.222	3.965

The values in this table were taken by the permission from Statistical Tables for *Biological, Agricultural and Medical Research*, by R.A. Fisher and F. Yates, Published by Oliver and Byod, Edinburgh, and from *Biometrika, vol. XXXII, April, 1942*.

18	1.330	2.445	1.734	2.101	2.878	3.197	3.922
19	1.328	2.433	1.729	2.093	2.861	3.174	3.883
20	1.325	2.423	1.725	2.086	2.845	3.153	3.850
21	1.323	2.414	1.721	2.080	2.831	3.135	3.819
22	1.321	2.406	1.717	2.074	2.819	3.119	3.792
23	1.319	2.398	1.714	2.069	2.807	3.104	3.767
24	1.318	2.391	1.711	2.064	2.797	3.090	3.745
25	1.316	2.385	1.708	2.060	2.787	3.078	3.725
26	1.315	2.379	1.706	2.056	2.779	3.067	3.707
27	1.314	2.373	1.703	2.052	2.771	3.056	3.690
28	1.313	2.368	1.701	2.048	2.763	3.047	3.674
29	1.311	2.364	1.699	2.045	2.756	3.038	3.659
30	1.310	2.360	1.697	2.042	2.750	3.030	3.646
40	1.303	2.329	1.684	2.021	2.704	2.971	3.551
60	1.296	2.299	1.671	2.000	2.660	2.915	3.460
120	1.289	2.270	1.658	1.980	2.617	2.860	3.373
∞	1.282	2.241	1.645	1.960	2.576	2.807	3.291

APPENDIX-V

Critical Values of χ^2

n	Level of Significance(P)					
	0.2	0.1	0.05	0.01	0.005	0.001
1	1.642	2.706	3.841	6.635	7.879	10.827
2	3.219	4.605	5.991	9.210	10.597	13.815
3	4.642	6.251	7.815	11.345	12.838	16.268
4	5.989	7.779	9.488	13.277	14.860	18.465
5	7.289	9.236	11.070	15.086	16.750	20.517
6	8.558	10.645	12.592	16.812	18.548	22.457
7	9.803	12.017	14.067	18.475	20.278	24.322
8	11.030	13.362	15.507	20.090	21.955	26.125
9	12.242	14.684	16.919	21.666	23.589	27.877
10	13.442	15.987	18.307	23.209	25.188	29.588
11	14.631	17.275	19.675	24.725	26.757	31.264
12	15.812	18.549	21.026	26.217	28.300	32.909
13	16.985	19.812	22.362	27.688	29.819	34.528
14	18.151	21.064	23.685	29.141	31.319	36.123

The values in this table were taken by the permission from Statistical Tables for *Biological, Agricultural and Medical Research*, by R.A. Fisher and F. Yates, Published by Oliver and Byod, Edinburgh, and from *Biometrika, vol. XXXII, April, 1942*.

15	19.311	22.307	24.996	30.578	32.801	37.697
16	20.465	23.542	26.296	32.000	34.267	39.252
17	21.615	24.769	27.587	33.409	35.718	40.790
18	22.760	25.989	28.869	34.805	37.156	42.312
19	23.900	27.204	30.144	36.191	38.582	43.820
20	25.038	28.412	31.410	37.566	39.997	45.315
21	26.171	29.615	32.671	38.932	41.401	46.797
22	27.301	30.813	33.924	40.289	42.796	48.268
23	28.429	32.007	35.172	41.638	44.181	49.728
24	29.553	33.196	36.415	42.980	45.558	51.179
25	30.675	34.382	37.652	44.314	46.928	52.620
26	31.795	35.563	38.885	45.642	48.290	54.052
27	32.912	36.741	40.113	46.963	49.645	55.476
28	34.027	37.916	41.337	48.278	50.993	56.893
29	35.139	39.087	42.557	49.588	52.336	58.302
30	36.250	40.256	43.773	50.892	53.672	59.703

APPENDIX-VI

Percentage points of the F-distribution, $\alpha=0.1$

	1	2	3	4	5	6	7	8	9	10	12	15	20	24
1	39.86	49.50	53.59	55.83	57.24	58.20	58.91	59.44	59.86	60.19	60.71	61.22	61.74	62.00
2	8.53	9.00	9.16	9.24	9.29	9.33	9.35	9.37	9.38	9.39	9.41	9.42	9.44	9.45
3	5.54	5.46	5.39	5.34	5.31	5.28	5.27	5.25	5.24	5.23	5.22	5.20	5.18	5.18
4	4.54	4.32	4.19	4.11	4.05	4.01	3.98	3.95	3.94	3.92	3.90	3.87	3.84	3.83
5	4.06	3.78	3.62	3.52	3.45	3.40	3.37	3.34	3.32	3.30	3.27	3.24	3.21	3.19
6	3.78	3.46	3.29	3.18	3.11	3.05	3.01	2.98	2.96	2.94	2.90	2.87	2.84	2.82
7	3.59	3.26	3.07	2.96	2.88	2.83	2.78	2.75	2.72	2.70	2.67	2.63	2.59	2.58
8	3.46	3.11	2.92	2.81	2.73	2.67	2.62	2.59	2.56	2.54	2.50	2.46	2.42	2.40
9	3.36	3.01	2.81	2.69	2.61	2.55	2.51	2.47	2.44	2.42	2.38	2.34	2.30	2.28
10	3.29	2.92	2.73	2.61	2.52	2.46	2.41	2.38	2.35	2.32	2.28	2.24	2.20	2.18
11	3.23	2.86	2.66	2.54	2.45	2.39	2.34	2.30	2.27	2.25	2.21	2.17	2.12	2.10
12	3.18	2.81	2.61	2.48	2.39	2.33	2.28	2.24	2.21	2.19	2.15	2.10	2.06	2.04
13	3.14	2.76	2.56	2.43	2.35	2.28	2.23	2.20	2.16	2.14	2.10	2.05	2.01	1.98
14	3.10	2.73	2.52	2.39	2.31	2.24	2.19	2.15	2.12	2.10	2.05	2.01	1.96	1.94
15	3.07	2.70	2.49	2.36	2.27	2.21	2.16	2.12	2.09	2.06	2.02	1.97	1.92	1.90
16	3.05	2.67	2.46	2.33	2.24	2.18	2.13	2.09	2.06	2.03	1.99	1.94	1.89	1.87
17	3.03	2.64	2.44	2.31	2.22	2.15	2.10	2.06	2.03	2.00	1.96	1.91	1.86	1.84

18	3.01	2.62	2.42	2.29	2.20	2.13	2.08	2.04	2.00	1.98	1.93	1.89	1.84	1.81
19	2.99	2.61	2.40	2.27	2.18	2.11	2.06	2.02	1.98	1.96	1.91	1.86	1.81	1.79
20	2.97	2.59	2.38	2.25	2.16	2.09	2.04	2.00	1.96	1.94	1.89	1.84	1.79	1.74
21	2.96	2.57	2.36	2.23	2.14	2.08	2.02	1.98	1.95	1.92	1.87	1.83	1.78	1.75
22	2.95	2.56	2.35	2.22	2.13	2.06	2.01	1.97	1.93	1.90	1.86	1.81	1.76	1.73
23	2.94	2.55	2.34	2.21	2.11	2.05	1.99	1.95	1.92	1.89	1.84	1.80	1.74	1.72
24	2.93	2.54	2.33	2.19	2.10	2.04	1.98	1.94	1.91	1.88	1.83	1.78	1.73	1.70
25	2.92	2.53	2.32	2.18	2.09	2.02	1.97	1.93	1.89	1.87	1.82	1.77	1.72	1.69
26	2.91	2.52	2.31	2.17	2.08	2.01	1.96	1.92	1.88	1.86	1.81	1.76	1.71	1.68
27	2.90	2.51	2.30	2.17	2.07	2.00	1.95	1.91	1.87	1.85	1.80	1.75	1.70	1.67
28	2.89	2.50	2.29	2.16	2.06	2.00	1.94	1.90	1.87	1.84	1.79	1.74	1.69	1.66
29	2.89	2.50	2.28	2.15	2.06	1.99	1.93	1.89	1.86	1.83	1.78	1.73	1.68	1.65
30	2.88	2.49	2.28	2.14	2.05	1.98	1.93	1.88	1.85	1.82	1.77	1.72	1.67	1.64
40	2.84	2.44	2.23	2.09	2.00	1.93	1.87	1.83	1.79	1.76	1.71	1.66	1.61	1.57
60	2.79	2.39	2.18	2.04	1.95	1.87	1.82	1.77	1.74	1.71	1.66	1.60	1.54	1.51
120	2.75	2.35	2.13	1.99	1.90	1.82	1.77	1.72	1.68	1.65	1.60	1.55	1.48	1.45

Source : From M. Merrington and C.M. Thompson, "Tables of Percentage Points of the Inverted Beta (F) Distribution", Biometrika, 1943, 33, 73-88. Reproduced by permission of the Biometrika Trustees.

APPENDIX-VII

Percentage points of the F-distribution, α=0.05

	1	2	3	4	5	6	7	8	9	10	12	15	20	24
1	161.4	199.5	215.7	224.6	230.2	234.0	236.8	238.9	240.5	241.9	243.9	245.9	248.0	249.1
2	18.53	19.00	19.16	19.25	19.30	19.33	19.35	19.37	19.38	19.40	19.41	19.43	19.45	19.45
3	10.13	9.55	9.28	9.12	9.01	8.94	8.89	8.85	8.81	8.79	8.74	8.70	8.66	8.64
4	7.71	6.94	6.59	6.39	6.26	6.16	6.09	6.04	6.00	5.96	5.91	5.86	5.80	5.77
5	6.61	5.79	5.41	5.19	5.05	4.95	4.88	4.82	4.77	4.74	4.68	4.62	4.56	4.53
6	5.99	5.14	4.76	4.53	4.39	4.28	4.21	4.15	4.10	4.06	4.00	3.94	3.87	3.84
7	5.59	4.74	4.35	4.12	3.97	3.87	3.79	3.73	3.68	3.64	3.57	3.51	3.44	3.41
8	5.32	4.46	4.07	3.84	3.69	3.58	3.50	3.44	3.39	3.35	3.28	3.22	3.15	3.12
9	5.12	4.26	3.86	3.63	3.48	3.37	3.29	3.23	3.18	3.14	3.07	3.01	2.94	2.90
10	4.96	4.10	3.71	3.48	3.33	3.22	3.14	3.07	3.02	2.98	2.91	2.85	2.77	2.74
11	4.84	3.98	3.59	3.36	3.20	3.09	3.01	2.95	2.90	2.85	2.79	2.72	2.65	2.61
12	4.75	3.89	3.49	3.26	3.11	3.00	2.91	2.85	2.80	2.75	2.69	2.62	2.54	2.51
13	4.67	3.81	3.41	3.18	3.03	2.92	2.83	2.77	2.71	2.67	2.60	2.53	2.46	2.42
14	4.60	3.74	3.34	3.11	2.96	2.85	2.76	2.70	2.65	2.60	2.53	2.46	2.39	2.35
15	4.54	3.68	3.29	3.06	2.90	2.79	2.71	2.64	2.59	2.54	2.48	2.40	2.33	2.29
16	4.49	3.63	3.24	3.01	2.85	2.74	2.66	2.59	2.54	2.49	2.42	2.35	2.28	2.24
17	4.45	3.59	3.20	2.96	2.81	2.70	2.61	2.55	2.49	2.45	2.38	2.31	2.23	2.19

18	4.41	3.55	3.16	2.93	2.77	2.66	2.58	2.51	2.46	2.41	2.34	2.27	2.19	2.15
19	4.38	3.52	3.13	2.90	2.74	2.63	2.54	2.48	2.42	2.38	2.31	2.23	2.16	2.11
20	4.35	3.49	3.10	2.87	2.71	2.60	2.51	2.45	2.39	2.35	2.28	2.20	2.12	2.08
21	4.32	3.47	3.07	2.84	2.68	2.57	2.49	2.42	2.37	2.32	2.25	2.18	2.10	2.05
22	4.30	3.44	3.05	2.82	2.66	2.55	2.46	2.40	2.34	2.30	2.23	2.15	2.07	2.03
23	4.28	3.42	3.03	2.80	2.64	2.53	2.44	2.37	2.32	2.27	2.20	2.13	2.05	2.01
24	4.26	3.40	3.01	2.78	2.62	2.51	2.42	2.36	2.30	2.25	2.18	2.11	2.03	1.98
25	4.24	3.39	2.99	2.76	2.60	2.49	2.40	2.34	2.28	2.24	2.16	2.09	2.01	1.96
26	4.23	3.37	2.98	2.74	2.59	2.47	2.39	2.32	2.27	2.22	2.15	2.07	1.99	1.95
27	4.21	3.35	2.96	2.73	2.57	2.46	2.37	2.31	2.25	2.20	2.13	2.06	1.97	1.93
28	4.20	3.34	2.95	2.71	2.56	2.45	2.36	2.29	2.24	2.19	2.12	2.04	1.96	1.91
29	4.18	3.33	2.93	2.70	2.55	2.43	2.35	2.28	2.22	2.18	2.10	2.03	1.94	1.90
30	4.17	3.32	2.92	2.69	2.53	2.42	2.33	2.27	2.21	2.16	2.09	2.01	1.93	1.89
40	4.08	3.23	2.84	2.61	2.45	2.34	2.25	2.18	2.12	2.08	2.00	1.92	1.84	1.79
60	4.00	3.15	2.76	2.53	2.37	2.25	2.17	2.10	2.04	1.99	1.92	1.84	1.75	1.70
120	3.92	3.07	2.68	2.45	2.29	2.17	2.09	2.02	1.96	1.91	1.83	1.75	1.66	1.61

Source : From M. Merrington and C.M. Thompson, "Tables of Percentage Points of the Inverted Beta (F) Distribution", Biometrika, 1943, 33, 73-88. Reproduced by permission of the Biometrika Trustees.

APPENDIX-VIII

Percentage points of the F-distribution, $\alpha=0.025$

	1	2	3	4	5	6	7	8	9	10	12	15	20	24
1	647.8	799.5	864.2	899.6	921.8	937.1	948.2	956.7	963.3	968.6	976.7	984.9	993.1	997.2
2	38.51	39.00	39.17	39.25	39.30	39.33	39.36	39.37	39.39	39.40	39.41	39.43	39.45	39.46
3	17.44	16.04	15.44	15.10	14.88	14.73	14.62	14.54	14.47	14.42	14.34	14.25	14.17	14.12
4	12.22	10.65	9.98	9.60	9.36	9.20	9.07	8.98	8.90	8.84	8.75	8.66	8.56	8.51
5	10.01	8.43	7.76	7.39	7.15	6.98	6.85	6.76	6.68	6.62	6.52	6.43	6.33	6.28
6	8.81	7.26	6.60	6.23	5.99	5.82	5.70	5.60	5.52	5.46	5.37	5.27	5.17	5.12
7	8.07	6.54	5.89	5.52	5.29	5.12	4.99	4.90	4.82	4.76	4.67	4.57	4.47	4.42
8	7.57	6.06	5.42	5.05	4.82	4.65	4.53	4.43	4.36	4.30	4.20	4.10	4.00	3.95
9	7.21	5.71	5.08	4.72	4.48	4.32	4.20	4.10	4.03	3.96	3.87	3.77	3.67	3.61
10	6.94	5.46	4.83	4.47	4.24	4.07	3.95	3.85	3.78	3.72	3.62	3.52	3.42	3.37
11	6.72	5.26	4.63	4.28	4.04	3.88	3.76	3.66	3.59	3.53	3.43	3.33	3.23	3.17
12	6.55	5.10	4.47	4.12	3.89	3.73	3.61	3.51	3.44	3.37	3.28	3.18	3.07	3.02
13	6.41	4.97	4.35	4.00	3.77	3.60	3.48	3.39	3.31	3.25	3.15	3.05	2.95	2.89
14	6.30	4.86	4.24	3.89	3.66	3.50	3.38	3.29	3.21	3.15	3.05	2.95	2.84	2.79
15	6.20	4.77	4.15	3.80	3.58	3.41	3.29	3.20	3.12	3.06	2.96	2.86	2.76	2.70
16	6.12	4.69	4.08	3.73	3.50	3.34	3.22	3.12	3.05	2.99	2.89	2.79	2.68	2.63
17	6.04	4.62	4.01	3.66	3.44	3.28	3.16	3.06	2.98	2.92	2.82	2.72	2.62	2.56

18	5.98	4.56	3.95	3.61	3.38	3.22	3.10	3.01	2.93	2.87	2.77	2.67	2.56	2.50
19	5.92	4.51	3.90	3.56	3.33	3.17	3.05	2.96	2.88	2.82	2.72	2.62	2.51	2.45
20	5.87	4.46	3.86	3.51	3.29	3.13	3.01	2.91	2.84	2.77	2.68	2.57	2.46	2.41
21	5.83	4.42	3.82	3.48	3.25	3.09	2.97	2.87	2.80	2.73	2.64	2.53	2.42	2.37
22	5.79	4.38	3.78	3.44	3.22	3.05	2.93	2.84	2.76	2.70	2.60	2.50	2.39	2.33
23	5.75	4.35	3.75	3.41	3.18	3.02	2.90	2.81	2.73	2.67	2.57	2.47	2.36	2.30
24	5.72	4.32	3.72	3.38	3.15	2.99	2.87	2.78	2.70	2.64	2.54	2.44	2.33	2.27
25	5.69	4.29	3.69	3.35	3.13	2.97	2.85	2.75	2.68	2.61	2.51	2.41	2.30	2.24
26	5.66	4.27	3.67	3.33	3.10	2.94	2.82	2.73	2.65	2.59	2.49	2.39	2.28	2.22
27	5.63	4.24	3.65	3.31	3.08	2.92	2.80	2.71	2.63	2.57	2.47	2.36	2.25	2.19
28	5.61	4.22	3.63	3.29	3.06	2.90	2.78	2.69	2.61	2.55	2.45	2.34	2.23	2.17
29	5.59	4.20	3.61	3.27	3.04	2.88	2.76	2.67	2.59	2.53	2.43	2.32	2.21	2.15
30	5.57	4.18	3.59	3.25	3.03	2.87	2.75	2.65	2.57	2.51	2.41	2.31	2.20	2.14
40	5.42	4.05	3.46	3.13	2.90	2.74	2.62	2.53	2.45	2.39	2.29	2.18	2.07	2.01
60	5.29	3.93	3.34	3.01	2.79	2.63	2.51	2.41	2.33	2.27	2.17	2.06	1.94	1.88
120	5.15	3.80	3.23	2.89	2.67	2.52	2.39	2.30	2.22	2.16	2.05	1.94	1.82	1.76

Source : From M. Merrington and C.M. Thompson, "Tables of Percentage Points of the Inverted Beta (F) Distribution", Biometrika, 1943, 33, 73-88. Reproduced by permission of the Biometrika Trustees.

APPENDIX-IX

Percentage points of the F-distribution, $\alpha=0.01$

	1	2	3	4	5	6	7	8	9	10	12	15	20	24
1	4052	4999.5	5403	5625	5764	5859	5928	5982	6022	6056	6106	6157	6209	6235
2	98.50	99.00	99.17	99.25	99.30	99.33	99.36	99.37	99.39	99.40	99.42	99.43	99.45	99.46
3	34.12	30.82	29.46	28.71	28.24	27.91	27.67	27.49	27.35	27.23	27.05	26.87	26.69	26.60
4	21.20	18.00	16.69	15.98	15.52	15.21	14.98	14.80	14.66	14.55	14.37	14.20	14.02	13.93
5	16.26	13.27	12.06	11.39	10.97	10.67	10.46	10.29	10.16	10.05	09.89	09.72	09.55	09.47
6	13.75	10.92	09.78	09.15	08.75	08.47	08.26	08.10	07.98	07.87	07.72	07.56	07.40	07.31
7	12.25	09.55	08.45	07.85	07.46	07.19	06.99	06.84	06.72	06.62	06.47	06.31	06.16	06.07
8	11.26	08.65	07.59	07.01	06.63	06.37	06.18	06.03	05.91	05.81	05.67	05.52	05.36	05.28
9	10.56	08.02	06.99	06.42	06.06	05.80	05.61	05.47	05.35	05.26	05.11	04.96	04.81	04.73
10	10.54	07.56	06.55	05.99	05.64	05.39	05.20	05.06	04.94	04.85	04.71	04.56	04.41	04.33
11	09.65	07.21	06.22	05.67	05.32	05.07	04.89	04.74	04.63	04.54	04.40	04.25	04.10	04.02
12	09.33	06.93	05.95	05.41	05.06	04.82	04.64	04.50	04.39	04.30	04.16	04.01	03.86	03.78
13	09.07	06.70	05.74	05.21	04.86	04.62	04.44	04.30	04.19	04.10	03.96	03.82	03.66	03.59
14	08.86	06.51	05.56	05.04	04.69	04.46	04.28	04.14	04.03	03.94	03.80	03.66	03.51	03.43
15	08.68	06.36	05.42	04.89	04.56	04.32	04.14	04.00	03.89	03.80	03.67	03.52	03.37	03.29
16	08.53	06.23	05.29	04.77	04.44	04.20	04.03	03.89	03.78	03.69	03.55	03.41	03.26	03.18
17	08.40	06.11	05.18	04.67	04.34	04.10	03.93	03.79	03.68	03.59	03.46	03.31	03.16	03.08

18	08.29	06.01	05.09	04.58	04.25	04.01	03.84	03.71	03.60	03.51	03.37	03.23	03.08	03.00
19	08.18	05.93	05.01	04.50	04.17	03.94	03.77	03.63	03.52	03.43	03.30	03.15	03.00	02.92
20	08.10	05.85	04.94	04.43	04.10	03.87	03.70	03.56	03.46	03.37	03.23	03.09	02.94	02.86
21	08.02	05.78	04.87	04.37	04.04	03.81	03.64	03.51	03.40	03.31	03.17	03.03	02.88	02.80
22	07.95	05.72	04.82	04.31	03.99	03.76	03.59	03.45	03.35	03.26	03.12	02.98	02.83	02.75
23	07.88	05.66	04.76	04.26	03.94	03.71	03.54	03.41	03.30	03.21	03.07	02.93	02.78	02.70
24	07.82	05.61	04.72	04.22	03.90	03.67	03.50	03.36	03.26	03.17	03.03	02.89	02.74	02.66
25	07.77	05.57	04.68	04.18	03.85	03.63	03.46	03.32	03.22	03.13	02.99	02.85	02.70	02.62
26	07.72	05.53	04.64	04.14	03.82	03.59	03.42	03.29	03.18	03.09	02.96	02.81	02.66	02.58
27	07.68	05.49	04.60	04.11	03.78	03.56	03.39	03.26	03.15	03.06	02.93	02.78	02.63	02.55
28	07.64	05.45	04.57	04.07	03.75	03.53	03.36	03.23	03.12	03.03	02.90	02.75	02.60	02.52
29	07.60	05.42	04.54	04.04	03.73	03.50	03.33	03.20	03.09	03.00	02.87	02.73	02.57	02.49
30	07.56	05.39	04.51	04.02	03.70	03.47	03.30	03.17	03.07	02.98	02.84	02.70	02.55	02.47
40	07.31	05.18	04.31	03.83	03.51	03.29	03.12	02.99	02.89	02.80	02.66	02.52	02.37	02.29
60	07.08	04.98	04.13	03.65	03.34	03.12	02.95	02.82	02.72	02.63	02.50	02.35	02.20	02.12
120	06.85	04.79	03.95	03.48	03.17	02.96	02.79	02.66	02.56	02.47	02.34	02.19	02.03	01.95

Source : From M. Merrington and C.M. Thompson, "Tables of Percentage Points of the Inverted Beta (F) Distribution", Biometrika, 1943, 33, 73-88. Reproduced by permission of the Biometrika Trustees.

APPENDIX-X

Critical Values of T_L and T_U for the Wilcoxon Rank Sum Test : Independent Samples

Test statistic is the rank sum associated with the smaller sample

1. α=0.025 one-tailed ; α=0.05 two-tailed

	3		4		5		6		7		8		9		10	
	T_L	T_U	T_L	T_U	T_L	T_U	T_L	T_U	T_L	T_U	T_L	T_U	T_L	T_U	T_L	T_U
3	5	16	06	18	06	21	07	23	07	26	08	28	08	31	09	33
4	6	18	11	25	12	28	12	32	13	35	14	38	15	41	16	44
5	6	21	12	28	18	37	19	41	20	45	21	49	22	53	24	56
6	7	23	12	32	19	41	26	52	28	56	29	61	31	65	32	70
7	7	26	13	35	20	45	28	56	37	68	39	73	41	78	43	83
8	8	28	14	38	21	49	29	61	39	73	49	87	51	93	54	98
9	8	31	15	41	22	53	31	65	41	78	51	93	63	108	66	114
10	9	33	16	44	24	56	32	70	43	83	54	98	66	114	79	131

2. α =0.05 one-tailed ; α =0.10 two-tailed

	3		4		5		6		7		8		9		10	
	T_L	T_U	T_L	T_U	T_L	T_U	T_L	T_U	T_L	T_U	T_L	T_U	T_L	T_U	T_L	T_U
3	06	15	07	17	07	20	08	22	09	24	09	27	10	29	11	31
4	07	17	12	24	13	27	14	30	15	33	16	36	17	39	18	42
5	07	20	13	27	19	36	20	40	22	43	24	46	25	50	26	54
6	08	22	14	30	20	40	28	50	30	54	32	58	33	63	35	67
7	09	24	15	33	22	43	30	54	39	66	41	71	43	76	46	80
8	09	27	16	36	24	46	32	58	41	71	52	84	54	90	57	95
9	10	29	17	39	25	50	33	63	43	76	54	90	66	105	69	111
10	11	31	18	42	26	54	35	67	46	80	57	95	69	111	83	127

Source : From F. Wilcoxon and R.A. Wilcox, "Some Rapid Approximate Statistical Procedures", 1964, 20-23. Reproduced with the permission of American Cyanamid Company.

APPENDIX-XI

Critical Values of T_0 in the Wilcoxon Paired Difference Signed Rank Test

One-Tailed	*Two-Tailed*	*n=5*	*n=6*	*n=7*	*n=8*	*n=9*	*n=10*
$\alpha = 0.05$	$\alpha = 0.1$	1	2	4	6	8	11
$\alpha = 0.025$	$\alpha = 0.05$		1	2	4	6	8
$\alpha = 0.01$	$\alpha = 0.02$			0	2	3	5
$\alpha = 0.005$	$\alpha = 0.01$				0	2	3

One-Tailed	*Two-Tailed*	*n=11*	*n=12*	*n=13*	*n=14*	*n=15*	*n=16*
$\alpha = 0.05$	$\alpha = 0.1$	14	17	21	26	30	36
$\alpha = 0.025$	$\alpha = 0.05$	11	14	17	21	25	30
$\alpha = 0.01$	$\alpha = 0.02$	7	10	13	16	20	24
$\alpha = 0.005$	$\alpha = 0.01$	5	7	10	13	16	19

One-Tailed	*Two-Tailed*	*n=17*	*n=18*	*n=19*	*n=20*	*n=21*	*n=22*
$\alpha = 0.05$	$\alpha = 0.1$	41	47	54	60	68	75
$\alpha = 0.025$	$\alpha = 0.05$	35	40	46	52	59	66
$\alpha = 0.01$	$\alpha = 0.02$	28	33	38	43	49	56
$\alpha = 0.005$	$\alpha = 0.01$	23	28	32	37	43	49

One-Tailed	*Two-Tailed*	*n=23*	*n=24*	*n=25*	*n=26*	*n=27*	*n=28*
$\alpha = 0.05$	$\alpha = 0.1$	83	92	101	110	120	130
$\alpha = 0.025$	$\alpha = 0.05$	73	81	90	98	107	117
$\alpha = 0.01$	$\alpha = 0.02$	62	69	77	85	93	102
$\alpha = 0.005$	$\alpha = 0.01$	55	61	68	76	84	92

One-Tailed	*Two-Tailed*	*n=29*	*n=30*	*n=31*	*n=32*	*n=33*	*n=34*
$\alpha = 0.05$	$\alpha = 0.1$	141	152	163	175	188	201
$\alpha = 0.025$	$\alpha = 0.05$	127	137	148	159	171	183
$\alpha = 0.01$	$\alpha = 0.02$	111	120	130	141	151	162
$\alpha = 0.005$	$\alpha = 0.01$	100	109	118	128	138	149
One-Tailed	*Two-Tailed*	*n=35*	*n=36*	*n=37*	*n=38*	*n=39*	*n=40*
$\alpha = 0.05$	$\alpha = 0.1$	214	228	242	256	271	287
$\alpha = 0.025$	$\alpha = 0.05$	195	208	222	235	250	264
$\alpha = 0.01$	$\alpha = 0.02$	174	186	198	211	224	238
$\alpha = 0.005$	$\alpha = 0.01$	160	171	183	195	208	221

One-Tailed	*Two-Tailed*	*n=41*	*n=42*	*n=43*	*n=44*	*n=45*	*n=46*
$\alpha = 0.05$	$\alpha = 0.1$	303	319	336	353	371	389
$\alpha = 0.025$	$\alpha = 0.05$	279	295	311	327	344	361
$\alpha = 0.01$	$\alpha = 0.02$	252	267	281	297	313	329
$\alpha = 0.005$	$\alpha = 0.01$	234	248	262	277	292	307

One-Tailed	*Two-Tailed*	*n=47*	*n=48*	*n=49*	*n=50*
$\alpha = 0.05$	$\alpha = 0.1$	408	427	446	466
$\alpha = 0.025$	$\alpha = 0.05$	379	397	415	434
$\alpha = 0.01$	$\alpha = 0.02$	345	362	380	398
$\alpha = 0.005$	$\alpha = 0.01$	323	339	356	373

Source : From F. Wilcoxon and R.A. Wilcox, "Some Rapid Approximate Statistical Procedures", 1964, p. 28. Reproduced with the permission of American Cyanamid Company.

APPENDIX-XII

The α values correspond to a one-tailed test of H0 : ps = 0. The values should be doubled for two-tailed test

N	$\alpha = 0.05$	$\alpha = 0.025$	$\alpha = 0.01$	$\alpha = 0.005$
5	0.900			
6	0.829	0.886	0.943	
7	0.714	0.786	0.893	
8	0.643	0.738	0.833	0.881
9	0.600	0.683	0.783	0.833
10	0.564	0.648	0.745	0.794
11	0.523	0.623	0.736	0.818
12	0.497	0.591	0.703	0.780
13	0.475	0.566	0.673	0.745
14	0.457	0.545	0.646	0.716
15	0.441	0.525	0.623	0.689
16	0.425	0.507	0.601	0.666
17	0.412	0.490	0.582	0.645
18	0.399	0.476	0.564	0.625
19	0.388	0.462	0.549	0.608

20	0.377	0.450	0.534	0.591
21	0.368	0.438	0.521	0.576
22	0.359	0.428	0.508	0.562
23	0.351	0.418	0.496	0.549
24	0.343	0.409	0.485	0.537
25	0.336	0.400	0.475	0.526
26	0.329	0.392	0.465	0.515
27	0.323	0.385	0.456	0.505
28	0.317	0.377	0.448	0.496
29	0.311	0.370	0.440	0.487
30	0.305	0.364	0.432	0.478

Source : From E.G.Olds, "Distribution of Sums of Squares of Rank Differences for Small Samples", Annals of Mathematical Statistics, 1938, 9. Reproduced with the permission of the Editor, Annals of mathematical Statistics.

APPENDIX-XIII

Metric System Conversion Rules

TO CONVERT	*Multiply by*	*TO CONVERT*	*Multiply by*
Inches to centimeters	2.540	Cub. Feet to Cub. Meters	0.02832
Centimeters to inches	0.3937	Cub. Meters to Cub. Feet	35.52
Feet to meters	0.3048	Cub. Yards to Cub. Meters	0.7646
Meters to feet	3.281	Cub. Meters to Cub. Yards	1.308
Yards to meters	0.9144	Cub. Inches to Litres	0.01639
Meters to yards	1.094	Litres to Cub. Inches	61.03
Miles to Kilometers	1.609	Gallons to Litres	4.535
Kilometers to Miles	0.6214	Litres to Gallons	0.2205
Sq. Inches to Sq. centimeters	6.452	Grains to Grams	0.0648
Sq. Centimeters to Sq. inches	0.1550	Grams to Grains	15.43
Sq. Feet to Sq. meters	0.0929	Ounces to Grams	28.35
Sq. Meters to Sq. feet	10.76	Grams to Ounces	0.03527
Sq. Yards to Sq. Meters	0.8361	Pounds to Grams	453.6
Sq. Meters to Sq. Yards	1.196	Grams to Pounds	0.002205
Sq. Miles to Sq. Kilometers	2.590	Pounds to Kilograms	0.4536
Sq. Kilometers to Sq. Miles	0.3861	Kilograms to Pounds	2.208
Acres to Hectares	0.4047	Tons to Kilograms	0.1015
Hectares to Acres	2.471	Kilograms to Tons	0.00096
Cub. Inches to Cub. Centimeters	16.39	Kilowatt to Horse Power	1.3409
Cub. Centimeters to Cub. Inches	0.06103	Horse Power to Kilowatt	0.7457

WEIGHT	*LENGTH*
200 miligrams = 1 carat 1 Centigram = 10 miligram 1 decigram = 10 centigram 1 gram = 10 decigram 1 Decagram = 10 grams 1 Hectogram = 10 decagram 1 Kilogram = 10 hectograms 1 Quintal = 100 kilograms 1 Metric Tonne = 1000 kilograms	1 Centimeter = 10 milimeters 1 Decimeter = 10 centimeters 1 meter = 10 decimeters 1 Decameter = 10 meters 1 Hectometer = 10 decameters 1 Kilometer = 10 hectometers
VOLUME	*CAPACITY*
1 sq. Centimeter = 1000 cu. millimeters 1 cu. Decimeter = 1000 cu. Centimeters 1 cu. Meter = 1000 decimeters	1 Centilitre = 10 millilitres 1 Decilitre = 10 centilitres 1 Litre = 10 decilitre 1 Decalitre = 10 litres 1 Hectolitre = 10 decalitres 1 Kilolitre = 10 hectolitres
AREA	*CONSTANTS*
1 sq. centimeter =100 sq. millimeters 1 sq. decimeter = 100 sq. centimeters 1 sq. meter = 100 sq. decimeters 1 sq. decameter = 100 sq. meters 1 sq. hectometer = 100 sq. decameters 1 sq. kilometer = 100 sq. hectometers.	$\pi = 3.1416$ $e = 2.71828$

Index